T0215174

The Home in the Digital Age

The Home in the Digital Age is a set of multidisciplinary studies exploring the impact of digital technologies in the home, with a shift of emphasis from technology to the people living and using this in their homes.

The book covers a wide variety of topics on the design, introduction and use of digital technologies in the home, combining the technological dimension with the cognitive, emotional, cultural and symbolic dimensions of the objects that incorporate digital technologies and project them onto people's lives. It offers a coherent approach, that of the home, which gives unity to the discussion.

Scholars of the home, the house and the family will find here the connection with the problems derived from the use of domestic robots and connected devices. Students of artificial intelligence, machine learning, robotics, big data and other branches of digital technologies will find ideas and arguments to apply their disciplines to the home and participate fruitfully in forums where digital technologies are built and negotiated in the home. Experts from various disciplines – psychologists and sociologists; philosophers, epistemologists and ethicists; economists; engineers, architects, urban planners and designers and so on – and also those interested in developing policies for the home and family will find this book contains well-founded and useful ideas to focus their work.

Antonio Argandoña is Emeritus Professor at IESE Business School, University of Navarra, Barcelona, Spain.

Joy Malala is a Lecturer at Aston University Law School, Birmingham, UK.

Richard C. Peatfield was Consultant Neurologist at Princess Margaret Migraine Clinic, Charing Cross Hospital and at Mount Vernon Hospital, Northwood.

Routledge Advances in Sociology

COVID-19
Volume II: Social Consequences and Cultural Adaptations
Edited by J. Michael Ryan

Prevent Strategy
Helping the Vulnerable Being Drawn Towards Terrorism or Another Layer of State Surveillance?
Edited by David Lowe and Robin Bennett

Regime Change in Turkey
Neoliberal Authoritarianism, Islamism and Hegemony
Edited by Errol Babacan, Melehat Kutun, Ezgi Pınar and Zafer Yılmaz

The Politics of Europeanisation
Work and Family Life Reconciliation Policy
Nazli Kazanoglu

Internet Dating
Intimacy and Social Change
Chris Beasley and Mary Holmes

Transcending Modernity with Relational Thinking
Pierpaolo Donati

Exploring Welfare Bricolage in Europe's Superdiverse Neighbourhoods
Jenny Phillimore, Hannah Bradby, Tilman Brand, Beatriz Padilla and Simon Pemberton

The Home in the Digital Age
Antonio Argandoña, Joy Malala and Richard C. Peatfield

For more information about this series, please visit: www.routledge.com/ Routledge-Advances-in-Sociology/book-series/SE0511)

The Home in the Digital Age

Edited by Antonio Argandoña,
Joy Malala and Richard C. Peatfield

LONDON AND NEW YORK

First published 2021
by Routledge
2 Park Square, Milton Park, Abingdon, Oxon OX14 4RN

and by Routledge
605 Third Avenue, New York, NY 10158

Routledge is an imprint of the Taylor & Francis Group, an Informa business

British Library Cataloguing-in-Publication Data
A catalogue record for this book is available from the British Library

Library of Congress Cataloging-in-Publication Data
Names: Argandoña Rámiz, Antonio, editor. | Malala, Joy, editor. |
Peatfield, R. C. (Richard C.), editor.
Title: The home in the digital age / edited by Antonio Argandoña,
Joy Malala and Richard C. Peatfield.
Description: Milton Park, Abingdon, Oxon ; New York : Routledge, 2021. |
Series: Routledge advances in sociology | Includes bibliographical
references and index.
Identifiers: LCCN 2020055414 (print) | LCCN 2020055415 (ebook) |
ISBN 9780367530174 (hbk) | ISBN 9781003080114 (ebk)
Subjects: LCSH: Home automation.
Classification: LCC TK7881.25 .H66 2021 (print) |
LCC TK7881.25 (ebook) | DDC 643/.6–dc23
LC record available at https://lccn.loc.gov/2020055414
LC ebook record available at https://lccn.loc.gov/2020055415

ISBN: 978-0-367-53017-4 (hbk)
ISBN: 978-0-367-53018-1 (pbk)
ISBN: 978-1-003-08011-4 (ebk)

Typeset in Times New Roman
by Newgen Publishing UK

Contents

Illustrations

Contributors

Mohamed Gamal Abdelmonem is the Chair in Architecture and the Director of the Centre for Architecture, Urbanism and Global Heritage at Nottingham Trent University. A Fellow of the Royal Society of Arts, Gamal is the university lead of the Strategic Research Theme, Global Heritage. He is the recipient of NTU 2020 Vice-Chancellor Outstanding Researcher Award and the 2014 recipient of the Jeffrey Cook Award of the International Association of the Study of Traditional Environments (IASTE). He serves as international expert on several international research associations, councils and funding panels in the United States, the United Kingdom and Europe. His research focuses on architectural and urban history, everyday homes, socio-spatial practices of urban communities, virtual heritage, medieval culture and post-conflict cities. His research has informed policy and practice of several governments and international organisations on aspects of heritage preservation, urban planning and architecture of home. His recent books include *Peripheries: Edge Conditions in Architecture* (2012), *Portush: Towards an Architecture for the North Irish Coast* (2013); *The Architecture of Home in Cairo* (2015); *Architecture, Space and Memory of Resurrection in Northern Ireland* (2019) and *People, Care and Work in the Home* (2020).

Maria Sophia Aguirre is an Ordinary Professor of Economics in the Department of Economics at the Catholic University of America. She is the founder of the Integral Economic Development methodology and Programs at this department. She earned her PhD in Economics from the University of Notre Dame and joined the Catholic University in 1994. Her professional background also includes degrees in accounting and banking finance, earned in Argentina. She also earned her undergraduate degrees, CPA and MBA, in Argentina. Dr Aguirre specialises in international finance and economic development. She has researched and published in the areas of exchange rates and economic integration, as well as on theories of population, human and social capital and family as it relates to integral economic development. She has been the recipient of several grants to support her research, and is a Fulbright Scholar. She is a member of several prestigious organisations and publications, in which she serves and has served as an officer in different capacities as well as a member of the editorial board. She has testified in front of Congresses on issues related to population, family and health, both nationally and internationally, and has advised several governments on women's education, family policy and health. She served as a presidential appointee to the US Advisory Commission on Foreign Diplomacy, 2003–2008, was a member of the Advisory Board to the Millennium Development Goals Fund (MDGF) evaluation and assisted the UN with the transition from the MDG to the Sustainable Development Goals.

Antonio Argandoña is Emeritus Professor of Economics and Business Ethics at IESE Business School. He got his PhD from the University of Barcelona (1969). He has taught in the universities of Barcelona, Málaga and Navarre. He is a member of the Real Academia de Ciencias Económicas y Financieras de España (Royal Academy of Economics and Finance), chairman of the Comité de Normativa y Ética Profesional (Committee of Standards and Professional Ethics) of the Association of Economists of Catalonia, member of the Commission on Corporate Social Responsibility and Anti-Corruption of the International Chamber of Commerce of Paris and of the deontological committees of various companies and institutions. He has published numerous books and articles on macroeconomics and monetary economics, the home and family issues, business and economic ethics, corporate social responsibility and related topics. He was the editor or co-editor and co-author of *People, Care and Work in the Home* (Routledge, 2020), *Work in a Human Economy. Business and Common Good in a Changing Society* (Edusc, 2018), *The Home. Multidisciplinary Reflections* (Edward Elgar, 2017), *The Social Dimensions of Employment. Institutional Reforms in Labour Markets* (Edward Elgar, 2002) and *The Ethical Dimension of Financial Institutions and Markets* (Springer, 1995).

Luisa Damiano (PhD) is an Associate Professor of Philosophy of Science at the IULM University (Milan, Italy), and the coordinator of the Research Group on the Epistemology of the Sciences of the Artificial (RG-ESA). Her main research areas include epistemology of complex systems, epistemology of the cognitive sciences and epistemology of the sciences of the artificial. On topics related to these domains she has written many articles and two books (*Unità in dialogo*, Bruno Mondadori, 2009, and *Vivre avec les robots. Essai sur l'empathie artificielle*, Seuil, 2016, with P. Dumouchel, published in English by Harvard University Press, 2017, in Korean by HEEDAM, 2019, and in Italian by Raffaello Cortina, 2019), and co-edited several journal special issues (among which are Artificial Empathy, *International Journal of Social Robotics*, with P. Dumouchel and H. Lehmann, 2014; What Can Synthetic Biology Offer to Artificial Intelligence (and Vice Versa), *BioSystems*, with Y. Kuruma and P. Stano, 2016; Synthetic Biology and Artificial Intelligence: Towards Cross-fertilization, *Complex Systems*, with Y. Kuruma and P. Stano, 2018).

Stephen Davies is the Head of Education at the Institute of Economic Affairs (IEA), London. He received his PhD from the University of St Andrews, Scotland, in 1984. Previously he was a Senior Lecturer in the Department of History and Economic History at Manchester Metropolitan University. He has also been a Visiting Scholar at the Social Philosophy and Policy Center at Bowling Green State University, Ohio. In his role at the IEA, he contributes to a wide range of publications and conferences on aspects of economic history and future planning. He has authored several books, including *Empiricism and History* (Palgrave Macmillan, 2003), *The Wealth Explosion: The Nature and Origins of Modernity* (Edward Everett Root, 2019) and *The Economics and Politics of Brexit: The Realignment of British Public Life* (AIER, 2020), and was a co-editor with Nigel Ashford of *The Dictionary of Conservative and Libertarian Thought* (Routledge, 1991).

Mei Lin Fung is the Chair of People-Centered Internet which she co-founded with Vint Cerf. She gave the closing keynote on Decade of Digital Transformation for the World Bank IFC Global SME Financing Forum on October 2020. She also presented at the World Economic Forum (WEF) Digital Economics launch. Mei Lin is an early pioneer of customer relationship management (CRM), which is now a $40 billion industry. She is the socio-technical lead for US Federal Health Futures initiative and sits on the WEF Cross Border Data flows, Payments and Genomics and Ethics working groups. She is the Chair of IEEE Standards Association Industry Connections Social Impact Measurement and sits on the Executive Committee for IEEE Humanitarian Activities Committee; she served as Vice Chair, Internet Inclusion for the IEEE Internet Initiative. Mei Lin is a Singaporean, living for decades in Silicon Valley working at Intel and then Oracle. She was a software programmer at Shell Australia. She served on the World Economic Forum Global Future Council on Digital Economy and Society. With a BSc in Mathematics from Australian National University (ANU) and an MBA from Massachusetts Institute of Technology (MIT), she convened the @GlobalHelpDesk network for pragmatic action response for the one billion children whose learning has been disrupted by COVID-19, connecting Tech communities with International Telecommunication Union (ITU), United Nations Development Programme (UNDP), World Bank and the WEF.

Deborah Gale is a gerontologist researcher, Apple Computer veteran and journalist. She is the Intergenerational Design Leader for two London-based social enterprises: The Age of No Retirement/The Common Room and the UK-based affiliate of encore.org, Encore Fellows UK. She holds a BA from Mercyhurst University, Erie, PA; an MBA from the University of Santa Clara, Santa Clara, CA; and an MA in Public Policy and Ageing from King's College in London. A dual citizen, Deborah, her British husband and five daughters have lived in the UK permanently since 2001. Deborah has written for the *American in Britain*, *Expatriate Living* and is a contributor to the *Huffington Post*. In addition to writing academic papers for peer-reviewed journals, she blogs for the British Society of Gerontology, the Age Equity Alliance and the Modern Elder Academy. She writes about ageing issues and current events surrounding policy, intergen collaboration and the future of work. More specifically, her research interests lie in the demographic transition currently underway and the potential longevity dividend that the world, via the boomer cohort in tandem with Gen X, Y, Z and upcoming C, could benefit from collectively.

Sonia Livingstone (DPhil (Oxon), OBE, FBA, FBPS, FAcSS, FRSA) is a Professor in the Department of Media and Communications at the London School of Economics and Political Science. Taking a comparative, critical and contextualised approach, her research examines how the changing conditions of mediation are reshaping everyday practices and possibilities for action. Much of Sonia's time these days is concerned with Children's Rights in the Digital Age. Sonia has published 20 books on media audiences, especially children and young people's risks and opportunities, media literacy and rights in the digital environment, including *The Class: Living and Learning in the Digital Age* (New York University Press, with Julian Sefton-Green). Her latest book is *Parenting for a Digital Future: How Hopes and Fears about Technology Shape Children's Lives* (Oxford University Press, with Alicia Blum-Ross). A recipient of many honours, she has advised the UK government, European Commission, European Parliament, UN Committee on the Rights of the Child, Organisation for Economic Co-operation and Development (OECD), International Telecommunication Union (ITU) and United Nations Childrens' Fund (UNICEF), among others, on children's Internet safety and rights in the digital environment. Sonia has served as Chair of the LSE's Truth, Trust and Technology Commission, Special Advisor to the House of Lords' Select Committee on Communications, Expert Advisor to the Council of Europe, President of the International Communication Association, and Executive Board member of the UK Council for Child Internet Safety. She currently directs the Digital Futures Commission (with the 5Rights Foundation) and the Global Kids Online project (with UNICEF).

Joy Malala is a Lecturer at Aston University Law School. She has a special interest in researching financial regulation and supervision, the legal accountability of regulators, corporate governance, as well as the regulation of financial innovation and technology. She particularly researched on the legal and regulation of mobile payments systems which she examines in her book, *Law and Regulation of Mobile Payment Systems: Issues Arising 'Post' Financial Inclusion in Kenya*. This book is a first of its kind, addressing the legal and regulatory issues arising out of the introduction of mobile payments in Kenya and its drive towards financial inclusion. It considers the interaction between regulation and technological innovation, with a particular focus on the regulatory tools, institutional arrangements and government decisional processes through the assessment as a whole of Kenya's regulatory capacity. It also addresses the vulnerabilities presented by technological innovation for consumers after financial inclusion. She researches financial sector reform through the consideration of the role of Central banks, and systemically important financial institutions and their impact on emerging economies.

Mia Mikic is a trade economist with a keen interest in sustainable development and with a proven track record and experience in academia and the international civil service. She served as Director, Trade, Investment and Innovation Division in United Nations Economic and Social Commission for Asia and the Pacific (ESCAP). She is currently an adviser and has previously coordinated the Asia-Pacific Research and Training Network on Trade (ARTNeT), an open network of research and academic institutions and think-tanks in the Asia-Pacific region covering all key means of implementation of the Sustainable Development Goals (for more details, see artnet.unescap.org). Prior to her UN tenure, she was Head of the Department of Economic Theory and Business International Program at the University of Zagreb, and Senior Lecturer at the University of Auckland. She is the author of many books, reports and papers, and has edited or co-edited several volumes on international economics, regional integration, and development. She oversaw preparation of the Asia-Pacific Trade and Investment Report (APTIR), a flagship publication in the area of trade and investment. Her current research and advisory work focus on the impact of the COVID-19 pandemic on trade and Global Value Chains, frontier technologies and inclusive future of work, advocating for women as influencers in policymaking, services trade, and promotion of evidence-based policymaking. She is collaborating with several universities on modernising trade curricula. She has a Doctorate in Economics from the University of Zagreb.

Ioana Ocnarescu is the Head of Strate Research, the Research and Innovation Department of Strate School of Design where she leads an active and multi-disciplinary research with other members of the team. She is also in charge of the "Master in Design for Smart Cities", a 2-year academic programme for international students at Strate School of Design. As a researcher and lecturer, Ioana promotes design research for design students, teaches courses on experience design, design research, and design & robotics. In

2019, with the support of five industrial partners and three academic partners, she launched "Robotics by Design Lab – AI, Robots & Humans –
ecologies of living together" (RbD Lab), a multidisciplinary lab hosting
four PhD students. The goal of RbD Lab is to question the fundamental
notions around the roles, interactions and, therefore, relations between
people and robots in order to design new ecologies of living together. At
Strate Research and within this laboratory, Ioana co-directs several PhD
projects in design, human sciences, robotics and AI. Before Strate, Ioana
studied Applied Mathematics at Ecole Polytechnique France and Design
at Strate School of Design. She obtained her PhD in design within the
User Experience team of Alcatel-Lucent Bell Labs France in collaboration
with Strate and the Product Design and Innovation Laboratory of Arts et
Métiers ParisTech.

Richard C. Peatfield was Consultant Neurologist at the Princess Margaret
Migraine Clinic, Charing Cross Hospital, and at Mount Vernon Hospital,
Northwood, from 1989 until his retirement at the end of 2019. He qualified
from the University of Cambridge and the Middlesex Hospital in 1973, and
was trained in General Medicine and Neurology in London and Leeds. His
main clinical and research interest was the diagnosis and management of
headache. He was the book review editor of the journal *Cephalalgia* from
2009 to 2019. In addition to 49 refereed papers, and 59 invited reviews and
chapters in books, he has written *Headache* in the book series "Clinical
Medicine and the Nervous System" published by Springer-Verlag, 1986;
Headache, a booklet for patients for the British Brain and Spine Foundation,
1998; *Headache* in the "Fast Facts" series, Health Press, Abingdon, 2000,
with J.K. Campbell (second edition, 2002, with D. Dodick), and Drug
Therapy for Migraine, *Current Medical Research and Opinion*, 2001, 17,
Supplement 1, pp. 1–99 (with P.J. Goadsby and S.D. Silberstein).

Matilde Santos received her BSc and MSc degrees in Physics (Computer
Engineering) and her PhD in Physics from the University Complutense
of Madrid (UCM). She is with the Institute of Knowledge Technology,
Computer Science School, at the UCM, where she is currently a Full
Professor in System Engineering and Automatic Control (since 2011).
She is a member of the European Academy of Sciences and Arts. She
has worked and led several national and European projects, focused on
the application of artificial intelligence techniques to control, mainly on
engineering and industrial problems. Over the last decades, she has worked
on autonomous vehicles (marine and aerial). She has also developed soft
computing applications for making decision systems and has applied
machine learning techniques for pattern recognition in different fields
(fusion signals, medical diagnosis, access detection and handwriting).
She is now working on modelling, simulation and control of wind energy
systems.

She has published many papers in international scientific journals and several book chapters. She has supervised 12 PhD and more than 60 Master projects.

She currently serves as a member of the editorial board of four Impact Factor (IF) scientific journals and as Programme Committee (PC) of numerous international conferences. Her major research interests include intelligent control, modelling and simulation, engineering applications of soft computing techniques, pattern recognition and renewable energies (modelling and control of floating wind turbines).

Dominique Sciamma is the Director and Dean of CY School of Design, CY Cergy Paris Université and President of APCI (France Design Promotion Agency). Holder of a Bachelor with Honours in Mathematics and a Master's degree in Theoretical Computer Science and after an eclectic career within international companies, Dominique is creating the first ever design school in a university (CY Cergy Paris University) opening September 2021. He directed Strate School of Design for seven years until September 2020. Before leading Strate, he successively created and led its "Intelligent Systems and Objects" department and its research activity. Always surfing on new technologies, he successively worked as an Artificial Intelligence (AI) researcher, software developer, marketing director, head of an AI business unit in Singapore, strategist (for Bull), head of a complex problem-solving team, multimedia marketing (for EDS), electronic editor (for La Tribune economic newspaper), multimedia author, Content Management Systems (CMS) author (as an independent digital consultant), before passionately investing on design pedagogy. A prominent figure in the design ecosystem in France, Dominique is a determined promoter of transformative design, through his actions, words and writings. As president of APCI, the main French design promotion association, he played a very active role in the Design National Conference (2019) for the implementation of a national design policy.

Francesca Toni is Professor in Computational Logic and Deputy Head in the Department of Computing, Imperial College London, UK, and the founder and leader of the Computational Logic and Argumentation (CLArg) research group. She graduated, summa cum laude, in Computing from the University of Pisa, Italy, in 1990, and received her PhD in Computing in 1995 from Imperial College London. She has coordinated two EU projects, received funding from EPSRC (in the UK) and the EU, and was awarded a Senior Research Fellowship from the Royal Academy of Engineering and the Leverhulme Trust. She is currently the Technical Director of the ROAD2H EPSRC-funded project and Co-director of the Centres of Doctoral Training in Safe and Trusted AI and in AI for Healthcare. She has co-chaired ICLP 2015 (the 31st International Conference on Logic Programming) and KR 2018 (the 16th Conference on

Principles of Knowledge Representation and Reasoning). She is a member of the steering committee of KR, Inc. and Agreement Technologies (AT), corner editor on Argumentation for the *Journal of Logic and Computation* and a member of the editorial board of the *Argument and Computation* journal and the *AI Journal*. She has published more than 200 publications. Her main research interests lie within the broad area of knowledge representation and reasoning and explainable AI, and in particular include argumentation, argument mining, logic-based multi-agent systems, logic programming, and non-monotonic/default/defeasible reasoning.

Foreword

The home is the place where the age-old and the brand-new meet. As each new generation is born and finds its place, the home remembers what went before, adapts to what is now and prepares for what is next. Ideally the home is the place where the tried and tested merges with the up and coming to create a thriving environment for all. It can be though the place where those different stories collide and the home becomes the frontline of any tensions that emerge.

The added element is the influence of those factors of change that come from outside the home and impact the life within. While a previous generation of parents worried about the effect of television on family life, today's parents are concerned by the Internet and streaming services embraced by their own children.

It is not only parents who are questioning the role of the new technologies in the home and in our lives. Challenges at all levels are currently being addressed to the Titans of Internet communication, entertainment and distribution. The challenge is also being extended to the less visible ways in which advanced technologies including artificial intelligence are taking up residence in our homes.

Asking questions now about the challenges and opportunities for the home from these new house guests – from SMART utilities to care-giving robots – is a key concern for Home Renaissance Foundation. This publication was put together during the coronavirus disease 2019 (COVID-19) pandemic, when, as never before, homes have needed to provide both basic shelter and high-performing e-work space.

From what follows in this important and pioneering study of these questions, it is clear that experts in this field see us only on the foothills of the great change that is ahead. The founding and guiding vision of Home Renaissance Foundation is the core value of the work of the home for the well-being of individuals and for the whole of society. Our commitment is to championing this value of home in a world that needs a fresh recognition of the attitudes and skills that build stable and secure homes, relationships and communities now and in the future.

Rigorous academic engagement with the implications for us all is vital if the next generations of both technology and humankind are to be prepared for what is already on the near horizon. Work is needed now to establish the ethics, values and the social and moral framework in which these new ways of interacting with machines can be shaped and guided for our benefit. As the need for the delineation of the contours of this new ethical landscape can hardly be overstated, its addressing as a part of this volume is to be greatly welcomed.

The contributors to this book show just that rigorous engagement, providing a step towards ensuring that this future is one in which the home and homemakers have not only an interest but an authoritative voice. I would like to take the opportunity here on behalf of Home Renaissance Foundation to thank all the contributors and the editorial team of Professor Antonio Argandoña, Dr. Joy Malala and Dr. Richard Peatfield for making this voice heard.

Bryan K. Sanderson, CBE
Chairman, Home Renaissance Foundation, London

Foreword

This volume is the fruit of the collaboration between two foundations that share fundamental aims.

The Home Renaissance Foundation's purpose is to shed light on the myriad ways in which the home serves as an irreplaceable building block for a human and thriving society.

The Social Trends Institute (STI) is a New York-based research centre that promotes, supports and disseminates the study of globally relevant social trends and their effects on human communities. It seeks to foster understanding of such trends, emphasising issues related to family, governance, civil society, culture and lifestyles, and bioethics.

The meeting of scholars that gave rise to this book approached three of those areas of interest, namely, how new cultural norms and lifestyle options (technologies) can be harnessed for the benefit of family dynamics. The end purpose is to understand how individuals can emerge from their home environments with the human capital that will ultimately contribute to a more robust and humane civil society.

The STI considers this to be a most worthy endeavor and is proud to have contributed to its fruition by providing financial and institutional support to the project.

This was the second such HRF initiative to which STI has lent a hand. The first was published as *The Home: Multidisciplinary Reflections* – another valuable contribution to treating the home with the respect and clarity it deserves – so necessary in today's society.

My colleague Professor Antonio Argandoña, along with Dr. Joy Malala and Dr. Richard Peatfield, has done an excellent work as the editor of this volume.

I am grateful for having had the opportunity to contribute to such a fine work with the resources of the STI, and am honored to have worked with

HRF Chairman Bryan K. Sanderson and his dedicated team of colleagues. Our two institutions already have other joint projects underway, and I look forward to a lasting cooperation.

Carlos P. Cavallé
President, Social Trends Institute, New York

Preface

Sonia Livingstone

"Home" is perhaps one of the most resonant words in the English language. "Home is where the heart is". "Home Sweet Home". "There's no place like home". Home is where you can be yourself, a place we hope to fill with peace and love. An intrusion into our home is an outrage, and being homeless is a tragedy.

By comparison with long-established ideas about "home", the idea of the "digital age" is very new and, thus, seemingly more urgent. But it is no less resonant. We think of "the digital" through the imagery of science fiction, often dystopian or, when more optimistically conceived, as somehow akin to magic; we don't understand how it works but it transforms our world and makes the impossible possible. Work transformed as robots do the menial jobs; surgeons save lives while, on the other side of the planet, children whose lives lack sanitation gain access to the best university libraries.

I begin with these thoughts because my research is grounded in ordinary people's experience – the people who live in homes rather than those who design them; the people who generally understand little about technology but love to buy the latest innovation. Thus, my starting assumption, when reading this book, was that, while technological innovation is undoubtedly reconfiguring the infrastructure of our society, we cannot grasp its meaning and consequences without attending to the public's imaginative, cultural and emotional investment in "the digital age". This includes their investment in the technologically mediated home.

The arrival of television led to a rearrangement of home and family – merging the "front" (more formal) and "back" (more domestic) spaces into open-plan living, replacing the kitchen or dining table with the "TV dinner", spawning family fights over the remote control and children's "screen time". The arrival of the PC led to another rearrangement – demanding that families create a "computer room" in the smallest bedroom or a workstation some-where, perhaps under the stairs, repositioning the children from the most ignorant to the most savvy and enabling adults to work from home 24/7 if they wanted to or had to. Also radical in its effects has been the portable device – the final straw in the coffin of the boring bedroom unused in the daytime, and enabling the family to sit together on the sofa yet multi-screening in individual entertainment bubbles, or to disperse around the house while messaging each other. While the media panicked about families who never spoke to each other or children addicted to video games, many families quietly found new ways to regroup around their favourite digital contents, some of them even managing to create their own.

But today's technological transformations are more radical yet, embedding themselves into every part of the home, and even our bodies, and connecting our every action to a datafied ecology through ever faster, yet more opaque systems that seem to promise greater agency with one hand as they take it away with the other. Opinion polls track plummeting trust in both the big tech companies and the governments that egg them on ahead of providing needed regulation or ethical reflection. Parents oscillate between a desperation to ensure their children can keep up and a fear of things to come. Marketers invest millions in enticing us to spend more, update quicker and live "smarter".

As a result, the home is being transformed in a multi-media and increasingly high-tech resource, accompanied by huge hopes about new arrangements for managing family, education, work and leisure, and growing fears about state surveillance, inequality and exclusion, commercial exploitation and the loss of privacy and agency. These transformations are both external – think of the transformed relation between home and the world outside, usually framed in terms of the blurring of private and public spheres – and internal, as technology mediates what happens within the home, exacerbating the renegotiation and individualisation of gender and generational relations, and the commodification of our daily lives.

Periods of rapid change tend to invite then-and-now thinking, positioning the immediate present as the pivot point of change (in our case, centred on today's latest technology), the future as radically uncertain and the past as a homogeneous blank ("life before the Internet", the pre-digital world, the unmediated home for which many are nostalgic). But of course there is nothing homogeneous or linear about human history. Family historians position the idea of "Home Sweet Home" – the private life of the nuclear family (often conceived in highly gendered and classed terms) strictly demarcated from the public sphere outside its door – as a historical aberration, briefly characteristic of Western post-war consumer society but with less relevance before or elsewhere. Through most of our history, and still in much of the world, the home has been a place of work and commerce as much or more than one of leisure and rest, and it has included many inhabitants beyond "family" (itself a historically and culturally contested term).

So when we – the public, policymakers, the academic community – imagine "home", we in the West tend to be swayed by that post-war image, and our often nostalgic response to it. But we must be careful. First, we must recognise the historical and cultural specificity of our expectations about home. Second, it is vital not to romanticise the home. Home can be a place of violence and other abuses of power, or a place of loneliness or suffering, unobserved and unaddressed. Homes also vary hugely, as a result of social class, ethnicity and other sources of inequality and discrimination in society. Technology enters into all of these problems, amplifying or ameliorating them in accordance with the intended or, often, unintended consequences of design, policy or practice. Third, we must not bracket off the home as concerned solely with our private lives. What happens at home has implications for the wider society. The popularity of first television, then video and then video streaming, necessitated parallel transformations by the cinema to retain its audience and revitalise its offering. Home shopping has challenged the High Street. Teleworking calls into question the need for the office. Home e-learning can make schools seem dull or dated. Medical centres complain that people have checked their symptoms online before consulting the doctor.

Three concepts must be distinguished: home, family and household. To use them interchangeably is to risk reproducing a heteronormative middle-class view of family in particular, and a romanticised view of the happy home. The household is the most neutral term – the unit of demography and social statistics; referring to a piece of real estate with a postcode, most people live in a household. But this may or may not be where their family lives. And they may or may not call it "home". The relation between family and home must be understood in historical and cultural context, for family may mean me and my cat, or me and my extended family spanning continents. Meanwhile, a household may contain within it several individuals or families, each applying the term "home" to different rooms. Or a household may not feel like home at all because of the trouble within it.

Digital technologies enter into all of these possibilities. They can be used to connect spaces or erect barriers and mark boundaries. They can be used to bring trouble to places that were previously safe and help to places that were previously troubled. But we need to pay attention. Demographers report on connectivity by focusing on households, notwithstanding the possibility that the wife or child may not be permitted to use it by an authoritarian father. Anthropologists explore how people can feel at home within digital networks, less defined by geographical location than by remediated cultural rituals. Psychologists think of family less in terms of space and more in terms of time, keen now to resolve difficult dynamics through digital storytelling or to trace how family biographies can be reimagined by constructing a digitalised family album.

I am a social scientist not a computer scientist, so perhaps I miss the nuance in the concept of "the user". But it worries me when mention of or assumptions about the users of technology, especially when designed into the very process of innovation, appear to neglect the social and contextual considerations that I have sought to explain above. As is now well known, technology embeds cultural values and social imaginaries of use and consequences into their origination. Too often the user is thought of as, tacitly, adult, male, middle-class, White, able-bodied, urban and so on. If not critically examined from the outset, the social scientists concerned with people's lives in the digital age find themselves having to document, expensively, the digital inequalities and exclusions can so often result from such assumptions. Then others must mobilise, usually with insufficient resource, to advocate retrofitting societal policies and practices to optimise what can be gained from available technologies and, especially, to mitigate the regrettably unanticipated risks of harm that accompany their roll-out.

These and many other thoughts were inspired by reading the chapters that follow. After reading this book, you will be better prepared for what may be to come. I hope, too, that you will be abler to imagine how it could be better, and more ready to join the struggle to ensure that our digital age meets everybody's needs and helps to realise their rights.

Chapter 1

Introduction

The home in the digital age

Antonio Argandoña, Joy Malala and
Richard C. Peatfield

> The car has left the highway. We are close to our house. Using our mobile phone, we send a message; the porch and entrance lights come on and the heating starts up so that when we arrive the temperature is adequate, which the device itself has learned is the one we prefer. The house is filled with soft music – we are coming to our smart home.

There are many definitions of smart home, and not all coincide (Aldrich, 2003). To introduce the readers to what they can find in this book, the definition of Balta-Ozkan et al. (2013, 364, cited in Hargreaves et al. 2017, 127) will help us: a smart home is a "residence equipped with a high-tech network, linking sensors and domestic devices, appliances and features that can be remotely monitored, access[ed] or controlled, and provide services that respond to the needs of [the] inhabitants".

> Computational agents have most definitely left the lab and entered daily life in a variety of forms. The Internet of Things (IoT) is incrementally making homes smarter by embedding networked, ambient technologies with varying degrees of autonomy into the physical and social fabric of domestic life ... As domestic service robot technologies advance and become more commercially accessible, the smart home will have already changed the domestic setting and laid the groundwork for robots to assimilate.
>
> (Urquhart et al., 2019, 247)

What a smart home now offers is much more than the devices that have been introduced in houses for decades, but it is still not within the reach of most users.

The literature on digital technologies has paid little attention to the home, beyond optimistic narratives about fabulous cleaning robots, integrated platforms and the information and communication capacity offered by mobiles, or pessimistic predictions about the negative impact of technology on employment, the dependency caused by screens, especially in children and adolescents, or the risks that smartphones pose to the privacy of citizens.

The home has always been a recipient and user of new technologies. The digital age is no exception: on the contrary, the process has been accelerating for decades. Technology promises comfort, convenience, companionship, security and leisure, among many other benefits. It does not always achieve this effectively and without causing inconvenience, among other reasons, because what the experts try to achieve with their machines and programs does not always coincide with what families expect or want, or with what they can achieve, given their material and human resources: learning to live in a smart home and get the most out of its technologies is not an easy task. It is not enough to bring technology to the house; it is not even enough to "embed" it in the house, because "these artefacts... are restructuring interactions, social order and relationships in the home" (Urquhart et al., 2019, 247).

This book is intended to offer various multidisciplinary views on the relationship between digital technologies and the home.

According to Argandoña:

> The concept of the home focuses on three internal elements: the person, the inner community or family, and shared living space with an intention of continuity. But there is also a fourth external element that cannot be excluded: the external social and material environment. These elements work together; the person is at the centre but the unifying concept is the home.
>
> (Argandoña, 2018, 11)

The social function of the home can be explained in terms of "why" the home exists, "for what" it exists and what is its "purpose". "The 'why' looks towards the past and seeks to give an explanation": it is an efficient and humane way to satisfy many needs.

> The "what for" looks towards the future... The "what for" invokes a function, first for its members, but later on for others outside of the home, and eventually reaching society as a whole ... A home without a "what for" can function for quite some time ... But it will be lacking a "purpose", which is the "what for" as defined, shared, and accepted by that particular community's members ... This "purpose" is not usually stated explicitly ... but this does not mean that they do not have an implicit "purpose" or "project". The lack of a "project", or the existence of several unshared "projects", implies a lack of unity, and this is a threat for the home's continued existence.
>
> (Abdelmonem and Argandoña, 2020, 6)

In Chapter 4, Professor Abdelmonem mentions a hierarchy of houses, according to the nature and intensity of the presence of digital technologies in them:

1. Homes which contain intelligent objects: homes contain single, stand-alone applications and objects which function in an intelligent manner.
2. Homes which contain intelligent, communicating objects: homes contain appliances and objects which function intelligently in their own right and which also exchange information between each other to increase functionality.
3. Connected homes: homes have internal and external networks, allowing interactive and remote control of systems, as well as access to services and information, both within and beyond the home.
4. Learning homes: patterns of activity in the homes are recorded and the accumulated data are used to anticipate users' needs and to control the technology accordingly.
5. Attentive homes: the activity and location of people and objects within the homes are constantly registered, and this information is used to control technology in anticipation of the occupants' needs.

Not surprisingly, the relationship between digital technologies and the home will vary considerably depending on the type of home, the location, the level of technological development and many other factors. Here we offer some general reflections that can guide the reading of this book; the specific content of each chapter is detailed at the end of this one.

The impact of digital technologies in the home

The common thread of this book is the home, broadly understood as a place for security and control, for activity, for relationships and continuity, and for identity and values (Gram-Hanssen and Darby, 2018). The community of people living in a physical space will always be the objective of our analysis, particularly when we consider the impact of technology on that space and on the objects. We will end up studying a particular aspect, to which the literature has given considerable attention: the impact of technology on work.

Physical space

The house is the material sphere of the home, including its facilities and its belongings and, therefore, the technologies incorporated into them. The home is not just a physical space (the house, abode, shelter or dwelling); it is also a cultural and psychological space (Argandoña, 2018; Buttimer and Seamon, 2015; Cuba and Hummon, 1993; d'Entremont, 2018). The home is not understood without the people who live in it and who personalize it: it is a place for human relationships (Karjalainen, 1993). "Thus, while the idea of home can be viewed as a universal concept, the experience of home is socially and culturally determined" (Fox O'Mahony, 2013, 165). The home also has a temporal dimension: it is "a unique place where a person's past, present, and future selves are reflected and come to life" (Graham et al., 2015, 346), and is also the place where many intergenerational relationships occur.

The home fulfils many functions: restaurant, hotel, leisure space, place of study and work, sometimes hospital, movie theatre, an area in which you learn to live and return to after years, but it is much more than that. Similarly, the impacts of digital technologies are related to that of functional dimension of home, but they also go much further. Chapter 4 offers interesting insights into those impacts, many of which are intangible but real. Technology provokes changes in lifestyles and, at the same time, allows people to adapt to them, an adaptation that is often more social and emotional than physical. Technology is not neutral. In turn, the social order of the home imposes conditions on the technologies that are appropriate, especially when it comes to aid and surveillance for the elderly, sick, disabled or children (Urquhart et al., 2019).

On top of this the furniture, ornaments and appliances in the home add to each individual's effective "reference plexus". Taken together, they make up the home's human world (Highmore, 2011; Miller, 2001). Chapter 6 discusses not only the physical or material dimension, but also the psychological, cognitive, emotional, cultural and symbolic dimensions of the objects that incorporate digital technologies and project them onto people's lives. This produces a recurrent conflict between commercial interests and efforts to improve the quality of life and empower home members. It is logical, therefore, that frequent changes take place, not only in the material dimension, but also in people and their relationships with machines and programs. The most important thing about home technology is that it changes the lives of its members.

Home management

An important, though not unique, motivation for the introduction and use of digital technologies in the home is to facilitate its management, as explained in Chapter 3. Domestic robots and connected devices (meters, sensors and alarms) are involved in this task. A robot is:

> [A]n actuated mechanism programmable in two or more axes with a degree of autonomy, moving within its environment, to perform intended tasks. Autonomy in this context means the ability to perform intended tasks based on current state and sensing, without human intervention.
>
> (ISO Standard 8373: 2012 on Robots and
> Robotic Devices, s2.08[1])

There are many types of robots that perform various tasks, such as vacuuming and floor cleaning (IFR, 2017, 14).

The interrelation between domestic robots and connected devices makes the communication of users with machines more intuitive, but it presents the risk of introducing biases that sacrifice the needs of users to the economic interests of producers (Leppënen and Jokinen, 2003). Wilson et al. (2015, 466) invite us to consider "how to use and meaning of technologies will be socially constructed and iteratively negotiated, rather than being the inevitable outcome of assumed functional benefits". Added to this are problems of user training and learning, security of the information collected by devices, interference of automation in people's pleasurable activities (Coskun et al., 2018) and in the autonomy of users (Coeckelbergh, 2012; Leenes and Lucivero, 2014), confidence in technology, and related problems, which are discussed in several chapters of this book, especially in Chapter 2.

Digital technology and people

As explained in Chapter 9, technology is a mediator, insofar as it influences people's actions and experiences (cf. Verbeek, 2006, 363ff), in that it not only allows agents access to reality, but also focuses, limits and conditions that access. Domestic robots also act as mediators for users and intermediaries for services (Urquhart et al., 2019, 249) – hence the relevance of human–computer interaction (Dautenhahn, 2018; Goodrich and Schultz, 2007). Chapter 5 explains that such interactions are not limited to human-powered machines, but rather involve processes of humanizing technology – when, for example, domestic robots are treated as if they were "someone" with emotions, intentions and beliefs – with the risk of distorting the nature of relationships between people and machines. In short, the human–computer interaction leads us to consider home robots as integral elements of the "ecology of the mind".

Chapter 9 also deals with the person–machine–person relationship, this time from an ethical point of view. Ethics is understood here not as a set of abstract principles, or as an extrinsic limitation to the initiative of the experts, or even as an ethics of action, which defines morality and meaning of concrete action. The proposed ethic is directed to the development of the character of the person, first of the user, but also, consequently, of the designer, producer, distributor or regulator: in short, an ethic of norms, goods and virtues. The ethical consequences of digital technologies are also discussed in other chapters.

The effect of disruptive technologies (automation, machine learning and artificial intelligence [AI]) on people is often focused on their impact on work. As explained in Chapter 8, in much of the literature on the subject this impact is limited to paid work outside the home: the home thus loses its function of unit of analysis. However, the loss of a job due to technological innovation,

an increase in the salary of a qualified employee due to technological progress, or the increasing uncertainty about future employment opportunities
due to that progress are not only problems of the people or societies affected,
but also problems of the home, which is the primary unit of economic
support, redistribution of resources and psychological and moral support for
the people affected. Chapters 7 and 8 present an independent analysis of the
social problems caused by technology through labour employment and remu-
neration, including reflections on the transition between a present that may
seem negative and a future that is full of opportunities and uncertainties; the
need for training and the development of specific skills; the promotion of
innovation and, above all, the creation of an awareness in political, economic
and social agents, which takes into account the role of home in the problem.

As we have already said, this book deals with how digital technologies
influence people who live in the home, their facilities and their physical structure, and also their relationships, the possibilities that the home provides, the
challenges that arise and their ability to exercise the social function attributed
to them (Argandoña, 2018). And this has a corollary: the home must play an
important role in the creation, management, use and development of digital
technologies that affect it – which, in short, are almost all of them.

There are many ways to put this into practice: putting the users and their
environment at the centre of device and program design, from its early stages;
establishing feedback mechanisms between designers, producers and users;
promoting the protocols, codes and principles that should govern these tasks;
making the assumptions underlying the designs explicit so that users are
aware of how they can restrict their freedom of decision and condition their
responses and so on. All this can be done through explicit regulations and
controls, but it also requires firm and credible commitments from all parties
interested. All this can be summed up in an idea that is present in all the pages
of this book: the home and its members must have a place of honour at the
table where technology passes from idea to design, from design to the product,
from the product to the program or machine, and from these to people's lives.

Home, technology and COVID-19

This book will be published while we are still suffering the coronavirus
(COVID-19) pandemic. The first drafts of the chapters were written before
the coronavirus made its influence felt on the homes of millions of people
around the world, especially when the slogan "stay at home" spread. In the
last review of the chapters, the editors offered the authors the possibility of
adding some comment on how they thought this affected the content of their
chapters. Some authors took advantage of this opportunity, but both those
who did and those who did not stated that the pandemic, first, did not sub-
stantially alter their conclusions; second, it underlined the importance of
the digital revolution in the home; and third, it reaffirmed the validity of the

comprehensive approach based on the home as a unit of analysis. Here we will only make some reflections on this topic.

Perhaps the image that the COVID-19 pandemic brought to many people is that of millions of people quarantined at home. Isolated? Not entirely, because they worked remotely together with others; enjoyed leisure and online information; shared messages, impressions and news through the media and social networks; and felt technologically protected and helped to carry out social tasks such as working, shopping, studying and managing their health problems. Somehow, in those weeks it became only too clear that digital technologies are changing almost everything in our lives, and that we are witnessing only the first steps of that transformation.

However, this does not sufficiently reflect the reality of home during the pandemic for millions of citizens. The economic impact was very different between countries, sectors and groups; for example, workers least likely to work remotely tend to be young, without a college education, working for non-standard contracts, employed in smaller firms and those at the bottom of the earnings distribution; all this suggests that the pandemic exacerbated inequality, precisely among those who are least likely to take advantage of the full potential of digital technologies (Brussevich et al., 2020). Once again the impact of automation, machine learning or AI on work and, therefore, on the home is highlighted. But the quarantine also revealed that technology is not within everyone's reach, that millions of people do not even have a home to take refuge in, and that for many others, especially the elderly, their home can be an inhospitable place to suffer in solitude.

Another example, also very close to the subject of this book, is teleworking, which received a major boost during the lockdown in 2020. Remote work has often been analyzed from the company's point of view, as a form of work organization that reduces costs and encourages innovation, although it also presents negative aspects, such as the possible loss of efficiency and coordination and the undervaluation of personal relationships and the organization's culture. It has also been studied from the point of view of people as a way to reduce the stress of workers, leaving them greater freedom of hours, the possibility of engaging in other tasks and minimizing the costs of commuting, although also recognizing the drawbacks of greater pressure on the results, the feeling of being controlled remotely by the boss or the difficulties to establish safe and comfortable relationships with their offices and colleagues.

However, the practice of teleworking during the pandemic revealed other dimensions little discussed in the previous literature, such as the availability of sufficiently isolated places to work at home and the need to create "barriers" that protect the domestic environment from work; the complex relationships with other family members in a coexistence that can be up to 24 hours a day; and the limitations to use technical means (computer, mobile, etc.) at the same time that the children attended classes online. It is here where the home is presented as a unit of analysis, in which people who live in it appear each with their own problems, limitations and challenges; the physical space in which everyone carries out their activities; the difficulties in relation to the immediate environment (the firms, in this case, but also the school and the local community); stress and loss of social contacts, etc.

There are many other examples of situations in which the home, and not just people or physical space, may be the appropriate framework for a problem. Work–family reconciliation, for example, affects not only the working woman or man and the company, but also couple relationships and children, external services, physical space, relations with schools, health, leisure possibilities and many other dimensions.

Similarly, caring for a child, an older or a disabled person using robots, sensors or other digital means is not just a matter of that person's relationship with the machine, but affects the entire family, now expanded to external caregivers, as well as the physical space, the household economy and other variables. And it presents new problems: how is a child's socialization affected by the fact that many of his first experiences take place with a robot and not with a human being? Are these problems broadened when the coexistence of several generations in the home is taken into account: for example, when designing a mobile, does it take into account its different impact on children, young, mature and older people? Are new technologies put at the service of everyone? Should humans learn to live with robots, or should robots be designed to suit the needs and capabilities of humans?

The same happens with the security of the home through digital controls and devices: it is not only relevant from a physical point of view, but also affects the function of the home itself as a place of rest, of privacy and of emotional support, "that most recondite, private, secure and comfortable place for the self, where it takes shelter from the natural world, to where it belongs as its innermost shelter, and where it addresses the world and the other, opening itself to transcendence" (Patrão Neves, 2018, 73).

Other forms of ambiguity arise in many of people's relationships with technologies in the home: cleaning robots or those that care for the elderly and children, home automation, surveillance and security gadgets or integrated platforms are opportunities to a safer, more comfortable humane life, but they also carry difficulties, risks and threats. The multiplication of the digital media is an opportunity to open up to the outside world, but it can also be a means of dispersion, or a lack of communication with those inside.

All this should not lead us to negative conclusions: the new technologies present in the home do not have to be *Terminator* or *Big Brother*; above all, they are opportunities for a better life. But they have a profound influence on behaviour and attitudes. That is why it is important that, in its future development, the problems that may arise are taken into account. The experts who design and develop machines and programs must be aware of the social function of the home – which is a place of rest, a nucleus of privacy, a place of learning for life, work and care, and so on – and try to avoid dangers such as isolation, loss of sense of belonging, security and privacy, fragmentation of home life, unfair treatment of some groups, lack of transparency, loss of autonomy (especially the most vulnerable: children and elderly) and many others.

The chapters of this book

"The Digital Home" is a safe place where we live, play, learn, earn, and develop the skills to care about other human beings. It is both a real and virtual space where families make healthy and responsible choices so that we can thrive together.

Thus begins Chapter 2, entitled "Digital Home: The missing element for a people-centered digital future". In it, Mei Lin Fung and Deborah Gale aim to define "what we want a digital family home to mean – when digital technology can now be embedded in every aspect of human life and when all the 'instants' in our lives seem to be encased in a digital wrapper". The authors invite the readers to reimagine the future of the home by examining the problems of the past, the challenges of the present and the opportunities of the future, under the lens of people, markets, regulators and the global system. From the point of view of people, the main challenge of the home at the present time is to protect it from the invasion of digital technologies, due to the impacts they have on mental health, the relationships between work and home and gender dynamics. From the perspective of business, regulators and communities, the main challenge is the decentralization of power that information technologies enable, but do not guarantee. And from the point of view of governments and societies, the future opens opportunities for cooperation to protect rights and make digital literacy accessible to all.

Chapter 3, entitled "Artificial intelligence-empowered technology in the home", provides an overview of the opportunities and challenges that AI presents for the home. Matilde Santos and Francesca Toni explain what is the impact of AI in the home and how its inhabitants benefit from AI along two dimensions: management of the home (including smart devices and domestic robots, which autonomously carry out household chores, and connected devices like smart sensors) and knowledge enrichment (including information gathering and question answering through linguistic interaction with humans). They discuss the challenges of AI at home, such as uncertainty about future developments, lack of explainability and standardization, and problems of communication and relationship, security, autonomy and privacy. And they list some helpful principles for ordering AI use at home, such as human agency and oversight, robustness and safety, privacy, transparency, diversity, intergenerational well-being and accountability.

In Chapter 4 entitled "Contested homes in the age of the cloud: The changing socio-spatial dynamics of family living and care for older people in the 21st century", Mohamed Gamal Abdelmonem faces two changes that are taking place in our environment and that affect the identity, meaning, practice and experience of the home: the changing demographics, with substantial increase of ageing population, and the encroachment of technologies in the way home functions on daily basis. The spatial configuration of the house is not a given, but is continually rebuilt according to the needs and changing their shape, uses and relationships, mainly depending on the stages of life. Digital technologies, integrated into the smart home, present new risks, challenges and opportunities in dialogue with people's lifestyles, generating engagement that is increasingly social and emotional and less spatial. The chapter also explores the role of embedded digital technologies in domestic operations and discusses the characters of AI at home: embedded, interconnected, adaptive, personalized, context aware, anticipatory and interactive. The chapter is enriched with two European research projects that looked at assistive technologies for older people, prior to the COVID-19 pandemic, that offer good insights on the readiness of European societies to help and support older people living independently at home.

Chapter 5 entitled "Homes as human–robot ecologies: An epistemological inquiry on the domestication of robots" deals with the integration of domestic robots in the home. The subject has been widely covered in the technical literature, but the author (Luisa Damiano) offers a different, epistemological view of the subject. Robots and platforms operationalize hypotheses about the human mind when it interacts with its environment (in this case, technology); these hypotheses are embedded in robots and in their design, installation and integration processes in the home so that the epistemological point of view that we have about the mind–technology relationship influences our way of understanding the domesticity of robots, and even the same conception of the human mind. Professor Damiano discusses the role of innovative robotic platforms, which spans from robotic furniture to autonomous agents co-inhabiting humans' domestic spaces based on "peer-to-peer" interaction skills. The chapter is divided into three parts. The first part is a brief survey of the work on domestic robots; these are understood as consumer products and their integration into people's homes is supported by theoretical frameworks describing the target domestic environments as "human–robot ecologies". The second part discusses the main related views of the mind–technology interaction grounded in the extended mind hypothesis and in the radically embodied characterization of mind. Based on the critical analysis of the implications of these frameworks, the third part takes position in favour of radical embodiment approaches, and advocates the urgency of theoretical and applicative endeavours articulating the ongoing process of domestication of robots around the "ecological" value of interconnection.

In Chapter 6 entitled "Homes through the design shift in the digital age", Ioana Ocnarescu and Dominique Sciamma give voice to design, understood both as science and art, that tries to make the world liveable, uniting the physical and material dimension with the psychological, cognitive, emotional, cultural and symbolic. Design is a bridge between the abstraction of research and the tangible requirements of real life, which is thought and action. The chapter presents the operationalization of the notion of robots as social connectors in domestic environments. The "speculative design" focuses on human–robot interaction; the "experience design" changes the focus to a broader and human-centred framework based on the human–[robot]–human interaction, inside and outside the home. The authors make a brief historical review of design throughout three ages: the Age of Making, the rational organization of things to improve people's quality of life; the Age of Having, with the emphasis on manipulating desires to make "the essential beautiful and the beautiful essential"; and the Age of Being, when users are considered critical, thinking people; this is the age of homogenization and, at the same time, of differentiation and of the continuous transformation of objects. The chapter studies the design shift, "from shape to function, from function to interaction, and from interaction to relation", through the history of two museum exhibitions on design, developed between 1950 and today, in which it is observed how the organization of the home has changed. Designers come into play as experimenters about what it can mean to live with smart technologies, playing with the interaction of people with the objects with which they live. In other words, research on robots becomes an opportunity to rethink how we live.

There is an abundant literature on the impact of automation and AI on work. In Chapter 7 entitled "Automation, the home and work", Stephen Davies and Maria Sophia Aguirre summarize the main currents of that literature and note that these studies mostly ignore the home. This derives from a blind spot of contemporary economics, which is the way it values paid employment at the expense of unpaid work, which mostly takes place within the home. This dominant approach also ignores the temporal nature of human experience and identity, taking as a model the middle age successful professional, ignoring the role of the home as an organizer of the distribution of efforts and results throughout life and the ways in which, because of that, the home and the work that takes place within it fit into the rest of economic life. The current economic model on work also omits factors such as food, childcare, the elderly and the sick, leisure and social activity as relational activities, which take place within the home. Technology is not exogenous, but results from the model of person, family and society that one has and, consequently, from the public policies and the private actions that are applied. Putting the home at the centre of thinking about automation and its impacts generates a range of new questions and leads to conclusions, however tentative, that would otherwise not be reached. The impact of AI will ultimately depend on how it affects the way people choose to live their lives.

Mia Mikic and Joy Malala explore in Chapter 8, entitled "The impact of artificial intelligence on the future of work", the nature of digital frontier technologies, mainly automation, machine learning and AI, and their impact on the home through employment and the nature of work, not only in developed economies but also in emerging and developing economies. They study the various channels of influence of technologies on work, mainly through productivity. Increased production has the effect of making paid work more casual and irregular as it reduces transaction costs and therefore the need for long-term and stable employment contracts. Furthermore, the automation of repetitive tasks has changed the demand for skills, which are rendered redundant as machines take over other analytical functions. Automation is decreasing the share of income flowing to labour so that the growth in aggregate income may be accompanied by greater inequality. The final impact on households will also depend on the availability of the necessary skills and the weight of the informal sectors in the economy, in which technological progress is much more uncertain; and the impact on other household services (transport, mobility, banking, education, energy, wealth, etc.), on security, on domestic violence, etc. The authors conclude that AI and automation are likely to be beneficial for the formation and stability of homes among professional and educated people, but not so among less educated and skilled households, which creates challenges for policymakers, mainly in technology transition policies, education, skills development and innovation.

Several chapters mention the ethical problems that appear when applying digital technologies in the home; Chapter 9, entitled "Ethics and digital technologies in the home", deals with this topic in more detail. In it, Antonio Argandoña emphasizes that ethics applies to people, not to things; therefore, it is the designers, producers, distributors, regulators and users who have the moral responsibility for the content and use of the programs and machines. Technology is a mediator in the relationship between people and things, which facilitates the human presence in the world, but also focuses and conditions the way we understand reality. Programs and machines are not moral agents: they are accountable, but not responsible because they have no intentions, meaning, wishing or wanting, and they are not consciously aware of their decisions. The chapter reviews the main ethical problems of technologies in the home: centrality of the person, security, comfort, privacy, fairness, impartiality, transparency, autonomy, freedom and sociability; it explains the role of ethical norms or principles in the elaboration and use of digital technologies in the home, and proposes the interdisciplinary collaboration of those involved in their elaboration and use, going from an "ethics by design" to a "pro-ethical design" in all stages of the process.

Note

1   www.iso.org/standard/55890.html (accessed 26 July 2020).

References

Abdelmonem, M.G. and Argandoña, A. (2020). Home and Care in a Changing Society. In M.A. Abdelmonem and A. Argandoña, eds., *People, Care and Work in the Home*. Abingdon, UK: Routledge, pp. 1–16.

Aldrich, F.K. (2003). Smart Homes: Past, Present and Future. In R. Harper, ed., *Inside the Smart Home*. London, UK: Springer, pp. 17–39. doi: 10.1007/1-85233-854-7_2.

Argandoña, A. (2018). The Home: Multidisciplinary Reflections. In A. Argandoña, ed., *The Home: Multidisciplinary Reflections*. Cheltenham, UK: Edward Elgar, pp. 8–31. doi: 10.4337/9781786436573.00009.

Balta-Ozkan, N., Davidson, R., Bicket, M. and Whitmarsh, L. (2013). Social Barriers to the Adoption of Smart Homes. *Energy Policy*, 63, pp. 363–374. doi: 10.1016/j.enpol.2013.08.043.

Brussevich, M., Dabla-Norris, E. and Khalid, S. (2020). Who Will Bear the Brunt of Lockdown Policies? Evidence from Tele-Workability Measures across Countries. IMF Working Paper No. 20/88. Washington, DC: International Monetary Fund.

Buttimer, A. and Seamon, D. (2015). *The Human Experience of Space and Place*. 2nd edn. London, UK: Routledge. doi=10.4324/9781315684192.

Coeckelbergh, M. (2012). Can We Trust Robots? *Ethics and Information Technology*, 14(1), pp. 53–60. doi: 10.1007/s10676-011-9279-1.

Coskun, A., Kaner, G. and Bostan, I. (2018). Is Smart Home a Necessity or a Fantasy for the Mainstream User? A Study on Users' Expectations of Smart Household Appliances. *International Journal of Design*, 12(1), pp. 7–20.

Cuba, L. and Hummon, D.M. (1993). A Place to Call Home: Identification with Dwelling, Community, and Region. *The Sociological Quarterly*, 34(1), pp. 111–131. doi: 10.1111/j.1533-8525.1993.tb00133.x.

Dautenhahn, K. (2018). Human Robot Interaction. In *The Encyclopedia of Human-Computer Interaction*. 2nd edn. Interaction Design Foundation. doi: 10.5555/2826087.

d'Entremont, A. (2018). Spatial Relationality and Domesticity: Reality and Functions of the Home from a Human Geography Perspective. In A. Argandoña, ed., *The Home: Multidisciplinary Reflections*. Cheltenham, UK: Edward Elgar, pp. 163–176. doi: 10.4337/9781786436573.00021.

Fox O'Mahony, L. (2013). The Meaning of Home: From Theory to Practice. *International Journal of Law and Built Environment*, 5(2), pp. 156–171. doi: 10.1108/IJLBE-11-2012-0024.

Goodrich, M.A. and Schultz, A.C. (2007). Human-Robot Interaction: A Survey. *Foundations and Trends® in Human-Computer Interaction*, 1(3), pp. 203–275. doi: 10.1561/1100000005.

Graham, L.T., Gosling, S.D and Travis, C.K. (2015). The Psychology of Home Environments: A Call for Research on Residential Space. *Perspectives on Psychological Science*, 10(3), 346–356. doi: 10.1177/1745691615576761.

Gram-Hanssen, K. and Darby, S.J. (2018). 'Home Is Where the Smart Is'? Evaluating Smart Home Research and Approaches against the Concept of Home. *Energy Research and Social Science*, 37, pp. 94–101. doi: 10.1016/j.erss.2017.09.037.

Hargreaves, T., Wilson, C. and Hauxwell-Baldwin, R. (2018). Learning to Live in a Smart Home. *Building Research & Information*, 46(1), pp. 127–139. doi: 10.1080/09613218.2017.1286882.

Highmore, B. (2011). *Ordinary Lives: Studies in the Everyday*. London, UK: Routledge.

IFR – International Federation of Robotics (2017). Executive Summary – World Robotics (Service Robots) 2017. *World Robotic Report – Executive Summary.* Frankfurt: International Federation of Robotics.

Karjalainen, P.T. (1993). House, Home and the Place of Dwelling. *Scandinavian Housing and Planning Research*, 10, 65–74. doi: 10.1080/02815739308730324.

Leenes, R. and Lucivero, F. (2014). Laws on Robots, Laws by Robots, Laws in Robots: Regulating Robot Behaviour by Design. *Law, Innovation and Technology*, 6(2), pp. 193–220. doi: 10.5235/17579961.6.2.193.

Leppënen, S. and Jokinen, M. (2003). Daily Routines and Means of Communication in a Smart Home. In R. Harper, ed., *Inside the Smart Home*. London, UK: Springer-Verlag, pp. 207–225. doi: 10.1007/1-85233-854-7_11.

Miller, D., ed. (2001). *Home Possessions: Material Culture behind Closed Doors*. Oxford, UK: Berg.

Patrão Neves, M.C. (2018). Self and Others: Home as a Cradle of a Non-Violent Relationship. In A. Argandoña, ed., *The Home: Multidisciplinary Reflections*. Cheltenham, UK: Edward Elgar, pp. 57–76. doi: 10.4337/9781786436573.00012.

Urquhart, L., Reedman-Flint, D. and Leesakul, N. (2019). Responsible Domestic Robotics: Exploring Ethical Implications of Robots in the Home. *Journal of Information, Communication and Ethics in Society*, 17(2), pp. 246–272. doi: 10.1108/JICES-12-2018-0096.

Verbeek, P.P. (2006). Materializing Morality. Design Ethics and Technological Mediation. *Science, Technology and Human Values*, 31(3), pp. 361–380. doi: 10.1177/0162243905285847.

Wilson, C., Hargreaves, T. and Hauxwell-Baldwin, R. (2015). Smart Homes and Their Users: Analysis and Key Challenges. *Personal and Ubiquitous Computing*, 19(2), pp. 463–476. doi: 10.1007/s00779-014-0813-0-

Digital Home

The missing element for a people-centred digital future

Mei Lin Fung and Deborah Gale

Introduction to the Digital Home

The Digital Home is a safe place where we live, play, learn, earn, and develop the skills to care about other human beings. It is both a real and virtual space where families make healthy and responsible choices so that we can thrive together. At this pivotal time, we must define what we want a digital family home to mean – when digital technology can be embedded in every aspect of human life and when all the "instants" in our lives seem to be encased in a digital wrapper.

> The joy of life discovered by the Greeks is not a profane type of enjoyment: it reveals the bliss of existing, of sharing — even figuratively — in the spontaneity of life and the majesty of the world. Like so many others before and after them, the Greeks learned that the surest way to escape from time is to exploit the wealth, at first sight impossible to suspect, of the lived instant.
>
> (As quoted in *Myth and Religion in Mircea Eliade* (Routledge 2002) by Douglas Allen, p. 90)

Technology has the potential to be pervasive from birth to death, for each of us. We face critical choices about how we let technology in, and via such addictive channels, how global institutions, ideas and insights enter unfiltered into our homes and change our families. The home is not just where people live. Humans learn what it is to be part of a larger society by observing, listening and interacting with family. Technology, where it is allowed in and where it is affordable, has become an integral part of every formative interactive relationship. Babies, adolescents, adults and elders are now wandering, as innocents might naively roam, on an ever-expanding and mostly unknown and unmapped digital frontier.

By 2019, half of the world's people were connected to the Internet. Geographic and cultural constraints forcing different cultures, languages, religions and customs to evolve separately are being bridged and broken down. Disruption in politics, business, health and education, transportation and housing, entertainment and the military is only now being recognized as both opportunity and threat to centuries-old human traditions and culture. The downsides of unrestrained technological growth are emerging: hate speech, bullying, fanning of tribal conflicts, including genocide in Myanmar, election fraud, loss of privacy and unchecked claims on personal data. As social, economic, legal, religious and cultural norms loosen their grip, new and increasingly unforeseeable risks, dangers and threats emerge, even as a few pioneers seize their chance to benefit themselves more than most. Positive and negative impacts on families are increasing and accelerating.

Home is where we get our first and deepest connections to other people and where we learn how to become a responsible person first within a family, then a community, then a country and then as a citizen of the world. Thus, the human family context of the digital home must now take centrestage and this section highlights the critical, civilizing function of the home. Meanwhile, convenient domestic appliances are extracting a formidable price in terms of privacy and safety.[1] A "Digital Wild West" has emerged where baby monitors connected to the Internet were taken control of by "bad actors". Concurrently, digital vendors rarely address diverse needs across ages and abilities and digital exclusion accelerates. This results in a few being more "digitally augmented" and savvy than others, outside and now within their own homes.

Domus sua cuique est tutissimum refugium translates to "every person's house is her/his refuge".[2] The human need for a place to be nurtured and grow, safely within a family, is being sorely tested. "Home" is audaciously evolving through a series of uninformed purchasing decisions by people viewed merely as consumers, rather than as stewards responsible for assuring the so far unbroken link of human evolution. Driven by profit-seeking, products and services are offered without sufficient consideration of their unintended consequences. Making the digital home the new building block of civilization will necessitate designating gateways for digital entry of trusted actors: remotely situated humans, remotely operated robots and "apps" also designed and distributed remotely. Digital design that can earn trust requires finding new ways to make participation in the shaping of the digital home everyone's responsibility.

In this chapter we will re-imagine the possible pathways to a better future for the digital home by examining the past conditioning, present challenges and future opportunities through the lens of individuals, regulators and commerce, and global systems.

The Digital Home: Individuals

In this section we will examine the evolution of the digital home.

Past: The origin of "home"

It was not until the 17th and 18th centuries that the division between personal and public spaces was formally defined, fuelled by the Industrial Revolution. Before then, most people were born, worked and died in the same place, and home represented the intersection of habitation, community and continuity.[3] When the concept of a workplace office was first conceived, it changed the dynamic between workplace and home forever. Home was no longer purely a function of birthplace. At the same time, a substantive mindset shift occurred with the purpose of work becoming the acquisition, maintenance and embellishment of the home.[4]

Modern life has therefore given us two meanings of home: a house in which to live and a place to feel attached. As the two meanings evolved with the emergence of the nuclear family, they became largely indistinguishable. In the past, the home was a retreat, a refuge and a place to build community, establish traditions and rest. In the digital home, these lines are becoming blurred and we are wrestling with the implications.

Present: A day in the life of the Digital Home

Let's run through a day in the life of Mei Lin Fung who lives in the heart of Silicon Valley in downtown Palo Alto, outside Stanford University. Living one of the most globally connected lives at this time, she is encountering perils and realizing that if home is to remain a refuge, it must *be guarded better*.[5] Technology has begun to change the daily rhythms of life. The counter to these extensive perils are the opportunities they present to individuals in helping them navigate their daily life with ease, stay connected to the world around them and play an active role in the development of technology (see Table 2.1).

Today, the digital home conflates the activities of daily living with being permanently attached to an external source. The digital home provides an entirely new dimension for creativity and utility for families and individuals. This new arena provides new economic and social opportunities for large groups of people who have hitherto been excluded from the global economy.

Next, we will explore how the digital home is already having impacts on the mental health of its residents, how working from home (WFH) is further blurring the lines between work life and home life and the significant impacts digitalization is having on women, their work and their place in the home.

Mental health and the Digital Home

A digital home on a desert island does not sound attractive to most of us. Human beings are social creatures – we see, hear, touch, smell and taste. Full interaction with another human being brings joy to our organic selves that

Table 2.1 Some perils of technology

Perils	Some examples
Peril 1 – We're easily disconnected or "locked out" of the Digital Home	Last night, I could not connect to Google, Amazon or Netflix. I didn't know why; stuck not knowing where to turn for help
Peril 2 – We experience fraudulence within the Digital Bank	A charge for "Hyperbaric Treatment" appears on the credit card statement. I did not sign for this
Peril 3 – Our personal information is unsafe	To search and make purchases, I have to reveal my identity, unaware of how information is protected and shared
Peril 4 – We aren't educated on the Internet of Things	My washing machine/dryer can send messages to their manufacturer. I don't know what they send or receive
Peril 5 – Our applications never sleep and work in unknown, mysterious ways	My mobile phone is connected to many applications and functions are in the background. What do they do?
Peril 6 – There is no user manual on the digital frontier	User-friendly instruction manuals are not available. We are learning by trial and error ignorant, too, of the digital dangers
Peril 7 – We lose power – of the electrical kind	Electrical power outages mean no credit cards can be used and more. We are too vulnerable to interruptions in power
Peril 8 – Who is collecting our data and who has access to it?	Doctors contract with information technology (IT) shops to maintain patient health records without trustworthy checking
Peril 9 – There is no protocol for empathy or compassion	Rules and regulations about accessing data do not prioritize empathy. Inhumane processes and procedures are increasing
Peril 10 – AI in fintech reproduces historical racist, gender bias	Financial service products are not fit-for-purpose and are trained on biased data, reproducing the bias and prolonging inequality
Peril 11 – Valuing profits over people	Corporate profit as society's overriding priority benefits the already wealthy at the expense of everyone else on earth
Peril 12 – Tech has no place for love, caring and empathy	Tech design leaves out small human gestures, caring, nurturing, compassion, love, meaning and empathy
Peril 13 – Elderly and vulnerable folks' needs are ignored	All people's needs could be richly met with technology: Tech designers are blind to this, designing for "people like me"
Peril 14 – There's little process for merging old and new technologies	Our abilities to merge old and new technologies are inadequate
Peril 15 – We sign contracts blindly	Click-to-agree contracts offer no alternatives: It would take someone 250 hours a year to read all US digital contracts

is irreplaceable. While the ultimate connection may be between a mother and her baby, a group of people playing music or singing together in a rock band, an orchestra or a jazz band allow the participants to reach an ineffable, transcendent feeling of joyous connection. Our digital world connects us in a way that has never historically been possible while also isolating us. We are increasingly devoid of in-person interaction both socially and professionally.

Notably, there are more people living alone today, many by choice. American census data from 2014 shows that 28% of homes comprised a single person, up from 13% in 1960.[6] This decline in social connections has been linked to a rise in depression and suicide. Older people, digitally excluded, feel even more abandoned by the society which they helped to build.

Isolation experienced by those living far from neighbours in rural communities is another shared problem. It also affects those with special needs and the physically and mentally challenged. Being able to remotely interact via video screens, with geographically distant people, is an improvement but is not the same experience. New technologies creating shapes, smells, touch and sound already exist, but such applications are not yet widely available. Compounding this problem, capital markets have shown limited interest in digital home opportunities, a missed growth opportunity with broad applicability to potentially benefit many people.

Then, there is hate speech, a regular feature of social media discourse. Hiding in anonymity, people's propensity to type without any filter is heightened. One research study suggests that the dopamine hit from Twitter or checking emails is stronger than cigarettes or alcohol.[7] Dopamine, a neurotransmitter, helps control the brain's reward and pleasure centres. It is argued that because giving into media desires over others bears less obvious consequences, people lose more time and social contact to reliance on the Internet.[8] This is an insidious and advancing problem impacting mental health. It is also a vulnerability that is being exploited by cyber criminals and those undermining public trust through misinformation.

To this point, Tim Berners-Lee has become increasingly outspoken about the impacts of individual disempowerment and what he refers to as cracks in human optimism. He maintains that social media are still being used to propagate hate.

> If you put a drop of love into Twitter it seems to decay but if you put in a drop of hatred you feel it actually propagates much more strongly. And you wonder: "Well is that because of the way that Twitter as a medium has been built?"[9]

In April 2018, following a torrent of criticism, Twitter embarked on a research project to make users more aware of the rules that promote civilised discussion.[10] In May 2019 after Facebook Live, the company's streaming service broadcast the mass shooting of 51 people in two New Zealand mosques; Facebook VP of Integrity Guy Rosen[11] wrote:

> From now on, anyone who violates our most serious policies will be restricted from using Live for set periods of time — for example 30 days — starting on their first offence. For instance, someone who shares a link to a statement from a terrorist group with no context will now be immediately blocked from using Live for a set period of time.

Addressing the mental health opportunities and implications of the digital home must be at the forefront of progress and innovation. Our lives, literally, depend on it.

Life and work collide in the Digital Home

What the mobile phone has enabled as new ways of working – the concept of on-demand work – has also furthered the blurring of lines between home and workplace.

In so doing, the digital home has already overlapped with the digital workplace. We are at the beginning of a major transition as work shifts to the digital home and the digital home shifts to wherever its potential increases. The implications for technological enhancements in transportation are enormous, as is the transformation of the built environment.

As traditional employment is complemented with on-demand work, the financial basis of the family's income is also diversifying. In turn, shifts in sources of income make it necessary for people to participate in lifelong learning, keeping skills relevant for changing marketplace demands.

> The Internet has already become the most important infrastructure of the world. And that's just the beginning. Soon it will also be the infrastructure of all of our other infrastructures. The airlines, the container ships, the power grids, telecommunication networks — they are all becoming increasingly dependent on a stable, secure and open global Internet.
>
> (Carl Bildt, former Prime Minister of Sweden[12])

Though digital nomads often come from developed countries and benefit from taxpayer-funded education, health, and social programs throughout their lives (and expect to in the future when they return to their home countries), they rarely feel an obligation to give back. Similar to tech libertarians, they minimize their tax burden by finding jurisdictions or countries with the lowest tax rate and, depending on the laws of their country of citizenship, move often enough that they aren't obliged to pay income tax.[13]

Concurrently, when cities and governments fail to invest in public housing, and the cost of living increases faster than wages, the possibility of remote work at first seems very attractive: to live in a place with a lower cost of living while being paid at a wage that is higher than the local norm is unsustainable.

When governments do not provide the social supports that are common in the developed countries, inequity between the haves and have-nots can be made even worse by those coming in to do remote work. Remote workers do not invest in building community, in being stewards of the place they are in. They take from those who have invested earlier, without feeling the responsibility to do the same for those who come after.

Women in the home and workplace

Women statistically live longer, make less per hour and spend more time out of the workforce than their male counterparts. Women have traditionally been homemakers and nurturers. In the United States of America (USA) today, single female homeownership exceeds that of single males by 17% to 7%.[14] This is all the more remarkable considering the persistent gender wage gap of over 20%. In the USA, 60% of the total wealth is concentrated in the hands of women, and globally the figure is 40%.[15] It has been estimated that over 80% of household expenditures are influenced by women.

Motherhood has traditionally had an isolating effect on women. Now that working women constitute over 47% of the workforce in the United Kingdom (UK) and 46% in the USA[16], the debate rages between stay-at-home mothers and working mothers in terms of the quality of infant care and how that impacts future development into children and young adults. New research suggests that it is not just the mother who is essential. The real need is that the people caring for the child are committed to positively communicating with the child. Caregiver sensitivity becomes the critical determinant of how a child learns to control their emotions, enabling them to operate properly in a social context.[17] This research is important because it liberates women from the guilt of leaving their children, while at the same time highlights the dearth of high-quality child care.

As rates of women participating in the workforce increase, the primary increase is among married women.[18] In 1900 the average US household spent 58 hours a week on housework (cleaning, cooking and doing laundry). In 1975 this fell to 18 hours and in 2015 it was under 8 hours given increased use of household appliances.[19] It has been estimated that if the work stay-at-home mothers provide was done in the business world, they would be paid an annual salary of up to $162K in 2018.[20] This is significant because stay-at-home mothers typically forfeit their chance to earn pensionable earnings.

With access to the power of the mobile phone, women have untapped powers as stewards for the families of the future. This puts women on an entirely different footing. Women who never would have been able to connect now have the ability to do so. This self-knowledge can breed confidence, which in turn imbues a sense of agency which did not previously exist. This, however, is not linear. It is dependent upon the degree of digital access and fluency as well as the woman's desire/impetus to employ this newfound agency.

Future: Can we utilize untapped resources and create an inclusive digital future?

Networked improvement communities

Even as the notion of an Internet of the people, by the people, for the people[21] becomes increasingly realizable, we need to develop new rules of the road for a world where information is decentralized and policy and decision-making can be participative. Current policies operate at a government level, business or organization level or at the individual level. The complexity of issues confronting an individual is overwhelming today and getting worse. The family unit is an entity from which we have traditionally drawn strength over generations, where the whole is greater than the sum of its parts. When faced with challenges at an individual level, when responding to threats and disasters, we have come together as families, in homes, and in the community – because together we find we can do better. Our lives, our families, our homes, workplaces and where we socialize are becoming increasingly digital. In the face of the common challenges, we need to develop a tactical response to design a future we want.

The networked improvement community (NIC) is an intentionally designed network of diverse stakeholders who come together in a purpose-driven, action-oriented and practitioner-led endeavour to make capability improvements. The roots may be traced to the 1950's ideas of W. Edward Deming and Dr. Douglas Engelbart. Deming gave us the Plan-Do-Study-Act cycle known as the Deming Wheel. Engelbart's work added a network information infrastructure. The NIC is the organizational structured information and coordination framework that unleashes and rapidly diffuses innovation with actionable results in a cycle – in effect, improving through improvisation. The following are the typical attributes of an NIC[22]:

1.   An engine for innovation through focus on specific objectives and actionable results
2.   Architecture for broad participation
3.   Not capital intensive
4.   Reveals bright spots and improvement targets from broadly sourced data
5.   Rapid learning through idea sharing and comparing results
6.   Accelerated adoption of innovations through emulation among network participants
7.   Easily measured success metrics – did network meet its target objective?

According to the Carnegie Foundation, which has embraced the NIC as the cornerstone of its educational reform initiative, some of the most successful efforts to learn, identify and solve problems occur within NICs. The Carnegie Foundation calls NICs "communities of common accomplishment."[23] They can be applied to the disruption and dilemmas of the Digital Home.

The NIC is a particularly valuable improvement paradigm when growth at scale cannot be realized unless a diverse community of stakeholders adopt shared concepts and practices. Digital Home NICs can engage communities in purposeful efforts, jointly testing and validating ideas, spreading the successful.

Tapping women to step forward in leadership

The rapid technological changes that we are facing require more diverse, inclusive workplaces to successfully and continually innovate. At the same time, the gender divide is growing in the tech industry. As the Fourth Industrial Revolution[24] is reshaping our world, transforming it socially, economically and politically, women have been excluded and are under-represented in leadership circles:

- Women hold 26% of computing jobs, only one in five senior management positions in tech firms and just 5% of leadership roles in the ICT industry.
- Female computer programmers are paid, on average, 28% less than males.
- Globally, the founder of a digitally driven business is five times more likely to be a man than a woman and, in many places, the ratio is closer to ten-to-one.
- Code developed by women is viewed as superior to that developed by men when gender is not revealed and as inferior when gender is known.
- Internationally, only 18% of computer science graduates are women and the numbers have fallen since 2000, or remain low in most countries.[25]

Despite some progress and efforts to integrate gender equality into national ICT policies, women are still less likely to have digital skills, take up formal computer science studies or hold technical or leadership roles in tech organizations. The profile of a technologist or tech chief executive officer (CEO) remains decidedly male, even though many women and girls are producing remarkable products and processes. Women are severely under-represented in board, strategy, design, sales and operational leadership circles.[26] These societal imbalances must be considered and corrected going forward.

The digital frontier: Regulators, businesses and communities

In this section, we will discuss how information sharing, starting with the printing press, has brought us to our present-day impasse regarding data privacy and how we will need to work together to ensure that data privacy can coexist with the global demands for information sharing.

Past: The evolution of information sharing

The introduction of the printing press in Europe led directly to the separation of Christianity into Catholicism and Protestantism. The Reformation allowed for widespread literacy when a much more affordable printed Bible replaced the handwritten version and became available in other languages. This eliminated dependence on priests and their control of this important information flow. Up to this point, it was only available in Latin.

After the Gutenberg press was introduced, the institutions of the day took time to change the social norms, and implicit beliefs. The telegraph was invented and in 1865 the forerunner institution of the International Telecommunication Union (ITU) was started in Paris, France.[27] In 1947 it became a specialized institution of the United Nations covering the whole Information Communications Technology sector, from digital broadcasting to the Internet, and from mobile technologies to three-dimensional (3D) TV. An organization of public–private partnerships, the ITU currently has a membership of 193 countries and some 700 private-sector entities. Coordination of regulation and protocols is increasingly challenging. This transition has taken decades for some institutions. We are presented with a challenge today. How do we adapt when our institutions and laws cannot protect our safety, political processes or the health or education of our children?[28]

The Digital Home NIC could be the global network that brings together regulators, policymakers, businesses and communities in a lab for a reality testing digitization affecting families and homes.

Present: Digital power decentralizes financial, political and academic power

> The longer we wait, the further we will fall behind.
>   (UN Secretary-General António Guterres[29])

Today, eBay, Amazon, Alibaba and Tencent are global marketplaces, connecting online buyers and sellers. Airbnb connects hosts and visitors enabling many more people to travel less expensively and hosts to earn income from sharing their homes. These are exciting and enabling technologies, but they are not equally accessible or regulated. For example, the laws for hotels that forbid discrimination, and require handicapped access, are not applied to Airbnb hosts.[30] In China, the payment ecosystem of WeChat is so pervasive that cash is not accepted by vendors. In a recent survey, 70% of Internet users in China polled found cash unnecessary.[31]

In 2018, suggestions for a Digital Bretton Woods have emerged.[32] Regulators for banking and the regulators for Telecom/Internet are strictly separated, but with digital money flowing through digital wallets "held" on mobile phones, the regulators are realizing that frameworks for joint regulation of digital money are urgently needed.

We are in an era of disruption and change to many foundational institutions. Social networks are disrupting politics, governments and international treaties and organizations including the World Bank, International Monetary Fund (IMF), Interpol and the UN agencies, each of which is separately pursuing digital innovation. The United Nations (UN) Secretary-General set up the UN High-Level Panel on Digital Cooperation and released its first report in June 2019.[33] The UN Secretary-General urged an "urgent and open debate between governments, the private sector, civil society, and others on how we move forward together safely in the age of digital interdependence".

He also expressed caution when he noted that the United Nations is "unprepared and needs to catch up", to address the disruption that digital technology can cause and the threats it can bring to the UN's mission. "The international community is failing to meet its responsibilities. The systems for the governance of digital technology are old, fragmented and reactive. The longer we wait to update these systems, the further we will fall behind".

This widespread lack of awareness and understanding of the impact of technology and the subset of artificial intelligence (AI) means that leaders are making decisions that can unwittingly have grave consequences for the governments[34], businesses, customers and the communities where they operate.

The two primary new challenges that AI gives to organizations are firstly that algorithms must be protected against manipulation by adversaries. If an adversary manipulates AI algorithms, it also manipulates the results and that is a problem. Secondly, data used for AI must be protected. If an adversary manipulates data, then, of course, the results are going to be wrong. Both of these require protection. Building up the security of enterprises is fundamental and requires ongoing extensive monitoring. In diversifying and decentralizing power structures within our communities and business landscapes, we have also opened ourselves up to unforeseen and unprecedented complications.

In addition, to this category of new AI risks is the complexity of the ethics surrounding AI. Bob Gourley, chief technical officer (CTO) and co-founder of OODA LLC, had this to say:

> We have seen example after example of AI that's fielded, then produces results that unintentionally are biased. It's a very serious security concern that increases risk. It's the same with ethics around AI. How do you know that your AI is performing ethically over time, if it's a machine learning algorithm that changes over time? Both are serious new risks.
>
> (Bob Gourley, 24 May 2019[35])

Future: What capacity and capabilities are we lacking that might help us respond better?

The knowledge that results from academic theory building may or may not develop capacity within a system. Douglas Engelbart, the founding father of information technology, whose inventions spread digital technology worldwide and who spent two-thirds of his career on this, noted this:

> [W]ith the useful cycle time of knowledge getting shorter and shorter, you're going to need to be coupling more closely with the rest of the world. This kind of networking stuff means that you can be part of a special new kind of knowledge conduit. For instance, there needs to be more of a constant connection between organizations and their user communities (...) It's like being in a vehicle going faster and faster through terrain that is rougher and rougher...and the vehicle has a very sluggish way of controlling where it is going. It is both sluggish and dumb, and the headlights don't shine very far in the future, so they don't show very much about what's coming. And it can't steer very well and there are barely brakes, and there is no reverse.[36]

While all these large-scale threats were in his focus, it is particularly attention-grabbing that he was warning us about the existential danger digital technology would pose to society and he passionately urged us to adopt a plan to protect humankind:

> It will be a survival issue for some countries and some companies, etc. But I'm also thinking of humanity. We just have to get smarter about the way we deal collectively with collective problems. So, if there's any chance, we should get going.[37]

At the World Summit on the Information Society (WSIS) in Geneva in April 2019, the high level Ministerial and Telecom regulatory Panel on Enabling Environment[38] recommended setting up an Innovation Lab Network to achieve the UN Sustainable Development Goals with interoperability. This would require integrated regulatory frameworks to provide enabling environments where people and businesses can flourish.

The final summary by the chair of the high-level panels at WSIS, His Excellency Mustafa Jabar, Minister of Posts, Telecom and Communication for Bangladesh, concluded: "[a]n integrated and citizen-centric framework that will support the digital transformation process and ensure digital identity is needed".

The Institute for Electrical and Electronic Engineers (IEEE) has a Standards Association arm which emerged to respond to the need for better self-regulation as electricity use became widespread. Hundreds of members of this global association came together in the IEEE Global Initiative on the Ethics of Autonomous and Intelligence Systems to develop the report on Ethically Aligned Design.[39] The ITU[40] has joined forces with the UN Foundation-funded Digital Impact Alliance[41] to create the Sustainable Development Goals Digital Investment Framework.[42]

The capacity to connect funding to projects that advance the UN Sustainable Development goals is necessary but not sufficient for us to achieve the promise of the Digital Home. Organizing ourselves so that human participation and human oversight are integral to the future of the digital home requires re-thinking how we invest in research, how we invest in business and how we modernize government. People must be at the centre of networks and frameworks that design the future digital home.

A digital world: Government and society

In this section, we will investigate the connection between information and power and pose questions that remain unanswered. The reality is that Internet protocols developed with US Military funding in 1974 initially allowed information to flow between academic and research institutions in the USA and then rapidly expanded globally. The implications are vast, and the questions raised are difficult. On our mobile phones right now, many of us have access to greater computing power than the technology that helped send people to the moon in 1969.[43] Does it matter that English is no longer the language of the Internet? What does it mean now that every supply chain for food, shelter and clothing is increasingly reliant upon data? And do we adopt the sense of urgency required to address digital exclusion and introduce regulated, ethical frameworks for data protection?[44]

Past: The origin of power

Top-down decision-making was necessary when information was scarce. Only the few, at the very top, could know enough of what was going on to make decisions for the rest. For example, in China, where culture has evolved over 6,000 years and despite enormous difference in wisdom, experience, knowledge, information and power, every person was expected to know the Five Virtues of Confucius by heart: *Li* (manners) considered the most important, *Ren* (kindness); *Xin* (loyalty), *Yi* (honesty) and *Zhi* (knowing the difference between right and wrong, moral knowledge).[45] Moral power in China since the time of Confucius became decentralized as a result, while political power remained firmly in the grasp of the Head of State – previously the Emperor, now the President.[46]

In Europe, monarchy prevailed until European immigrants to America, seeking a better life, fought for the right to govern themselves. They declared independence as the 13 United States of America. The US Constitution, developed by soldiers (Washington, Hamilton), at least one inventor (Franklin) and many lawyers (Jefferson, Madison)[47], laid the foundation for an educated citizenry with rights and responsibilities to govern as a democracy, with a careful balance of powers: the Executive branch, the Supreme Court and the Legislature. This participative basis of democracy was tested in the American Civil War 1860–1865, giving rise to a concept of Government of the People, by the People, for the People[48] articulated by Abraham Lincoln in the Gettysburg address and inspiring many other countries to follow suit. One hundred fifty years later, participative democracy is the political model for over half of the world's population.[49]

Present: Redefining language, systems and supply

The loss of language and culture

> In 2016, Rosa Andrade Ocagane, the last female speaker of the Amazonian language was murdered in Peru at age 67. She and her brother, Pablo — now Resígaro's last known speaker, making it one of the most endangered languages — were the children of a Resígaro mother and Ocaina father. They spoke their mother's language to honor her and were also among the last 40 speakers of Ocaina.[50]

Language and home are closely tied – the language you speak when growing up shapes your worldview. Yet of the 7,000 languages in the world, over half may go extinct in the 21st century. What will that do to the culture of the people who grew up in those homes and families? Decisions about what "character sets" Vodafone, Telefonica, Google, Alibaba, Tencent and Facebook support can lead to the next generation of speakers no longer wanting to learn the language of their birthplace, if they cannot use it to communicate over their mobile phones. The impact of these decisions on the diversity of cultures of the world and the loss of cultural history is not being considered in the economic decisions taking place in small conference rooms around the world.

We tend to think that English is the language of the Internet but that has been steadily declining over the past 20 years. Asian people dominate Internet use with over 2 billion users, Europe its closest rival with 705 million, Africa 645m, Latin America and the Caribbean 438 million and North America in fifth position with 345 million.[51] As of 2017, English continued to dominate at 25.4%, but Chinese followed closely at 19.3%.[52]

For Chinese users, there is also an interesting problem for some 60 million Chinese with "unusual characters" in their names. The Chinese government only recognizes 8,105 standard Chinese characters that are allowed to be used to register births. This disadvantages a large portion of the population. Millions are impacted, particularly ethnic minorities outside of the majority

Han Chinese, who represent 92% of the population.[53] This complicates very basic but essential components of life, including applying for credit cards, booking online flights or getting a social security number. This has serious consequences for keeping track of China's massive citizenry.

Research also highlights the fact that voice assistants are suppressing regional accents[54], and that children aged 7–9 years are more inclined to take direction from a robot and even accept an incorrect answer if provided by a robot. With the use of smartphones as "babysitters", keeping children occupied while adults are not able to nurture, we need protective measures to minimize risks to children during interactions with digital voices.[55] These basic, while complex, issues demand thoughtful consideration and response.

Agriculture and food systems in the digital world

As the Internet of Things (IoT) spreads, agriculture will be one of the major beneficiaries. In San Diego, a community of gleaners,[56] originally the people who gathered any produce left behind in fields after harvest, are "gleaning" fruits and vegetables from home gardens, then bringing them to targeted homeless shelters and other distribution points for the needy.[57] In an additional development, the information that can be tracked about food from farm to table to nurturing human life is now being tracked by technologies from the IoT. Here, trucks and pickers can arrive at the appropriate fields and time the harvest with greater efficiency.[58] The new technology, 5G,[59] will be 20 times faster and also provide a much greater sense of "instant" or real-time response.

Better methods for planting food and cooperatives for growing food also make it possible to grow food closer to the point of consumption, thereby enhancing nutritional benefit while reducing transportation and processing costs. This could not be more welcome. In 2015, the

> EPA estimated that more food in the US reached landfills and combustion facilities than any other single material in our everyday trash. This represented 22 percent of the total amount in landfills and 22 percent of the amount combusted with energy recovery.[60,61]

When food is not harvested in a timely manner, stored improperly and over-bought or oversold, the resulting wastage increases costs and at the same time those who could have been nurtured by food that had been sold at a lower price only suffer more.

There are also benefits for people with disabilities who can now enjoy gardening with design adaptations and special tools.[62] Improved methods for planting food, cooperatives for growing at home or in community allotments, make it possible to farm closer to the point of consumption. Not only does this reduce transportation and processing costs, but it also gives the housebound and others with varied disabilities a new pathway into productive living and community involvement.[63] As we continue to learn about loneliness and mindfulness, the more we can appreciate the positive impacts a community gardening programme can exert on everything from dietary choices to personal relationships and improvements in well-being.[64,65]

Supply chains in the digital world

Bruno Pieters, former art director at Hugo Boss, started the world's first 100% transparent luxury clothing brand, Honest By.[66] Pieters makes it possible for the public to know the provenance of every raw material, fabric and trim. This extends to publishing cost break-downs for each garment including his brand's retail mark-up.[67]

The technology blockchain, often described as a ledger for assuring transparency and accountability, is an exciting development but few people understand what it does, how it works or why it matters. One way to think about this is like a Google doc, something that multiple people can edit with a system that tracks when and who makes each edit, that no one can change.

Blockchains log transactions like the transfer of money, goods or services in a ledger. The ledger keeps a record of each blockchain transaction. That ledger is replicated and stored in the blockchain network, which right now resides on over 200,000 computers around the world. Blockchain is not owned by a single entity even though many people can work with blockchain, and this "decentralized ownership is what makes it tamper-proof in the sense that no one can alter it and then cover their tracks."[68] Why blockchain matters is that until now only large organizations or governments were capable of maintaining a ledger used by millions of people. Blockchain can be part of a human network that operates without the hierarchy or centralized authority that lies behind today's large organizations and governments.

There are many use cases, for example, clothing and housing and all have relevance in the digital home.[69] In these supply chains, components are brought together in intermediate products and later reach the endpoint as a piece of clothing, a house or a building. Blockchain can give all participants in the supply chain visibility into all the other parts of the supply chain. Like Pieter's Honest By, the value lies in transparency for the end consumer as well as for the people operating in the supply chain. This includes inventory control, shipping particulars, dates, and modes of transport, temperature and humidity readings in storage and transit; in fact, everything that could affect the quality of the end product. Transparency in the supply chain can help all producers create better products with less waste and less energy, which arrive on time, in the right condition and the right quantity.

Provenance[70] and SourceMap[71] are blockchain companies that work on ensuring that every fashion or beauty product has traceable, transparent origins and helps accomplish that with blockchain-based tamper-resistant record-keeping.

> SourceMap has developed a social network that allows everyone from the farmer, to the textile mill, to the cut-and-sew factory, to communicate directly with the brand that buys from them using Provenance's blockchain technology to verify those communications. The benefit arises from the fact that organic[72] or Fair Trade[73] certifications can't be faked; brands can't deny having worked with factories after news of human rights abuses[74]at certain factories surface and auditors can essentially trace any claim about a product straight back to the entity who first made that claim. And it can do all of this while keeping certain sensitive details — like someone's salary — private. Data privacy is a major concern for those looking to create radically transparent supply chains, without violating individuals' privacy.[75]

With respect to housing, the lack of affordable housing[76] for families in the USA and around the world has generated much hand wringing. This shortage is blamed for the homeless crisis as well as the anxieties that people encounter when they want to ensure that their families have safe, reliable shelter. Applying digital technology[77] to the construction industry could potentially contribute to better quality housing at lower costs.

Katerra, a modular construction project, has raised over $1 billion in venture funds[78] and is developing repeatable "kit-of-parts" designs which can be easily configured, constructed in offsite factories and, finally, integrated onsite. Using digital technology modelling building information (BIM) "recipes" or design scripts are produced for projects that plug into its global supply chain, integrating design and materials sourcing. Home buyers can look forward to the innovations in fashion being replicated in housing construction. One day, people can know the provenance of every material used in building their home.

Future: How do we build a foundation for global humanity to thrive?

Digital laws and regulations

When faced with the challenges of managing a global industrial revolution, it is imperative that individuals, businesses and governments are playing by the same rules, using common protocols.

> The scale, spread, and speed of change brought about by digital technology is unprecedented, and the current means and levels of international

cooperation are unequal to the challenge. Digital technologies make a significant contribution to the realization of the 2030 Agenda for Sustainable Development and cut uniquely across international boundaries, policy silos and professional domains. Cooperation across domains and across borders is therefore critical to realizing the full social and economic potential of digital technologies, mitigating the risks they pose, and curtailing any unintended consequences.

(United Nations High Level Panel on Digital Cooperation)

Convened by the UN Secretary-General and chaired by Melinda Gates and Jack Ma, this High-level Panel on Digital Cooperation[79] advanced proposals in 2019 to strengthen cooperation in the digital space among governments, the private sector, civil society, international organizations, academia, the technical community and other relevant stakeholders. To cooperate requires raising awareness about the transformative impact of digital technologies[80] across society and the economy by instigating public dialogue and discussion on how to ensure a safe and inclusive digital future for all. This requires taking into account cultural sensitivities and human rights norms for everyone.

Internet justice of the peace

As people are living substantial portions of their lives interfacing with digital ecosystems, people and governments alike are struggling to determine how to effectively translate the protections, rights and laws of the physical world into the digital world. Individuals and communities across the planet are unable to have responsive representation with regard to their digital rights and freedoms. Most countries lack robust data protection law and a corresponding centralized enforcement body. Even where these exist, we have yet to see institutions accountable to the health of digital communities. To analogize to the healthcare context, while emergency response (ER) mechanisms for egregious digital harms exist in some countries, virtually nowhere do we see clinics capable of administering digital preventative care.

The Justice of the Peace in the UK provides an example of an institution created to allow new law to take root among people in disparate regions of the country. It is worth considering what we may be able to glean from this model in attempts to consider how to consolidate top-down (legal-driven) and bottom-up (community norms-driven) structures for data governance and well-being of digital communities.[81]

Digital literacy for everyone

The potential of every human being is a precious asset for humanity, and the homes of the future should be engines for harnessing that potential. This should be true for all who live in the home: male and female, parent and child, the old and the very young, and able and less able.

The 17 UN Sustainable Developments Goals for 2030[82] require global reminder so that we can all play our part in reaching them. Digital technology will play a key role in identifying, teaching and learning the skills necessary for people to be full participants in this essential humanitarian endeavour.

The education of citizens of the digital age will be vastly different from the industrial scale education that was necessary when information could only be communicated in person and face to face. Firstly, education will be across the life course – the skills needed at different stages of life will be different, and education will be accessible in the workplace, as well as in the home to facilitate lifelong learning.

On a related point, some things are better learned in groups in real time – collective problem solving needs teamwork free-flowing discussion. Other things require personal concentration and can be done alone, in a self-paced manner. With digital technology, people like teachers, peers and teaching assistants don't have to be at the same place at the same time in order for education and learning to take place. At this time of the COVID-19 pandemic, the transition although rocky has begun in earnest.[83]

The transition to a digitally augmented society has begun, and education is the way we can make sure that we preserve the assets we have inherited and understand our responsibilities to the future.

Conclusion

The digital home has integrated into all aspects of our lives: home, work and government. Through the lens of history, we have arrived at a new frontier, a new industrial revolution. It is upon us in ways we understand and ways we never could have anticipated. Instead of asking "when or will it?", we must ask "how?". The all-encompassing impact of the digital home touches each person in a family. People must be at the heart of every decision in the home because each action has a consequence pertaining to their individual and family livelihood, rights and privacy. These consequences include but are not limited to misinformation, education, commerce, work–life balance, information sharing, equal opportunity, sustainability and also joy.

Within the digital home, the entire world has a seat at our dining room table. An unprecedented amount of data and information is at our fingertips, yet we still have very little understanding and control over how data and information are used, and for what purpose and for whose benefit. This cannot continue.

Through regulators and open communication channels – such as the UN's High Level Panel on Digital Cooperation, the Sustainable Development Goals, NIC, the EQUALS Women in Tech Taskforce, the Sustainable Development Goals Digital Investment Framework, People-Centered Internet, the Internet Society, the IEEE and the WEB Foundation – we are at the very earliest stage of an important dialogue. We have to construct a narrative, foundation and incentives to make sure that the emerging digital home is inclusive and brings all voices forward to design and shape it. This must include women. It is our most important responsibility to take our knowledge and awareness and ensure that the homes of the future nurture all who live within them. It is up to every one of us to become responsible digital citizens of the world, and stewards for our shared humanity.

Addendum 25 April 2020

The 2020 COVID-19 pandemic has served to accelerate many of the topics which were only considered briefly when the first draft of this chapter was originally written in February 2019.

The COVID-19 crisis has made a significant portion of the connected world more digitally knowledgeable by the day. Billions of people and millions of households have shifted to remote work, online learning and social convenings on Skype and Zoom.

With this increasing embedding of technology – some might see it as invasion – into our homes, there is a renewed sense of urgency regarding data oversight and privacy in the time of COVID-19. This development is particularly critical with respect to sharing personal health data. Interest in the notion of data trusts, first considered in research conducted at Southampton University in 2017, is escalating.[84]

General Data Protection Regulation (GDPR) is a start but conflicts of interest, non-existent governance criteria and a lack of an internationally agreed ethical framework hamper progress. We have huge amounts of data as well as huge silos. We are collecting this data under pressure during the crisis in the absence of data consistency, and the immediate need for it is paramount. Public trust is on the wane.

It is clear that a strong public international voice must affirm that this is the time for every technology company, with data, to come together and share resources for the benefit of global humanity. It is in the interest of every current and eventual digital citizen, in every home, to be offered confidence building, ethical measures. Only by gaining public trust can we help turn the current crisis into an opportunity.

Notes

1 www.rapid7.com/docs/Hacking-IoT-A-Case-Study-on-Baby-Monitor-Exposures-and-Vulnerabilities.pdf
2 www.duhaime.org/LegalDictionary/D/DomusSuaCuiqueEstTutissimumRefugium.aspx
3 Beckman, Jonathan. "The Roaming Empire", *The Economist*, 1843, April and May 2018, p. 94.

4   Beckman, Jonathan. "The Roaming Empire", *The Economist*, 1843, April and May 2018, p. 95.

5   www.techemergence.com/snuggle-up-with-technology-but-dont-leave-empathy-in-the-cold-a-conversation-with-dr-sherry-turkle/;   www.sciencenews.org/article/machines-are-getting-schooled-fairness;   www.thestreet.com/video/14455574/women-control-over-50-of-household-wealth-says-schwab-s-liz-ann-sonders.html; https://webfoundation.org/2018/05/measuring-the-digital-divide-why-we-should-be-using-a-women-centered-analysis/;   www.economist.com/leaders/2012/04/28/bit-rot;   www.theguardian.com/technology/2017/mar/03/terms-of-service-online-contracts-fine-print

6   Beckman, Jonathan. "The Roaming Empire", *The Economist*, 1843, April and May 2018, p. 94.

7   www.theguardian.com/technology/2012/feb/03/twitter-resist-cigarettes-alcohol-study

8   www.theguardian.com/technology/2012/feb/03/twitter-resist-cigarettes-alcohol-study

9   www.theguardian.com/technology/2018/nov/01/tim-berners-lee-says-says-tech-giants-may-have-to-be-broken-up?CMP=Share_iOSApp_Other

10   www.theverge.com/2018/4/6/17207566/twitter-rules-behavior-test-abuse

11   https://newsroom.fb.com/news/2019/05/protecting-live-from-abuse/

12   www.huffingtonpost.com/carl-bildt/who-govern-Internet_b_7922948.html

13   https://medium.com/s/story/digital-nomads-are-not-the-future-be360c7911b4

14   www.bloomberg.com/news/articles/2017-01-31/why-single-women-are-buying-homes-at-twice-the-rate-of-single-men

15   www.credit-suisse.com/corporate/en/articles/news-and-expertise/global-wealth-report-2018-women-hold-40-percent-of-global-wealth-201810.html

16   https://data.worldbank.org/indicator/SL.TLF.TOTL.FE.ZS

17   www.youtube.com/watch?v=7NX7TIvLCqw&fbclid=IwAR1BqjCVHrocXc4rbNhB5f8wuC-KMGQRT0pC4pSGwy_jukzZ7g7HT0kyUiA

18   https://ourworldindata.org/female-labor-force-participation-key-facts

19   https://ourworldindata.org/working-hours#as-productivity-in-the-household-increased-working-hours-in-the-household-declined

20   www.salary.com/articles/stay-at-home-mom/

21   apc.org/en/pubs/community-networks-internet-people-people

22   IEEE Industry Connections Social Impact Measurement working paper on Networked Improvement Communities. https://docs.google.com/document/d/1Rt03c2LNzQp_cGrXs9ClldIXL8DZp18Qy06M9vUkWWw/edit?usp=sharing

23   www.carnegiefoundation.org/newsroom/improvement-voices/what-were-reading-paul-lemahieus-why-a-nic/

24   https://whatis.techtarget.com/definition/fourth-industrial-revolution

25   https://drive.google.com/file/d/1OMvZAZRJ9KKfN3mm1kzYQFvDqqw2SEj6/view?usp=sharing

26   www.equals.org/

27   www.itu.int/en/about/Pages/history.aspx

28   www.forbes.com/sites/forbestechcouncil/2018/05/21/fakenews-as-an-information-security-problem/#5f80465d6dcc

29   www.uniindia.com/~/longer-we-wait-further-we-will-fall-behind-un-chief/World/news/1627675.html

30 www.economist.com/gulliver/2018/07/20/the-case-for-treating-disabled-travellers-better

31 https://motherboard.vice.com/en_us/article/53n9ka/china-cashless

32 www.weforum.org/agenda/2016/05/yanis-varoufakis-imagining-a-new-keynesian-bretton-woods

33 https://news.un.org/en/story/2019/06/1040131

34 www.scmp.com/news/world/united-states-canada/article/3002093/us-transportation-department-probes-faa-approval

35 www.aitrends.com/executive-interview/executive-interview-david-bray-and-bob-gourley-technology-entrepreneurs-and-thought-leaders/

36 1995 Lecture at UC Santa Barbara, Glen Culler Honorary Event

37 Ibid.

38 www.itu.int/net4/wsis/forum/2019/Agenda/ViewSession/173

39 https://ethicsinaction.ieee.org/

40 www.itu.int/en/Pages/default.aspx

41 https://digitalimpactalliance.org/

42 www.itu.int/dms_pub/itu-d/opb/str/D-STR-DIGITAL.02-2019-PDF-E.pdf

43 www.nasa.gov/audience/foreducators/diypodcast/rocket-evolution-index-diy.html

44 www.nasa.gov/audience/foreducators/diypodcast/rocket-evolution-index-diy.html

45 www.ancient.eu/article/890/daily-life-in-ancient-china/

46 www.britannica.com/place/China/Social-political-and-cultural-changes

47 http://law2.umkc.edu/faculty/projects/ftrials/conlaw/marryff.html

48 http://rmc.library.cornell.edu/gettysburg/good_cause/transcript.htm

49 www.pewresearch.org/fact-tank/2017/12/06/despite-concerns-about-global-democracy-nearly-six-in-ten-countries-are-now-democratic/

50 www.weforum.org/agenda/2018/03/15-languages-around-the-world-that-are-going-extinct

51 https://Internetworldstats.com/stats.htm

52 www.statista.com/statistics/262946/share-of-the-most-common-languages-on-the-Internet/

53 *The Economist*, 1843, DISPATCHES; A real character, August/September 2018, p. 21.

54 https://news.sky.com/story/regional-accents-suppressed-by-voice-assistants-says-study-11473853

55 https://news.sky.com/story/children-more-at-risk-from-being-told-what-to-think-by-robots-say-researchers-11473798

56 https://en.wikipedia.org/wiki/Gleaner

57 www.sdfsa.org/gleaning/

58 Private conversation of Mei Lin Fung with Robert Tse, National Broadband Coordinator for the US Department of Agriculture, June 2018.

59 www.nytimes.com/2018/12/31/technology/personaltech/5g-what-you-need-to-know.html

60 www.epa.gov/sustainable-management-food/united-states-2030-food-loss-and-waste-reduction-goal

61 Combusted with energy recovery refers to the waste that was used to generate heat through combustion and the resulting heat was used to create energy that could be stored for later use.

62 www.rhs.org.uk/advice/Profile?pid=812

63 www.gardeningfordisabledtrust.org.uk/
64 www.ncbi.nlm.nih.gov/pmc/articles/PMC3661291/
65 www.theguardian.com/lifeandstyle/gardening-blog/2016/sep/01/if-you-want-to-practice-mindfulness-the-garden-is-the-place-to-be
66 www.honestby.com
67 www.segura.co.uk/newsroom/conscious-consumers-transparent-supply-chain-and-ethical-sourcing/
68 https://fashionista.com/2018/04/what-is-blockchain-explained-ethical-fashion-supply-chain
69 www.bain.com/insights/build-a-digital-supply-chain-that-is-fit-for-the-future/
70 www.provenance.org/
71 www.sourcemap.com/
72 https://en.wikipedia.org/wiki/Organic_certification
73 https://en.wikipedia.org/wiki/Fair_trade_certification
74 https://fashionista.com/2016/12/forced-labor-report-2016
75 https://fashionista.com/2018/04/what-is-blockchain-explained-ethical-fashion-supply-chain
76 www.mckinsey.com/featured-insights/future-of-cities/housing-affordability-a-supply-side-tool-kit-for-cities
77 www.cbinsights.com/research/future-of-housing/
78 www.nytimes.com/2018/01/24/business/dealbook/katerra-softbank-vision-fund.html
79 https://digitalcooperation.org/
80 www.un.org/en/newtechnologies/
81 Acknowledging the contribution of Justin Bryant Olivier who assisted in drafting this, based on Justice of the Peace by Esther Moir, Penguin Books 1969. www.amazon.com/justice-peace-Esther-Moir/dp/B007ELZ6Q6
82 www.undp.org/content/undp/en/home/news-centre/speeches/2017/financing-the-2030-agenda--the-role-of-the-un.html
83 www.zdnet.com/article/online-learning-gets-its-moment-due-to-covid-19-pandemic-heres-how-education-will-change/
84 https://eprints.soton.ac.uk/428276/1/WSI_White_Paper_1.pdf

Chapter 3

Artificial intelligence-empowered technology in the home

Matilde Santos and Francesca Toni

Introduction

Artificial intelligence (AI) has been around at least since 1956, but has only relatively recently made its way into everyday life, outside the research labs around the world where it predominantly belonged for most of its existence. In particular, the home has become host to several forms of AI, embedded into technology that support in particular the management of the home (e.g., for energy saving via smart devices and for cleaning and companionship by domestic robots) and knowledge enrichment for the inhabitants of the home (e.g., with chatbots for information gathering and question answering).

But can all technology in the home be deemed to be empowered by AI? In order to answer this question, we first need to understand what AI is.

Several definitions of AI have been proposed in the literature, many of which are focused on studying and developing systems that can be deemed to *think* or *act* intelligently (Russell and Norvig, 2016), where "intelligent" may be interpreted as *rational*, as understood in philosophy or economics, or *human-like*, as understood in cognitive psychology or neuroscience. Thinking is an internal activity, whose "intelligence" may or may not be verifiable. Actions are instead verifiable from the outside, as observers may judge whether these actions are indeed "intelligent". The two interpretations of "intelligence" are not equivalent, as humans may be irrational, in particular in the sense that their activities may not be – strictly speaking – about maximising utility or achieving goals. Other important features of AI systems are their *social skills*, in being able to relate to humans as well as other AI systems within their environment of operation, and their *autonomy*, in being able to function without or with limited human intervention. However, autonomy alone does not suffice for a system to fall under the AI umbrella (Pajares and Santos, 2005). For example, not all autonomous vacuum cleaners may be deemed to be AI empowered: if they are just moving blindly and randomly in a room, without any vision or planning skills (essential manifestations of human-like intelligence and rationality), then they would just be autonomous tools, no more than mere toys. Similarly, chat systems that mechanically provide information without engaging with their users, without the ability to understand speech and incapable of reasoning so as to understand what the users require, cannot be deemed AI.

AI has undergone several phases since its onset: a first phase focused on reasoning powered by formal models and knowledge representation; a second phase focused on machine learning powered by large data availability and high computational power; more recently, a third wave of development is undergoing focusing on a mixture of reasoning and learning.[1]

The first two phases had specific, somewhat narrow foci (e.g., expert systems and perception, respectively) within the scope of the so-called weak AI, characterised by technological solutions applicable to specific domains and with a narrow focus (e.g., speech recognition). But in order to deal with more generic and complex settings, such as the home, a combination of several AI technologies, meeting potentially very diverse challenges, is needed. For example, a service robot may need to be able to navigate unknown environments, and thus be capable of sophisticated vision, to speak with a variety of human stakeholders, and thus be capable of sophisticated speech, as well as to integrate expertise and reason with knowledge it learns or acquires via interaction with human users.

In this chapter, after giving a brief introduction to the AI discipline in its short history, we will overview some recent technologies for the home, focusing on management and knowledge enrichment. We will emphasise the AI components of these technologies and any future directions for augmenting their AI. We will conclude with a brief analysis of challenges that AI-empowered technologies face when deployed in the home, and with an analysis of ethical issues posed by the use of AI in society.

AI: A very brief introduction

The term "artificial intelligence" was coined in 1956 at a research workshop at the Dartmouth College in New Hampshire, USA.[2] The document resulting from this seminal event defines AI as aiming towards "how to make machines use language, form abstractions and concepts, solve kinds of problems now reserved for humans, and improve themselves". This is a very broad definition, encompassing several very different tasks identified as manifestations of intelligence when performed by humans. Earlier influential works, predating the Dartmouth workshop, include "[a] Logical Calculus of the Ideas Immanent in Nervous Activity", by McCulloch and Pitts (1943), introducing the concept of a "perceptron", that is, an artificial neural network (consisting of artificial neurons computing logical expressions and mathematical functions), and Alan Turing's "Computing Machinery and Intelligence" (Turing, 1950), bringing up the question as to whether machines could be made to think: "I believe that at the end of the century the use of words and general educated opinion will have altered so much that one will be able to speak of machines thinking without expecting to be contradicted". These works brought a first wave of AI enthusiasm during the 1960s and 1970s. The UK Lighthill Report (Lighthill, 1973) identified three categories of contributions:

(a) Advanced automation – replacing human beings by machines for specific purposes (e.g., for assisting humans in the home) – requiring pattern and speech recognition, speech synthesis, and complex spatial reasoning and optimisation (e.g., for identifying shortest paths and for packing things optimally), logical deduction, inductive generalisation and analogical reasoning, common-sense reasoning, information retrieval);

(c) Building nature inspired models (e.g., artificial neural networks, inspired by the brain) and evaluating these models experimentally with (neurobio-logical and psychological) data, for example, for scene analysis, classifica-tion and generalisation;

(b) (Bridging the gap between a and c): building robots as advanced automated systems inspired by humans (and thus nature): "each robot is designed to mimic some group of human functions, including functions such as eye-hand co-ordination, scene analysis, use of natural language, problem solving, etc., within some limited universe of discourse such as we may exemplify by a game (chess, draughts, etc.), a puzzle, a table top on which blocks are moved about, or a drawing-book".

The outputs from this first wave of AI systems were, however, to a large extent disappointing, and:

> [C]laims and predictions regarding the potential results of AI research had been publicised which went even farther than the expectations of the majority of workers in the field, whose embarrassments have been added to by the lamentable failure of such inflated predictions.
>
> (Lighthill, 1973)

A cause for the perceived failure was the limited availability of computational power at the time to deal with the combinatorial explosion underpinning the majority of the tasks underlying the AI vision. The disappointment led to a first "AI winter", followed in the 1980s by a new hype, as indicated, for example, by the Fifth Generation Computer Systems (FGCS) initiative by Japan's Ministry of International Trade and Industry that begun in 1982, to create machines using massively parallel computing/processing to increase performances in knowledge processing via a specific programming paradigm, Prolog, based on automated inference of solutions from specifications in symbolic logic of problems (Warren, 1982). Other countries followed suit, for example, the United Kingdom (UK) government with the Alvey Programme 1983–1988. Again, the expectations behind these efforts were too inflated, and the computational resources available at the time were too limited. So, this second hype was followed by a second "AI winter" (Crevier, 1993), followed in turn by the currently ongoing hype, mostly fuelled by large data availability and increasingly more sophisticated statistical methods drawing patterns from the data, making use of increased computational power available nowadays.

The current AI landscape is supported by considerable investments, by industry[3] and governments[4] alike. AI applications have come to play a role in people's lives, for example, in smartphones, with voice recognition and image processing, in information retrieval by smart search engines, in medicine with image recognition, in autonomous driving with navigation and scene recognition, and in natural language processing in general and machine translation in particular. Some of AI's recent achievements can indeed be deemed impressive, but there is widespread agreement that more cohesion between different methodologies[5] and a push towards explicability and ethical forms of AI are crucial[6] for AI to play a beneficial role in society.

AI for the management of the home: Domestic robots

Domestic robots are robots that can autonomously perform household chores in domestic environments, for example, cleaning, butlering or shopping. Special kinds of domestic robots, referred to as "assistive" robots, can support independent living of users (e.g., elderly or disabled). The environments within which domestic (assistive) robots need to operate are typically unknown and unpredictable. Indeed, even when the layout is known and stable (as in the case of an apartment or house) objects may change their position and new objects may appear at any time. Moreover, humans within these environments may be highly unpredictable. Thus, domestic robots pose more challenges than service robots used, for example, in industrial settings such as factories, as these have a rather stable and controllable set-up. Another important difference between domestic robots and industrial robots is that the former need to socially interact with humans.

The last decade has witnessed a hive of activity in the design and realisation of domestic robots in general and assistive robots in particular. RoboCup@ Home[7] is the most well-known benchmark competition for domestic robots, having been running since 2006, and showcasing the state of the art in this field, with a focus on human–robot interaction and cooperation, navigation and mapping in dynamic environments, computer vision and object recognition, object manipulation and adaptive behaviour, among others. The competition tests robots' capabilities in performing domestic tasks (different ones in different years), such as shopping in a supermarket whose layout and product availability and positions are unknown beforehand. Several commercial domestic robots for cleaning are available on the market, including but not limited to the Dyson 360 eye[8], capable of navigating unknown environments and avoiding obstacles by exploiting sophisticated computer vision mechanisms, and iRobot Roomba[9], using intelligent sensors to guide the robot and preventing it from falling and tumbling. Whereas these commercial products focus on vision and sensing alone, other, non-industrial research-driven endeavours also integrate further capabilities, such as manipulation, to explore, interact with and possibly modify objects in the environment within which the robots operate. Strong correlations exist between these different "physical" capabilities, in that vision and sensing empower manipulation while manipulation benefits scene understanding via vision. Manipulation may be needed, as in the case of RAMCIP – a service robot for mild cognitive impairments patients at home[10] – to handle medicines, for example.

But how much AI, understood as in the Introduction section, is used in these domestic robots? According to the final report on Automatica 2018, the latest exhibition on smart automation and robotics[11], not much:

> Artificial Intelligence (AI) is the next technological leap. [...] AI-based data analyses can give industry an enormous increase in growth. Interdisciplinary dialog is crucial here. To use business potential success-fully, automation and IT providers must collaborate much more closely together with AI experts in future.
>
> (Ralf Bucksch, Technical Executive of Watson IoT
> Europe, IBM Sales & Distribution, Software Sales)

Some of the research challenges addressed by academics in AI to support domestic robots are:

- Empowering domestic robots with the ability to decide which actions to perform (Iwata et al., 2018), by reasoning as to which tasks they con-tribute to. For example, the movement of certain joints may contribute to cooking, whereas the movement of other joints may contribute to picking up medicines.
- Equipping domestic robots with human-friendly interactive features. A first challenge is proxemic to determine how close a robot should be to a human: whereas approaching other people is a natural task for humans, it is very complex for robots (Repiso et al., 2018). Further challenges include the ability to follow humans and human–robot collaboration, for example, to enable robots to work with humans to share tasks within dynamic environments (Lee et al., 2018).
- Empowering domestic robots with cognitive abilities. Cognition amounts to the mental action or process of acquiring knowledge and reasoning with it, through thought, experience and the senses. A robot equipped with cognitive abilities may be able, for example, to work out, while attempting to prepare a hot chocolate, that milk can be found in the fridge and how this can be opened, knowing how a door can (Haidu et al., 2018).

Despite the plethora of research efforts in academia, the goal of obtaining fully AI-empowered domestic robots is still unachieved:

> Full robot autonomy, including natural interaction, learning from and with human, safe and flexible performance for challenging tasks in unstructured environments will remain out of reach for the foreseeable future. In the envisioned future factory setups, home and office environments, humans and robots will share the same workspace and perform different object manipulation tasks in a collaborative manner.
>
> (Kragic et al., 2018)

AI for the management of the home: Connected devices

Several technological advances in recent years have empowered a transition to the use of AI for the management of the home. These advances include a variety of connected devices, such as smart sensors, smart actuators and smart meters, which can all be embedded in the home to identify and "optimise" human activities. An example of device available on the market is the Nest thermostat[12], integrating forms of AI to learn and adjust to the behaviour of the inhabitants of homes. Other commercial enterprises, such as Centrica[13], envisage connected homes, integrating connected smart sensors and smart actuators. The UK government envisages that all homes should be equipped with smart meters by 2020.[14] The data collected by smart meters could be used for visualisation of consumption and cost by different providers, for example, as in Makriyiannis et al. (2016).

The output of smart meters could also empower AI-based recommender systems, for example, as in Makriyiannis et al. (2016): based on user consumption and information on various tariffs by the energy provider, an AI device can argue as to why a change of behaviour by the inhabitants of the house or a change of provider altogether may be beneficial, in terms of lowering energy expenditure, while causing the least possible disruption to the inhabitants. Here AI has a clear role to play, in combination with technology. Albeit not yet on the market, and still within the academic research sphere, this kind of AI usage could be deployable in the near future.

AI for knowledge enrichment in the home

Modern technology offers many opportunities for knowledge enrichment in the home, in particular by means of information retrieval over the web and other documents, in some cases supported by tools capable of answering questions. The latter include commercial products such as Alexa/Echo[15] and Google Assistant,[16] which in turn can connect to several devices, are able to understand and generate speech and are endowed with natural language processing and generation abilities. These devices depart from other means of interactions with machines, such as web browsers or static pull-down menus, in that they are capable of linguistic interactions with humans. They are empowered by AI, in the form of machine learning abilities, for example, to draw patterns from known interactions with humans or between humans, and to use these patterns to generate responses. In some cases, these machine learning methods use examples of interactions (e.g., context-response pairs) as training data to draw response patterns.

These technologies pave the way for the so-called conversational AI, including intelligent chatbots that rely on machine learning and natural language processing techniques to engage in conversations of increasingly higher quality, depending on the availability of suitable data for training. They often focus on eliciting information (e.g., preferences) from human users, usually to maximise some utility function, either relative to easing human life or, oftentimes, external to the humans (e.g., relative to selling products to them). Despite impressive recent advances in conversational AI, little effort has been devoted to trying and equip these devices with reasoning capabilities, for example, to infer information not explicitly conveyed in dialogue as well as to endow conversational AI with common sense (Young et al., 2018). Even when common-sense knowledge is made available to intelligent chatbots, this is often limited to simple facts, such as that "Paris is the capital of France", as represented in simple semantics networks.[17] An additional issue with most conversational AI, shared with other AI methodologies and tools[18], is the inability to explain its outputs: early studies (Cocarascu et al., 2019) envisaged instead dialogical exchanges between human users and machines whereby users can question automated recommendations, and machines can provide the reasons behind these recommendations, incrementally and on demand.

Challenges

AI in the home provides many benefits, but it also poses some threats. Indeed, the digital home can put at risk some core human values, for example, considerate, supportive behaviour and relationships. Is an AI-empowered home really a "sweet home", or just a "swAIt smart house"?

In the previous sections we have seen how AI-empowered technology can be applied and used at home. Particularly, robots can help us manage our home, perform some tasks, and some AI applications can even help us enrich our knowledge and broaden our views. We do not envisage a future without AI, and we do not envisage real AI if it is not in our future.

But still, are these devices and apps "intelligent"? Even with all various connected appliances, virtual assistants and copious sensors that can be installed in a modern smart home, the "smart" side of things is still in its infancy in many ways. Would we consider someone with the basic skills of today's smart homes really "smart"? Will fully AI-equipped smart homes emerge in the distant or near future, say, by 2025, or even sooner? Considering that some aspects of the smart home are already here, and others are likely to develop further given the amount of interest in smart homes, it is worth to consider what AI has brought us so far and the challenges it poses in the home.

Explainability and standardisation

We have touched upon the predominant lack of explainability of AI systems and methodologies. Recent legislation, notably European Union General Data Protection Regulation (GDPR)[19], is linked to sanctioning a "right to explanation" (Goodman and Flaxman, 2017) for outputs generated algorithmically. In the specific case of AI for the home, it is necessary to acquire a clear understanding of what explainability means, in collaboration with psychologists and social scientists. In particular, given that different types of humans co-inhabit the home, different types of explanations will be required to suit different cognitive abilities and ages.

Another risk emerges from the lack of standardisation. It is a fact that there are many different brands in the market for the same families of technological products, so we can find ourselves surrounded by many different small incompatible devices. A quick glance at a handy list of "intelligent" devices available on the market today will give us some idea of what can be done using these large number of new age devices. But if you look carefully, you will notice that there are a whole lot of different companies making these hardware devices.

Is this a problem? What is the issue with a lack of standards? The devices will not simply plug and play and would need additional software before they can start functioning. They will not play nicely with each other because of competing standards and a lot of complexity would arise for the end user.

Brands do not always work well together. Currently, devices from different brands or even from one single brand, models and generations are incompatible at the data level. Still today you cannot transfer your data from an older version of a smart device or from a device by another manufacturer; for example, if you are using an Apple Watch, you will have trouble transferring the information to a Microsoft Band. As a result, you lose data continuity.

Smart homes and their environment, that is, Internet of Things (IoT), as it stands today, is still in its simplest stage. Basically, we have a myriad of devices that are connected to the Internet that we can control remotely and receive notifications from. Are we talking about AI or IoT when we refer to the future smart home? There is a subtle difference and a strong relation between AI and IoT. AI provides a crucial role by making sense of data streamed from smart devices. AI serves to detect patterns in this data from which it can learn to adjust the behaviour of IoT services. A good example of

AI and IoT successfully working together at home is a smart thermostat solution. It allows to check and control temperature from anywhere. The device analyses temperature preferences and work schedule of its users and adapts temperature accordingly. Applications where IoT works together with AI are only growing, creating new markets and opportunities and they are highly unlikely to lose ground in the near future. Interoperability is the key to the viability and long-term growth of the entire ecosystem, especially consumer IoT. But interoperability has many layers. We may have already solved key issues on the physical connectivity level, such as wireless standards, in making sure that devices can communicate with each other within a system. Nevertheless, on the service level, can devices talk to each other and share information to offer higher level offerings? Think of the smart home where you might have connected things – lighting, home security, refrigerator, washing machine, entertainment system and more – from different manufacturers and systems, working together to bring greater energy efficiency, comfort or convenience. These different companies have apps that enable the users to interact with the hardware and they all use a different technology or platform. There is no IoT standard established yet and of the companies making IoT products, most would choose anything they would feel comfortable with.

We badly need standardisation to advance IoT and thus fulfil the dream of an intelligent home and environment. What AI promises is that all of your boring "things", such as refrigerators, air-conditioners, light bulbs, microwave ovens, washing machines and even cars, will become "smart connected devices" and will be able to talk to each other using some sort of technology, like Bluetooth, infrared, Wi-Fi and more. But they need to speak the same language, or at least, they must be able to connect and share data and information.

Some countries are taking charge. For instance, a new industry alliance is forming in China to set up standards and protocols in areas of data, human–machine interface (HMI), knowledge and service interoperability. But there needs to be a global response because these issues on interoperability are the same in every market. Standards, industry and consumer organisations can all play a role in defining these protocols. Despite the fact that there has been some agreement lately between companies and agreement on common standards and technology, there are competitors and no universal body has formed yet. The big obstacle of the lack of standardisation still stands, the biggest hurdle facing the industry and hindering its acceleration. The ecosystem will develop faster and we will see a lot of innovative ideas and integrations coming to fruition sooner. It is high time the bigger industry players realise this and agree on focusing their energy at standardisation to push the industry forward on the right track.

We believe that standardisation will definitely make things easier for the end user. By enabling every manufacturer to integrate the devices in an open platform compatible with different systems and devices, easily supporting the interchanges of services, knowledge, data and communications, they could be controlled from a single app instead of multiple apps and the end user will not have to worry about competing standards or any other complexities.

Also, the manufacturers will be able to sell the hardware easily once they are compliant to global standards and integrate with popular services like If This Then That (IFTTT). The unified protocols will help manufacturers to save costs and other resources in developing their hardware and supporting software and speed up the manufacturing process.

In short, unified standards will push smart home development further and will be a boon for both manufacturers and consumers.

Relationships in the Digital Home

At present, any home in the West, even if not a "smart" one, has at least a smart TV, or a smart phone, tablet, computer, etc., and its inhabitants interact with their peers via social networks, while enjoying the free web service If This Then That (IFTTT).

Do these communication technologies foster connectivity or isolation? Since these tools generate virtual worlds among the people that use them, they allow people to be close to others who are in a different physical location, possibly even closer than to people physically nearby. But that does not mean that they are interacting together. Those intelligent communication devices also cause evolution of vocabulary, with new words flourishing, unintelligible acronyms emerging, social trends leading to new behaviours, etc.: a dark language is generated; indeed, if you are not in, you are completely out.

These means of communications give rise to some paradoxes. For example, they may lead to hyper-activism while being a couch potato: you can be just sitting for hours and, at the same time, having many apps opened and actually doing a lot of stuff (answering, commenting on some pictures, arranging some meeting, sending emails, etc.). Another contradiction that smart devices can bring us is real isolation while being connected to thousands of people: you are multi-connected but on your own, alone. You may be communicating with a wide network of friends, while having no time to cultivate face-to-face friendship. Are these virtual relationships real ones? Virtual relationships can also be time consuming – it takes time to write, to choose an image to send, to forward a message, etc.

Let us take another example. Smart TV is present in most western homes. Is it impacting the home? Definitely! First, who chooses what we see? Though we believe we watch contents on demand, it is the TV set that suggests us films and series that we may like, and shows us commercials related to our interests. So there is this strong bias over content that narrows our choices. Also, we may be missing interesting and enriching contents that go beyond our narrow sphere of interest. Even more, sometimes smart TV may create tension over its access and weaken authority at home. The fact that in most western homes there is a TV or personal computer (PC) in every room may foster individualism and laziness.

Concerning AI for knowledge enrichment, our relationship with other people changes when we replace "our aunty" for AI-based personal assistants. For sure, we have experienced what it is to have someone to wake us up, to tell us about the weather forecast, to play some music they think we would like, or someone who cooks for us. All this can be replaced by personal assistants that provide more to-the-point and dedicated-info more easily and rapidly accessible. But ... it is not the same!

Security, autonomy and privacy

There are already commercial robots that are a good aid to help in the management of the home, doing some of the house chores: vacuum cleaning, floor-washing, ironing, cooking, watering plants, lawn mowing, feeding puppies and many more.

These variety of intelligent devices have been proved efficient, time and energy saving, effortless, less noisy, 24/7 with no need for coffee breaks, snacks, etc. Definitely, they make life easier – or more entertaining.

But not all that glitters is gold. Software adds an additional layer of things that can fail. A toaster that can short-circuit is bad enough, but a toaster that can refuse to serve you toast because its firmware is being updated is something else entirely. Besides, these devices can also act as domestic spies, they learn everything about our habits, timetables, likes and dislikes, etc. This opens the door to security vulnerabilities.

There is a further added problem: if any of these devices, doing tedious chores, breaks, do we still know how to carry out the chore ourselves? Some people, mainly young ones, may not know the effort that it requires because they have never done it (clothes washing, for instance). Moreover, personal assistant may influence what we do, make decisions for us and even generate dependencies on them (we have only to remember how we use Google Maps to get anywhere). We would not allow anyone to control our life but personal assistants threaten to do it.

It is true that domestic robots and personal assistants are a good aid at home. But is that all we want to ask AI to do for us? We gain time when we are released from these tasks but do we really gain quality time?

On the other hand, there are a lot of smart devices that keep us in contact with other people, and this allows us to have quick access to information, etc. They provide a lot of advantages that improve our quality of life. They can stimulate our curiosity, motivate us to do some sports or lead a healthier life, foster empathy with other people getting to know others' life, etc.

This usually means enrichment but there is also the risk of it contributing to our impoverishment. First, because of the bias on contents, loss of privacy is becoming a huge problem nowadays. The multitask capacity is a source of dispersion. This creates the need for immediacy and instant communication, and the sense that everything should be effortless, hiding the inevitable effort that it is behind everything. The social networks present us unreal models as something close and easy. And they take us out of our physical space to live in an unreal virtual world.

Ethics guidelines for trustworthy artificial intelligence

Given that intelligent systems are transforming our lives, AI is just as much a new frontier for ethics and risk assessment as it is an emerging technology. There are many questions related to the development of AI in society that need to be answered, and the responsibility lies with all stakeholders – companies, associations, governments and the public. The European Commission has taken a step forward and the High-Level Expert Group on AI published the Ethics Guidelines for Trustworthy Artificial Intelligence on 8 April 2019.[20] We will briefly summarise some of these guidelines to later present ethical challenges that arise from introducing AI into our homes. According to the guidelines, trustworthy AI should be:

- lawful: respecting all applicable laws and regulations;
- ethical: respecting ethical principles and values;
- robust: both from a technical perspective while taking into account its social environment.

The guidelines put forward seven key requirements that AI systems should meet in order to be deemed trustworthy. A specific assessment list aims to help verify the application of each of the key requirements:

1) Human agency and oversight: AI systems should empower human beings, allowing them to make informed decisions and fostering their fundamental rights. At the same time, proper oversight mechanisms need to be ensured, which can be achieved through human-in-the-loop, human-on-the-loop and human-in-command approaches.
2) Technical robustness and safety: AI systems need to be resilient and secure. They need to be safe, ensuring a fall-back plan in case something goes wrong, as well as being accurate, reliable and reproducible. That is the only way to ensure that also unintentional harm can be minimised and prevented.
3) Privacy and data governance: besides ensuring full respect for privacy and data protection, adequate data governance mechanisms must also be ensured, taking into account the quality and integrity of the data, and ensuring legitimised access to data.
4) Transparency: the data, system and AI business models should be transparent. Traceability mechanisms can help achieve this. Moreover, AI

systems and their decisions should be explained in a manner adapted to the stakeholders concerned. Humans need to be aware that they are interacting with an AI system, and must be informed of the system's capabilities and limitations.

5) Diversity, non-discrimination and fairness: unfair bias must be avoided, as it could have multiple negative implications, from the marginalisation of vulnerable groups, to the exacerbation of prejudice and discrimination. Fostering diversity, AI systems should be accessible to all, regardless of any disability, and involve relevant stakeholders throughout their entire life cycle.

6) Societal and environmental well-being: AI systems should benefit all human beings, including future generations. It must hence be ensured that they are sustainable and environmentally friendly. Moreover, they should take into account the environment, including other living beings, and their social and societal impact should be carefully considered.

7) Accountability: mechanisms should be put in place to ensure responsibility and accountability for AI systems and their outcomes. Auditability, which enables the assessment of algorithms, data and design processes, plays a key role therein, especially in critical applications. Moreover, adequate and accessible redress should be ensured.

But what are the real risks people are afraid of?

Privacy. The smart devices that surround us know our tastes, likes, dislikes, preferences, etc. They know what our favourite food is, and what cannot be missed in the fridge. They know our habits, the time we get up, when we leave home and come back from work. They can calculate how many people are living in the house or are there at a certain time. They know the programmes, movies and TV series we see, the ads that interest us because we do not flip channels, the music we listen to depending on the time of the day. And a long et cetera. Are we aware?

At the end of the day, who owns the data? Because this information is recorded and available (cameras, sound, data, excel sheets, etc.), who can use it? Is it used only for our benefit or does it benefit companies, stores, etc.? We may think that everyone wins something, but who really gets the most benefit?

There needs to be a higher level of awareness for consumers about their stake in smart devices, especially regarding their data and privacy. Directives and guidance regarding these issues should be set and be clearer. The GDPR goes somewhat in this direction, but is just a first step.

I am not alone. Another scary aspect of being surrounded by smart devices is that one is never alone. Big Brother is continually watching, with many eyes and ears. What you do, say, comment, etc., can be passed on to other people as it is being stored. This may make you feel vulnerable and exposed. This is especially worrying when it comes to the elderly or children, who are unaware that they are always under the eye of a device that is watching them.

In addition, this allows knowing the lives of other people, relatives or not so close acquaintances. Should getting to know about others be so interesting for us? We know a lot through social networks, but in that case it is information shared by the owner, in a more or less conscious way. With smart devices at home, we could potentially have access to the conversations that others have had; that could be the dream of some gossip people but it may also be dangerous. And definitely, even if people may not be interested in getting to know about others, companies may still do.

AI systems could potentially cause damage if used maliciously, for example, if sensitive information and confidential data fall into the wrong hands. We should not forget that AI systems are created by humans who can be biased and judgmental. Once again, if used correctly, or if used by those who strive for social progress, AI can become a catalyst for positive change.

Artificial mistakes. How can we guard against misinformation, misunderstandings and mistakes? Intelligence comes from learning, whether you are human or machine. Systems usually have a training phase in which they "learn" to detect the right patterns and act according to their input. Once a system is fully trained, it can then go into test phase, where it is hit with more examples and we see how it performs.

Obviously, the training phase cannot cover all possible examples that a system may deal with in the real world. These systems can be fooled in ways that humans would not be. For example, random dot patterns can lead a machine to "see" things that are not there. If we rely on AI to bring us into a new world of labour, security and efficiency, we need to ensure that the machine performs as planned, and that people cannot overpower it to use it for their own ends. Or they can reach the wrong conclusion or take the wrong decision based on false or incorrect information. In the case of a machine, there is unlikely to be malice at play, only a lack of understanding of the full context. As an extreme example, imagine an AI system that is asked to eradicate cancer in the world. After a lot of computing, it spits out a formula that does, in fact, bring about the end of cancer – by killing everyone on the planet. The computer would have achieved its goal of "no more cancer" very efficiently, but not in the way humans intended it.

Dependency on machines. Artificially intelligent bots are becoming better and better at modelling human conversation and relationships. In 2015, a bot named Eugene Goostman won the Turing Challenge for the first time. In this challenge, human raters used text input to chat with an unknown entity, then guessed whether they had been chatting with a human or a machine. Eugene Goostman, portrayed as a 13-year-old boy, fooled more than half of the human raters into thinking they had been talking to a human being.

This event is only the start of an age where we will frequently interact with machines as if they are humans, for example, in customer service or sales. While humans are limited in the attention and kindness that they can expend on another person, artificial bots can channel virtually unlimited resources into building relationships. Even though not many of us are aware of this, some AI techniques are used to optimise the content of some video games, mobile applications and series so that they become addictive. Tech addiction is the new frontier of human dependency.

Besides, who has not heard someone saying that he/she is not able to find his/her way without Google Maps or any similar type of application? We are lost without these new technologies. Nowadays, we do not need to remember any phone number, to do any calculation, to memorise anything. All of this is close at hand, just typing or clicking the keyboard of our computer, writing some words in our mobiles or even just using Amazon Alexa to control your entire house with only your voice. Not to say the time we spend with those "smart" friends. This indiscriminate use of intelligent devices is also related to the critical thinking and the moral authority that comes from the knowledge that people have. Earlier the authority regarding knowledge was based on the wisdom of certain people, who were consulted when we wanted to know or learn something. Now everything is questioned and we rely on search engines or apps rather than on people. It is even more important what a search engine says than the experience of someone.

Besides that, does continually questioning the reliability of everything help us to better learn the use of these technologies? Or on the contrary, does it lead us to depend on the knowledge stored in a machine, which can be erroneous or may have been introduced by a human person who can be wrong?

Different jobs, different wealth distribution. The automation of work, which could be in most of the cases tedious, repetitive, mechanical and even risky and dangerous, shows the progress that has benefited our society since the industrial revolution. It is true that workforce is replaced by machines, but this creates new types of jobs and, besides, we live better and safer. Let us take the example of the millions of individuals that work as truck drivers. What will happen to them if the self-driving trucks promised by Tesla's Elon Musk become widely available in the next decade? But on the other hand, if we consider the lower risk of accidents, self-driving trucks seem like an ethical choice. The same scenario could happen to office workers, as well as to the majority of the workforce in developed countries. This poses new win-win situations.

As we have invented ways to automate work, we could create a space for people to assume more complex roles, from the physical work that dominated the pre-industrial world to the cognitive work that characterises the strategic and administrative work in our globalised society.

Our economic system is based on compensation for contribution to the economy, often assessed using hourly wages. The majority of companies are still dependent on hourly work when it comes to products and services. But by using AI, a company can drastically cut down on relying on the human workforce, and this means that revenues will go to fewer people. Consequently, individuals who have ownership in AI-driven companies will be better-off.

We are already seeing a widening wealth gap, where start-up founders take home a large portion of the economic surplus they create. If we are truly imagining a post-work society, how do we structure a fair post-labour economy?

This is where we come to the question of how we are going to spend our time. Most people still rely on selling their time to have enough income to sustain themselves and their families. We can only hope that AI will enable people to find meaning in non-labour activities, such as caring for their families, engaging with their communities and learning new ways to contribute to human society. If we succeed with the transition, one day we might look back and think that it was barbaric that human beings were required to sell the majority of their waking time just to be able to live. While we consider ethical questions on AI, we should also keep in mind that, on the whole, this technological progress has the potential to bring better lives for everyone. AI has vast potential, and its responsible implementation is up to us.

Conclusions

AI is entering the home, and has a lot to offer to its inhabitants, in support of management of the home as well as cognitive enrichment. We have provided a brief, and by no means exhaustive, overview of the state-of-the-art efforts and challenges in this setting: a lot more is required to equip technology with AI abilities, but there are already several AI-empowered devices running around us. The home of the future cannot stay away from AI, and more efforts are required to face some of the possible threats that AI may bring.

Now is the right moment to stop and think about what AI has done and could do for our homes. The digital era of smart homes is already here. We can foster some of the benefits it brings and change whatever needs to be changed. The next generation will control intelligent homes in 20, 30 or 50 years, but it will not be the current generation. Unexpected outcomes from advances that are to come can make people change habits, with younger people able to adapt to new paradigms more easily. The current generations, with knowledge and experience spanning old and new, are suited to understand the advantages, disadvantages, risks and mitigating factors of the technological home. This will require close-knit collaboration between computer scientists and engineers on one hand and philosophers, psychologists, social scientists and legal experts and policymakers on the other.

Notes

1 See www.darpa.mil/news-events/2018-09-07.
2 See www-formal.stanford.edu/jmc/history/dartmouth/dartmouth.html.
3 For example, see https://ai.google/ and www.research.ibm.com/artificial-intelligence/.

4 For example, in the UK see www.gov.uk/government/publications/artificial-intelligence-sector-deal/ai-sector-deal and in France see www.aiforhumanity.fr/en/.
5 For example, see www.darpa.mil/about-us/darpa-perspective-on-ai.
6 See Ethics Guidelines for Trustworthy Artificial Intelligence, published on 8 April 2019 by the European Commission (https://ec.europa.eu/digital-single-market/en/news/ethics-guidelines-trustworthy-ai).
7 See www.robocupathome.org/.
8 See www.dyson.co.uk/robot-vacuums/.
9 See www.irobot.com/for-the-home/vacuuming/.
10 See https://ramcip-project.eu/.
11 See https://automatica-munich.com/press/newsroom/press-releases/automatica-beats-all-records-again.html.
12 See https://nest.com/uk/thermostats/.
13 See www.centrica.com/about-us/what-we-do/centrica-hive.
14 www.ofgem.gov.uk/gas/retail-market/metering/transition-smart-meters.
15 See www.amazon.co.uk/b?ie=UTF8&node=14100223031.
16 See https://assistant.google.com/.
17 One example is ConceptNet, see http://conceptnet.io/.
18 For example, see www.imperial.ac.uk/enterprise/issues/explainable-ai/ for a presentation of some examples of explainable AI in general.
19 See https://ec.europa.eu/commission/priorities/justice-and-fundamental-rights/data-protection/2018-reform-eu-data-protection-rules_en.
20 See Ethics Guidelines for Trustworthy Artificial Intelligence, published on 8 April 2019 by the European Commission (https://ec.europa.eu/digital-single-market/en/news/ethics-guidelines-trustworthy-ai).

References

Cocarascu, O., Rago, A. and Toni, F. (2019). Extracting Dialogical Explanations for Review Aggregations with Argumentative Dialogical Agents. In *Proceedings of the 18th International Conference on Autonomous Agents and MultiAgent Systems*. International Foundation for Autonomous Agents and MultiAgent Systems. Montreal: Canada, pp. 1261–1269. http://hdl.handle.net/10044/1/71424.

Crevier, D. (1993). *AI: The Tumultuous History of the Search for Artificial Intelligence.* New York, NY: Basic Books.

Goodman, B. and Flaxman, S. (2017). European Union Regulations on Algorithmic Decision-Making and a "Right to Explanation". *AI Magazine*, 38(3), pp. 50–57. doi: https://doi.org/10.1609/aimag.v38i3.2741.

Haidu, A., Beßler, D., Bozcuoğlu, A.K. and Beetz, M. (2018). KnowRobSIM—Game Engine-Enabled Knowledge Processing Towards Cognition-Enabled Robot Control. In *2018 IEEE/RSJ International Conference on Intelligent Robots and Systems (IROS)*. Institute of Electrical and Electronics Engineers, pp. 4491–4498. doi: 10.1109/IROS.2018.8593935.

Iwata, K., Aoki, T., Horii, T., Nakamura, T. and Nagai, T. (2018). Learning and Generation of Actions from Teleoperation for Domestic Service Robots. In *2018 IEEE/RSJ International Conference on Intelligent Robots and Systems (IROS)*, Institute of Electrical and Electronics Engineers, pp. 8184–8191. doi: 10.1109/IROS.2018.8593892.

Kragic, D., Gustafson, J., Karaoguz, H., Jensfelt, P. and Krug, R. (2018). Interactive, Collaborative Robots: Challenges and Opportunities. In *Proceedings of the Twenty-Seventh International Joint Conference on Artificial Intelligence (IJCAI-18)*. International Joint Conferences on Artificial Intelligence, pp. 18–25.

Lee, B.J., Choi, J., Baek, C. and Zhang, B.T. (2018). Robust Human Following by Deep Bayesian Trajectory Prediction for Home Service Robots. In *2018 IEEE International Conference on Robotics and Automation (ICRA)*. Institute of Electrical and Electronics Engineers, pp. 7189–7195. doi: 10.1109/ICRA.2018.8462969

Lighthill, J. (1973). *Artificial Intelligence: A Paper Symposium*. London: Science Research Council. www.chilton-computing.org.uk/inf/literature/reports/lighthill_report/contents.htm.

Makriyiannis, M., Lung, T., Craven, R., Toni, F. and Kelly, J. (2016). Smarter Electricity and Argumentation Theory. In *Combinations of Intelligent Methods and Applications*, 46, New York, NY: Springer, pp. 79–95. doi: 10.1007/978-3-319-26860-6_5.

McCulloch, W.S. and Pitts, W. (1943). A Logical Calculus of the Ideas Immanent in Nervous Activity. *The Bulletin of Mathematical Biophysics*, 5(4), pp. 115–133. https://doi.org/10.1007/BF02478259.

Pajares, G., and Santos, M. (2005). Inteligencia Artificial e Ingeniería del Conocimiento, RA-MA. www.ra-ma.es/libro/inteligencia-artificial-e-ingenieria-del-conocimiento_48238/.

Repiso, E., Garrell, A. and Sanfeliu, A. (2018). Robot Approaching and Engaging People in a Human-Robot Companion Framework. In *2018 IEEE/RSJ International Conference on Intelligent Robots and Systems (IROS)*. Institute of Electrical and Electronics Engineers, pp. 8200–8205. doi: 10.1109/IROS.2018.8594149.

Russell, S. and Norvig, P. (2016). *Artificial Intelligence: A Modern Approach* (3rd edn.), Upper Saddle River, NJ: Prentice Hall.

Turing, A.M. (1950). Computing Machinery and Intelligence. In *Parsing the Turing Test 2009*. Dordrecht: Springer, pp. 23–65. www.csee.umbc.edu/courses/471/papers/turing.pdf.

Warren, D.H. (1982). A View of the Fifth Generation and its Impact. *AI Magazine*, 3(4), pp. 34–34. doi: https://doi.org/10.1609/aimag.v3i4.380.

Young, T., Cambria, E., Chaturvedi, I., Zhou, H., Biswas, S. and Huang, M. (2018). Augmenting End-to-End Dialogue Systems with Commonsense Knowledge. In *Thirty-Second AAAI Conference on Artificial Intelligence*. Association for the Advancement of Artificial Intelligence, Palo Alto, CA, pp. 4970–4977.

Chapter 4

Contested homes in the age of the cloud

The changing socio-spatial dynamics of family living and care for older people in the 21st century

Mohamed Gamal Abdelmonem

Introduction: Changing homes, changing culture of living

The power of home lies in its enduring practices, conventions, everyday rituals, social interactions and communications, either within the household or with the outside world. Spatial configurations of homes are not, in this sense, limited to the physical characteristics of the domestic space; rather, people reconstruct domestic spheres based on sociocultural and temporal needs that transcend the limitations of the physical space (Mallet, 2004; Lawrence, 1987; Lefebvre, 1991). Homes are socially constructed and have consistently been changing in forms, uses and meanings (Smith, 1986; Smith, 1994; Saunders and Williams, 1988). While houses are built with the capacity to serve a wide range of family social engagements and needs that differ through generations, homes are constructed out of continuities of social activity, interaction, attitudes and conduct (Abdelmonem, 2011; Saunders, 1989). With online communications and social media interactions becoming essential part of everyday lives, homes are facing new affront, namely, the confrontation of uncontrolled access to private spaces, challenges to family attitudes and social-training, and above all, vanishing privacy. Homes are becoming increasingly contested between the controlled physical and the uncontrolled virtual, between the tangibility of one's presence and the intangibility of alien influences (such as social media, online friendship groups and shopping websites). From smart TV, smart phones, surveillance cameras, to social interaction and care, smart home systems do exchange much of our personal information with service providers, including information that defines personalities and personal consumption or needs profile (Smart Home, 2009).

Recent demographic analysis of western societies shows that the profile of older people is changing. In the United Kingdom (UK) there are 4 million people over the age of 75, which is projected to increase to 5.9 million by 2025 (Tinker, 1997, p. 274). In Europe it is predicted that in 2025 the total of number of people over 65 years will be 173 million, and will reach 27.6% of the total population. Population ageing brings with it a number of challenges to aspects of life in the home and the way the home is connected to society, most notably a rise in the proportion of the population in need of care. By 2010, 36 million people globally were recognised as having dementia and, by 2050, this number is expected to rise to 115 million (Mihailidis et al., 2012). The proportion of that population living alone at home is also increasing, and approximately one-third of older people living at home also live alone (Wild and Boise, 2012). Such predictions highlight the importance of pursuing research on information and communication technologies (ICTs) and housing design for older people and those who care for them; to respond to the needs of aging at home, and of those who care for them (Mieczakowski and Clarkson, 2012; Pragnell et al., 2000). The impact ICT has on the lives of older individuals are still a topic of debate and discussion (Mordini and de Hert, 2010), although more issues such as privacy, security, social isolation and dependence are coming to the fore. Homes developed for the need of older people have fundamental difference from those used by young families or those with multiple generations. The responsive capacity and connectedness of those homes are critical to the support, care and social engagement of older adults.

Much of the attention over the past few decades has focused on the 'work–family conflict' being a key operational hurdle with suspicion of negative impact on work rate and efficiency (MacDermid, 2005; Edwards and Rothbard, 2000). The result is a home–work interface that is a "socially constructed" boundary between the life domains of work and home, which remain at the core of human history (Holliss, 2012). The development of Skype, Zoom and virtual meeting rooms and workspaces, and e-shopping have made it much easier to overlap private and public domains, compared to time, cost and health risks of commuting on busy transport, as we learnt during the 2020 pandemic. Yet, the home holds more significance for older people. Recent data suggest that elders spend on average 80% of their daytime at home (Rowles and Chadhury, 2005, p. 25) and 89% of older people live in a mainstream family home (Hanson, 2001, p. 14). Within the Futurage Road Map, the home's centrality to everyday life is important with increasing age, and particularly in very old age, people spend most of their time in the home with incremental need for monitoring, support and care (Futurage, 2007).

In the UK, the global coronavirus (COVID-19) pandemic has impacted all sections of society and resulted in close to 124,419 victims between March 2020 and March 2021, with older adults being most vulnerable, forming over 80% of fatalities. The government's preventive measures such as "social distancing" and household quarantine and closure of schools and universities have been critical in reducing the total number of deaths by at least 78%, with the capacity to reduce the viral infection reproduction rate to below one (Ferguson et al., 2020; Long, 2020). On 16 March 2020 the British Prime Minister announced that it was "time for everyone to stop non-essential contact with others", instructing people to work from home and avoid "social venues" such as pubs, clubs and theatres (Long, 2020). Such measures led to aspects of technology-driven and e-communications (e-shopping, e-medicine and e-learning) become overnight mandatory practices by Monday 24 March 2020, when the British government enacted a national lockdown, altering the way we work, communicate, educate and care. TV and playrooms have become workplaces, classrooms, meeting rooms or a virtual-coffee room to socialise with colleagues or elder relatives. iPads and computers with cameras have enabled work devices and facilitated such instant transition, allowing more flexible working hours, and open access to workplaces round the clock.

The critical importance of technology for older people makes technology an essential factor at home, which would come to be critical during the COVID-19 preventive measures and during the stay-at-home. With growing ageing population and associated vulnerability to such external factor as the coronavirus, the growing influence of technology on domestic environments, mixing work with life could mark the beginning of a new pattern of living. The effectiveness of e-shopping and e-medicine was therefore involuntarily tested during March 2020 – March 2021 to a great success, with millions of older people being self-isolated, ordering supplies online and receiving care and medication via e-medicine and e-care support without any physical contact.

Researchers argue that technology is favourable in increasing the level of control an older person can feel within his or her home. Barlow and Venables (2004, p. 1) argue that technology can increase control grasped in the home as the level of security felt is improved, in reference to technology that can "deliver more control over the domestic environment and provide an 'electronic blanket' for those being cared for and for carers". By contrast, control could be lost if technology is taken in unwillingly, and tensions can arise. ICTs have become structurally integrated with the home environment. Our understanding, design and architecture of home need to equally change to suit such conditions and active communication arenas. This chapter, hence, looks at the challenges, risks and opportunities that modern technology poses for the domestic sphere, specially testing the effectiveness of existing ICT systems and assisted living to support older people ageing at home.

The architecture of home in the digital era: Space and identity of domestic atmosphere

Louis Kahn once argued that architecture "is the thoughtful making of spaces". The continual renewal of architecture comes from those changing concepts of space (Norberg-Schultz, 1971). While architecture is able to provide the multi-dimensional experiences of space and time, home corresponds those experiences to the human actors in a structured and synchronised organisation (Abdelmonem, 2016). The idea of home lies in its organisation of space over time, in its capacity for memory or anticipation (Douglas,

1991). The home is capable of anticipating future events through coordinating actions and planning consumption, not only through efficient response to memory and the regularity of experiences, but also regarding swift changes and adaptation to unpredictable events, such as the COVID-19 worldwide pandemic.

In this context, homes have been one of the most rewarding experimental missions of humans in their negotiation with nature and technology. Philosophers have related the process of building a shelter, dwelling or a home to the state of being in the world. Norberg-Schultz argue that "architectural space may be understood as a concretization of environmental schemata or images, which form a necessary part of man's general orientation or 'being in the world'" (Norberg-Schultz, 1971). From Nietzsche to Martin Heidegger and Hannah Arendt, the act of building and inhabiting space is a process of mediation with nature, culture and technology and contextualised to meet the always changing human needs (Abdelmonem, 2012). The change of those aspects forces a change in form, spatial configuration and social processes. Humans have always created spaces as a medium of their understanding of the world. The architectural space, its inhabitation and use have changed over time (Junestrand and Tollmar, 1998).

The underlying meaning of modern living, however, suggests a temporal condition that is largely time-flexible, thereby situating the understanding of modern homes peculiar to their contemporary relevance, and more increasingly technology (Kern, 2003; Bauman, 2000). The use and management of domestic space to accommodate modern and technologically led lifestyles have become symptoms of mobile communication as a driving force for social engagement; physical space became less critical; emotional engagement became more volatile. The necessity of attachment, confrontation and mutual co-habitation are increasingly vulnerable to forces of efficiency, detachment and redundancy as epitomised by the stark scenes of high-rise concrete forests of apartment blocks in the downtowns of contemporary cities.

Yet, the intervention of smart, digital and virtual technologies has largely altered these patterns within the domestic space. The face-to-face contact in protected environment has largely been challenged by multiple online influences on children and young generation into an increasingly boundary-less environment. Access to social media, reliance on smart devices and online resources by schools have created generational gap in communication skills and accessibility at home. But, equally, same devices have enabled critical access to older people by family, neighbours and carers from remote locations. In addition, devices that may pose risks to some family members at certain age become very important to reduce those risks to different age groups. The dichotomy of risk and opportunity has largely been debated in technology-centred intellectual debate. Here, I will try to explore how ICT devices at home are increasingly essential and integrated components of domestic operations and family life.

Smart homes: Technologies, systems and infrastructure

Despite their predominance in everyday homes, research lacked critical evidence on how technology in domestic environments has an impact on people's everyday life (Demiris and Hensel, 2008), at least until the 2020 pandemic. Research demonstrates the viability of technological solutions of essential social and medical needs either in a laboratory or limited community-based settings (Demiris and Hensel, 2008, p. 40). The co-design of technology with the input of the end user balances technological challenges with the cultural context of practice and needs in domestic environments. (Weiner et al. 2003, p. 430). While these are driven by technology companies, they remain universal in their applications and context neutral for commercial purposes. The input of users or the impact of technology on different user groups is very small, leaving our understanding on this evolving integrative environment quite limited.

The concept of a "smart home" has existed for many years. Referred to as intelligent homes or home networking, it involves the introduction of networked devices into the house, or "the integration of technology and services through home networking for a better quality of living" (Bierhoff et al., 2005). There are two elements that require further discussion. First, the capabilities of the technology are always expanding through increasing networks speeds. Second, the introduction of entirely new devices, the rapid pace of development means that the smart home paradigm must be periodically assessed and adjusted to reflect new capabilities, opportunities and challenges. Smart homes can also be classified from a functional perspective, as illustrated by Aldrich's (2003) five hierarchical classes:

1) Homes which contain intelligent objects: homes contain single, stand-alone applications and objects which function in an intelligent manner.
2) Homes which contain intelligent, communicating objects: homes contain appliances and objects which function intelligently in their own right and which also exchange information between each other to increase functionality.
3) Connected homes: homes have internal and external networks, allowing interactive and remote control of systems, as well as access to services and information, both within and beyond the home.
4) Learning homes: patterns of activity in the homes are recorded and the accumulated data are used to anticipate users' needs and to control the technology accordingly.
5) Attentive homes: the activity and location of people and objects within the homes are constantly registered, and this information is used to control technology in anticipation of the occupants' needs.

Each stage of the hierarchy requires increasingly complex technology, both in terms of hardware and software, as well as increased need for efficient

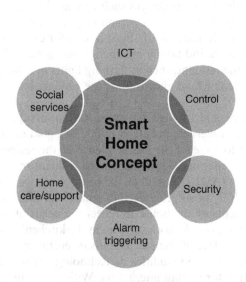

Figure 4.1 Home technologies: Functions.

networking and data collection, particularly with respect to tiers 4 and 5, where the needs and preferences of users are anticipated.

Smart home technologies (SHT) can perform a wide variety of functions and incorporate many different devices as listed in Figure 4.1:

- **ICT**: Although many elements in the smart home are networked, ICT in the context of smart homes refers to those that allow for direct, controlled access to the outside world and includes devices such as the telephone, TV, and services provided by an Internet connection.
- **Control**: Control refers to the ability of the resident to manipulate the environment through the use of switches and panels for lights or heating. The degree and comfort with which a resident is able to control or operate the different parts of the smart home is an important factor for the devices being deemed acceptable or desirable to the wider public and older people. Control also includes smart meters, and remote control of security cameras, energy consumption and lights, among others.
- **Security**: Security refers to security from intrusion and from potential hazard. It may involve the use of "smart" locks, which can be operated via smart phone or alarms that indicate the presence of a water leak or fire, among other information.
- **Alarm Triggering**: Although the six categories listed here describe various aspects of the smart home, it is important to note that these distinctions are not impermeable, as evidenced by the links between security and alarm triggering, which both feature alarms for a variety of purposes.

Alarm triggering however also includes devices such as wearable alarms and sensors that detect where in the house a person may be. The alarm may trigger for the resident or, in the case of smart homes for elderly or vulnerable people, for caregivers and family members. Alarms may also be tailored to the needs of the resident, such as flashing lights or a wearable alarm that vibrates in lieu of loud alarms for those who are hard of hearing.

- **Home Care/Support**: Devices and services for home care and support are designed with elderly or vulnerable people in mind. The goal of the elements in this category is to increase the independence of the resident through the use of measures that make it easier for the resident to perform activities of daily living (ADL). Not all of the solutions in a smart home need to be based on ICT. In some cases, the "smart" solution is a redesign of traditional elements of the house to reflect the needs of the resident. This could include adjustable work surfaces in the kitchen, seats in the shower or ramps in the place of steps at the outside entrances.

- **Social Services**: Regardless of the possibilities of technology, it should enhance not replace potential for human interaction. With this in mind, the social services aspect of the smart home concept focuses on the services which can encourage independence and enable ageing in place. Although advances in technology may assist in this aspect (such as easier access to reliable information on buses or other services), it is primarily focused with the infrastructure that surrounds the smart home, emphasising that the concept is not merely about the physical structure of the house, but in providing an environment that is supportive of the resident, especially in the context of the older people. This aspect of technology was paramount in older people's ability to engage with their families, friends and social networks during the strict lock down in 2020, as was recommended by many health and ageing groups as frequently appeared on ABC News, and the BBC. Such engagement was critical for mental health and well-being of older adults during several weeks of self-isolation (Gill and Munbodh 2020), as grandparents were able to see grandchildren and socially engage with siblings and family.

To be truly effective, smart homes must be responsive to the needs of the user, increasing their comfort, independence, security and quality of life. This is equally true of smart homes for older people. Smart homes are designed to address needs based on three main areas: comfort, leisure and healthcare (Chan et al., 2008). The potential of smart homes to address the healthcare needs is however of greatest relevance. The smart home itself is not a technology per se, but rather a concept incorporating many different devices and services. While some of those aspects are digital and virtual, critical elements of smart home design remained physical and spatial (Value Ageing, 2010–2014). Beyond a network connection through which technology can communicate both to each other and to the outside world, there is no rigid formula for making a home smart. They need to be curated and designed for the use of specific individual needs and require expertise in architecture and construction, ICT, hardware design, psychology, healthcare, medicine and robotics.

Smart, responsible and intelligent homes can be classified under the umbrella of "Ambient Intelligence" (ETICA D5.7.c, 2010). The ETICA Project identified and defined seven features of artificial intelligence (AI) environments:

- **Embedded**: The technology is not conspicuous in its presence, but is rather in the background as a network of sensors and devices.
- **Interconnected**: The different devices and sensors are wirelessly connected to each other, forming a single system.
- **Adaptive**: The system can operate (with varying degrees of efficiency) even with incomplete data. This is important for users who wish to restrict the collection or use of personal data.
- **Personalised**: The system can be tailored to the needs and wishes of the user (user centred).
- **Context-Aware**: The system can recognise and react in an appropriate manner to the circumstance, such as switching on a light (in the evening or at night) when a person enters the room.
- **Anticipatory**: Through the collection and analysis of user data, the system can anticipate user preferences and act accordingly, such as automatically adjusting the room temperature based on prior behaviour and settings.
- **Novel human–technology interaction paradigms**: How users interact with AI environments is always changing or developing in directions. What began as interactions with a computer through the use of a keyboard and mouse has moved to touchscreens, voice and motion control.

Smart homes can also incorporate "e-health" technologies as emerging applications in the intersection of medical informatics, public health and business, which provide health services with flow of information enhanced through the Internet and related technologies. These are series of applications of telehealth technologies and services, both for the user and for society, from National Health Service (NHS) individual account of checking personal records, appointments or tests, with record of medications and reviews, to the Trace and Track applications in the case of monitoring infection diseases and their spread within society, like 2003's Severe Acute Respiratory Syndrome (SARS) or the new 2020's COVID-19 (Robinson et al., 2020). The former reduces the need for patients to leave their houses and travel to the hospital for check-ups, while the latter detects the spread of virus through big-data monitoring system of contacts, advising people to stay away from contagious areas (Firth et.al., 2020). As such, for e-health applications the cost on the patient is lowered and the burden on hospital facilities is reduced (European Commission, 2010). Telehealth is not only remote monitoring and communication with doctors, it is more of an increase in information available for the patient as well as the doctors, with some new application providing live data on patients' biological conditions. Weighing scales are, for example, capable of monitoring and recording heart rate data, as well as calculating body mass index (BMI) and providing environmental information.

Most arguments against ICT within the home are concerned with the acceptability of technology, ethics and the negative connotations of "substituting 'warm' hands with 'cold' technology" (Aanesen et al., 2011). The aim of SHT is defined by Demiris and Hensel (2008, p. 35) in their paper, "Technologies for an Ageing Society", as

[a] smart home aims to enable non-obtrusive monitoring of residents and involves different levels of technological sophistication, ranging from stand-alone intelligent devices to home that continuously monitor residents' activities and physical status and adapt to residents' needs, often providing proactive measures.

The degree to which an older person living at home accepts technology depends on numerous factors. A major influence in the use of technology is the motivation of the older person, desire for control, sense of privacy and understanding of its potential connectivity. Below, I will try to shed more focus on the impact of smart technologies on the lives of older people in everyday life by analysing the findings of two research projects: the first one is Value Ageing (2010–2014) that looked on the impact of artificial and assistive technologies on enhancing the design and quality of life for older people at home. The second project (2012–2017) focused on the analysis of older peoples' reaction to the use of smart technologies at home for care purposes.

As demonstrated above, while this work has been conducted much earlier than the disruptive occurrence of COVID-19 pandemic between March 2020 and March 2021, much of the research and analysis in those projects pave the road for in-depth understanding on how ICTs were already available and in good operation for some time. Hence, once coronavirus spread and lockdown enacted by the British government, households across the UK and abroad have swiftly used the very present technologies and infrastructures to operate as smoothly and as efficiently as possible, helping millions of families across the globe to stay safe at home, while e-care and work from home continued at large.

Investigating smart homes of older people: Methodology, data and findings[1]

The understanding of smart homes from older people's perspective is centred around how they accept, react and co-inhabit a domestic environment dominated by electronic systems, communication devices and flow of personal information within their homes, and the impact of such inter-activity on their sense of security, privacy and well-being. To gather the data for this research, two methods were deployed: first, gathering information on technologies and systems that shape our active and responsive homes, and, second, in-depth face-to-face semi-structured interviews with user groups (with and without access to technologies) to enable the collection of rich data on the meaning and perception of smart homes to older people. Technology in those homes comprises motion sensors, lux sensors, door and window sensors, Internet-connected TV, temperature sensors, electricity water and heating usage sensors and emergency alarm devices including pull cord alarms in the bathroom and bedroom and a push alarm in the hall entrance, all connected to an outside security call centre. The participants without technology were sampled considering the number of years they had been living in their homes. No self-identifying data has been included in any material presented in this research and confidentiality of all participants was maintained throughout.

There are a number of themes that emerged from the research and analysis that predominate the impact and feeling towards the use of smart technologies at home. While some of these themes embrace the use of technologies, others underline the need for co-design of smart technologies. These include security from intruders, security for assistance, control, independence and privacy.

a. Safety (security from intruders): Safety was the most frequent topic when discussing the meaning of home and what they consider important. Participants discussed the importance of locking their doors, not only at night but also during the day. The front door was seen as a link to outside but more importantly a link for intruders to enter. Fear was mentioned along with security, emphasising the fact that many older people were vulnerable. Participants recognised their limited involvements in the operation of smart technology used for their security or its use. The findings revealed that feeling secure is the greatest benefit and acceptability factor of having technology, and the major motivation. When asked if they feel secure in their home, one participant stressed it as the greatest benefit of assistive technologies: "[t]hat is the biggest, the security ... you see the security that gives you the peace and tranquility" (RW3).

Another participant lived with such technology referred to being burgled once and had been unable to sleep in her room ever since. Instead she sleeps on a sofa in complete fear. Having moved to a new home with assistive tech-nologies, she asserted: "I have security everywhere, nobody is going to get me" (RW3). One symptom of such appreciation of technologies is the psych-ology of vulnerability and fear, as older adults become more frail, espe-cially when living alone. Safety in this sense affects the motivation of use and acceptability of technology, helping older people live more peacefully as security is becoming more prominent in their lives.

b. Security for assistance: Security is fundamental and the most influencing factor for accepting SHT. Older people mostly live alone and some feel fragile – therefore, feeling more secure can help them dwell more peacefully. Participants agreed that they would and do feel more secure if they knew that at the pull of an alarm cord or the push of a button they would receive help quickly. The presence of such simple devices offers assurances and sense of external help should it be needed: "Well I suppose the one good thing…, you only have to press a button if something happens to you and I'm sure that's the greatest benefit of all" (RW2).

Yet technology can also disappoint and fail to enhance security for some. One participant was sceptical about the effectiveness of technology in this regard. He referred to incidents when he fell, lying for hours as the motion sensor could not pick up a movement of an arm while he lay on the floor:

> If you move your leg, it couldn't distinguish - I'm sure it can't distinguish a movement of your leg, lying on the floor or standing… It breaks the infrared or whatever it is. It breaks the signals that's all it can do. It doesn't show you anything, if I move my hand like that, it thinks you're moving normally.
>
> (RW1)

When asked whether the technology made him feel secure in the home, one participant asserted: "I don't know, I suppose the windows can still be broken" (RW1).[2] Scepticism, however, prevails on the back of loss of control of your own security. Some participants stressed that having technology could make them feel less secure as control would be taken away from them; it could be given to wrong or less caring people, without control from the resident's side.

c. Control, independence and privacy are key elements that separate our private sphere from that of institutional and public domain. Territoriality and control within the home are intrinsically linked and this was made clear through ownership of items and autonomy over the home. Adoption of technology is uncontrollable in some instances as participants expressed their desire to control all devices in the home with nobody to answer to: "Very important, it's my home and I like to think I'm in charge (laughs)" (RWO2).[3] Autonomy is also significant as freedom and control to act is key to their independence and living at home, not in the over-controlled care homes. Autonomy is evidently a motivational factor in using technology when compared to the other alternative:

I think it's just you can do what you like, move around, you're independent, answering to nobody, there's nobody saying right be down for your tea at 4 or 5 o'clock. I can have my tea at 7 o'clock if I like. I think it's just the independence in the place of your own.

(RWO3)

Technology could both hinder and enhance the control over home. The device which directly enhanced control for all SHT participants was the videophone which gives authority and control to the resident. Indirectly, sensors that detect intruders improved the feeling of safety and control and assured some older adults of the continued monitoring of healthcare provision, and hence instil more confidence and freedom to move about and activate their life knowing that a backup and responsive system is in place should it be needed. One participant stressed that some compromise and two end controls will enhance the sense of ownership by older people, which could be achieved if there was an "off" and "on" button, and one participant felt that this would replenish control: "Maybe that I could control the technology, in other words, it's nice knowing you can switch it off as well" (RW1).

d. Independence: Independence is another motivational factor especially as the thought of altering the home and embedding assistive technologies would aid those who are fragile. In way, there was a predominant feeling that altering the house physically to accommodate assistive technology would make residents feel more dependent and fragile who needs continuous monitoring, in comparison to the average person in their home, and hence, letting go of their independence. According to one resident living without assistive technology:

[T]hey're more or less cries for help anything that I've seen there, which I don't think, you know, up to now that I need... It needs a whole lot I suppose but I refuse to turn it into a disabled person's home... I can manage it at the moment.

(RWO1)

Participants recognised that technology helped them age in place, through increased security and peace of mind with a trade-off of part of their independence. One participant stressed that having responsive technology actually made them feel more independent as it helped to look after herself. Future capacities such as self-monitoring blood pressure and heart rate ensure that such autonomous feeling is well placed: "And it's going to stop me from [going to] hospitals, from [seeing] doctors; you know it's given me a greater quality of life" (RW3).

e. Privacy: The idea of remote monitoring of people's safe movement without actual presence and seeing them in person breaks down the barriers of what home means. Technology which is simply placed in the home for your benefit, which does not involve someone else keeping an eye on your actions and movements, was seen as viable, such as light sensors or alarms. However, in direct monitoring by a stranger through motion sensors, queries arise. Participants viewed it as an invasion of privacy: "Actually, I wouldn't like it at all because to me it's a bit like big brother is watching you. The more I think about it" (RWO1). Another asserted the same point: "I don't think I would like that … Yeah, no, no not really, that would be sort of intruding on your privacy, do you know what I mean. It doesn't appeal to me at all" (RWO2).

Participants have different opinions due to their personal experiences and health problems. One with healthy conditions and no prior incidents values privacy over being monitored by someone else. By contrast, those with previous history of falls and need of assistance support it. One supporting participant had suffered two falls within her home and this left her feeling afraid of it happening again. Participants RW2 and RW3 took to the technology immediately and put that down to the fact that they feel it is beneficial and also the fact that it appears physically did not disturb how rooms felt: "Not at all, no, I wouldn't pass any remarks, you just go around and as you walk they'll light up but you pass no remarks" (RW2). "Well for me, other people might see them intrusive, I don't. I honestly don't" (RW3).

The consideration of the future development of such technology was also an acceptability factor, as SHT participant RW1, who felt that monitoring could become recorded in the future, having devastating effects on privacy and the meaning of home.

> Well I don't think it's doing any damage at the moment but it has the potential to do it… It can change the meaning of home, from a place where you should be able to sit back, relax, feel your own comforts in, to you know, jail. It's not a jail, they [are] not putting people into jail and I say I know people can feel that, go to some of the homes and older people are in prison, they can't get out.
>
> (RW1)

Impact of smart technologies in improving older people homes

Research indicates there are two stages of user motivation: "felt-need" and "perceived benefits" (Mahmood et al., 2008, p. 108). The degree to which an individual feels they need technology will affect their acceptability of it (McCreadie and Tinker, 2005); they state that, "the assessment of objective need has to be balanced by reference to the individual's perception of his or her own needs" (p. 105). "Independence is also a factor for motivation, if an older adult is strongly determined to live independently despite his/her physical or mobility limitations; motivation is likely to be high to find ways to achieve that goal" (Mahmood et al., 2008, p. 108).

While considering the impact of ICT on an older person's living conditions and environment, it is necessary to consider such impact on different functions and aspects of a person's life that takes place in these conditions. Three different spheres of influence can be distinguished: cognitive function, physical function and social, cultural and emotional life. Different ICT solutions will vary in terms of their impact, benefits and risks for different spheres of a person's life, usually influencing more than one sphere. They may also affect differently the space older people's lives take place in – only home or home and a wider community. ICT solutions can also play different roles for various phases of the ageing process: they can help to delay the effects of ageing, such as cognitive decline, assist in managing specific conditions, such as physical disability or dementia, or open up social, cultural and economic opportunities for older adults. The basic cognitive functions that are most affected by ageing are attention and memory. Among other cognitive functions that may decline with age are the following: perception, mainly due to deteriorating sensory capacities, language processing and decision-making. Maintaining cognitive health allows older people to live independently longer, postponing or in some cases reducing the need for carers or being moved to residential care.

Although in most cases the impact of ICT on cognitive functions is positive, there are some ICT solutions that reduce cognitive functions if designed or applied inappropriately. One of the key risks associated with SHT is removing the user's need for thinking and decision-making (ActiveAge, 2010). Safer walking technologies, including alarms and tracking devices, are used to inform the carer that the user is outside the set boundary or to track the movements of older people with memory problems and particularly with "wandering" tendencies. Although such technologies are potentially beneficial for both the user and the carer, the use of such solutions is feared to lead to the loss of civil liberties and privacy, as well as stigmatisation as such devices often have negative connotations. Issue of the user consent is also important in this context (Alzheimer's Society, 2013).

Similarly, like in the case of cognitive functions, ICT developments have a significant role to play in maintaining and improving the physical abilities of older people. ICT solutions, such as Vital Mind, support participation in physical exercises by allowing users to choose from a range of different exercises (from repetitive to fun), carry them out at home and with friends if desired, and while doing so to receive feedback and monitor their physical performance. Although Vital Mind is a purposefully built system, other systems available on the mass market, for example, game console Wii or XBox Kinect may be used for exercises.

Challenges and opportunities of technology at home

This research into older people's perception of assistive technology has been shaped by availability and access to assistive technologies, which change over time and vary from one country to another. While assistive technology changes with the evolution of systems, applications and infrastructure, the sudden impact of COVID-19 has meant that self-isolation has significantly pushed and tested the boundaries and use of simple and more commercial technologies that activated the responsive functions of homes, making simple interaction like Skype/Facetime video calls, regular medical appointments over the phone (e-medicine), and shopping orders (e-shopping), among others, a normal everyday practice. In fact, such activation of SHT emerged from essential need and context of which all age groups, families and society had to change their lifestyle into more technologically adept (Gill and Mundobh, 2020). Older people's swift acceptance of technology in this sense was informed by overarching societal change in response to an existential and universal health crisis. In other words, while those technologies were available for long time, they became commonly used, when normal family and societal context used them equally.

In the long term, once the dust of this crisis settles, we do not expect to go back to our way of living pre-pandemic, instead effective technologies will remain in active use. But, while families go back to work and children go back to school, older people will be left with similar challenges of being alone. Hence, some of these concerns remain valid and important to address in the transformative culture of living in post-pandemic homes. These are discussed under a number of topics:

a. Social isolation: Social isolation can manifest itself as loneliness in the individual, and is reflective of dissatisfaction with the frequency or closeness of social relationships they have, when compared against what they would like to have (Steptoe et al., 2013). It has social, psychological and even physical implications for those who experience it, particularly those in need of care and assistance. A person is or is not deemed to be isolated based on contact with other people, while the feeling of loneliness is one of the psychological implications of the isolation and it has been associated with higher mortality in older men and women (Steptoe et al., 2013). Loneliness does not have a measurable, direct impact on the mortality of older people (isolation had an impact regardless of the individual's own perceived satisfaction), it stressed that they were both important for quality of life and well-being (Steptoe et al., 2013). In 2010, a Eurostat study "Social Participation and Social Isolation" noted that the likelihood of social isolation tended to increase with age. Within half of the countries in the European union (EU), 10% of respondents over the age of 65 years had no contact with friends for weeks, either in person or remotely. In the cases of Hungary and Lithuania, this increased to 25%.

Addressing social isolation is one of the core areas of implementing "successful" ageing in place and one aspect where ICT and SHT show a lot of promise. The connectedness of smart homes allows users access to new forms of communication, which may assist in mitigating some of the impact of social isolation, particularly the feeling of loneliness. ICT serves a social need by connecting family and friends, but to do so it must be available and accessible to all, as we saw between March 2020 and March 2021 in the UK and around the globe. It also should be viewed as a tool to augment, not replace, human contact. This was highlighted in the "Report on Best Practices and Roadmap towards the Roadmap" published as part of SENIOR (2009), which warns that "new communication tools may become a substitute for face-to-face contact and make social isolation worse" (SENIOR D4.1, 2009).

b. Sense of identity: The home is reflective of the individual's experiences and personality, and the environment can possess a strong sense of identity for residents. This identity is drawn from tradition, social cohesion and history, and it is important that any modifications have a minimal impact on this aspect of the home. This sense of identity has numerous positive implications on older people, particularly those with cognitive or physical impairments. Familiarity with the place, home and its features enables those who are frail to navigate spaces that would normally require greater effort and even those with dementia are documented to be able to perform tasks otherwise outside their capabilities when performed at home (Mihailidis et al., 2012).

AAL technology may be of benefit in this respect, as the sensors employed are often embedded and unobtrusive. However, AAL technology can interfere with individual's space, particularly affecting the relationship between public and private space, where the distinction between the two becomes blurred. As Jennings describes it, "someone outside your home knows what's happening, totally breaking down the privacy of the home. That can be troublesome for some older adults" (Abdelmonem and Krawczyk, 2013). It is important that SHT and home modifications do not erode the sense of identity of the home environment with over-dependence on technology. However, they must also find a balance between providing the distinction of the public and private space, while not making the residents feel like they are closed off from society.

c. Privacy: For those that are physically or cognitively impaired, ageing well at home is made significantly more achievable through the use of ICT and communications technology. However, technology must be deployed in a manner that both feels comfortable to the user and is effective in conducting its assigned task. Even though monitoring is a function of the ambient assisted living (AAL) and a potential benefit for assisting ageing in place, we must be careful to ensure that the privacy and autonomy of the resident is respected. Privacy also involves the shielding of people from unnecessary or excessive categorisation, which can have a negative impact on the lives and quality of life of older people (de Hert and Mantovani, 2010). While social networks can have a positive impact on the well-being of older people, they must also shield the user from unwanted contact (such as spam) and take all necessary measures to ensure that the data provided by the user are protected. Failure to properly respect the privacy and private lives of older people can have serious negative consequences to their quality of life (ibid.). It remains important to consider while older people adapt to new technology effectively, they remain more vulnerable and easier target to digital piracy and their data could be stolen at much more frequent basis than other age groups.

d. Control: Smart homes can act independently of active user input, triggering an alarm in the event of a fall, for example. Their systems, such as sensors for monitoring motion, heat, electricity usage, etc., are designed to operate in the background, at all hours of the day. However, while this may enhance the effectiveness of the technology, it can also have a significant psycho-logical impact on the resident. Smart home technology can be divided into two groups: active and passive. The issue of control and the level of control provided to the resident is one of the most important factors influencing user acceptability of smart home technology. According to Lisa Jennings:

> Active technology seems to be much more acceptable, because it is tech-nology that they are used to, and they can turn on or they can turn off. They can use the phone if they want to, they can turn on their house alarm if they want to, or they can push the button on the wearable alarm around their neck.
>
> (Abdelmonem and Krawczyk, 2013, Annex A)

The issue of control is strongly connected to that of privacy and personal space. The need to maintain an awareness of user preference in finding the balance, and the ability to manage it in a way that is dynamic and responsive to changing user needs and attitudes, is vital. According to Capurro (2013):

> Freedom is not a fixed parameter but depends on the personal degree of openness to others and the shared world. This balance, particularly in the context of smart homes, should be thoroughly reflected, evaluated and dynamically adapted to persons and their respective worlds, including physical and digital places, within a relation of mutual care and respect.
>
> (Abdelmonem and Krawczyk, 2013, Annex A)

e. Frustration and abandonment: Although the number and capabilities of assistive technologies is increasing, older people may still be reluctant to adopt them. Even when they begin to use them, however, there is the potential for them to abandon the technology, resulting in benefit to the user's quality of life. One of the greatest reasons for user abandonment is frustration

(Abdelmonem and Krawczyk, 2013). Frustration occurs when the device or service is a "poor fit" for the user. This poor fit is of particular concern with emerging technologies, where the user may have no prior experience with a device and no initial comfort can be assumed. The inability of the user to adapt the device to their specific needs, either as a result of inflexible design or poor training, increases the risk of the user growing frustrated with the technology and either actively choosing not to engage with it, or using it with less frequency. Frustration with a device may also occur if it is not comfortable to use, for example, if a wearable sensor weighs too much, or an installed ramp is too steep.

Conclusions: Implications of smart homes and housing design for the elderly

Smart homes are designed to improve the quality of life of older people, family or households. Measuring, evaluating and improving the home of an individual or a group is a complex process. There is no standard or universally accepted definition of quality of life at home, nor is there universal consensus on what elements should be considered under its umbrella. This is particularly problematic in the context of smart homes for older people. Traditionally, assessing older people's quality of life has focused on diminishing capabilities and the subsequent loss of independence. Functional capacity, care, health status, psychological well-being, social support, morale, dependence, coping and adjustment are all examples of indicators used as "proxies" for quality of life at home (Fernandez-Ballesteros et al., 2010). However, there are attempts to develop definitions and concepts of ageing well at home for older people as to "facilitate older people in living independently longer and support their active involvement and contribution to society. Such conditions also have the potential to reduce health risks and consequently lead to lower costs of healthcare for elderly" (Abdelmonem and Krawczyk, 2013, p. 1).

As we emerge from the COVID-19 pandemic, most of these functions were facilitated by technology using mobile technologies, online applications and e-services from all types of trades: banking, grocery, care and shopping. Hence, quality of life for the near future will be reviewed and assessed differently and with technology and smart system at the centre. Yet, human aspects and sense of identity, privacy and control will remain paramount. For the majority of people, the house they reside in is their "home", an environmental space, threaded with memories and meaning, informing and informed by the identity of the resident. This is especially true for older people, where the home is a symbol of their independence. The proportion of time spent in the home also increases as a person ages, reinforcing its importance as a place of comfort and security to the resident. The links between the home and smart technologies are well established in contemporary everyday life. Such is the importance of the environment, that there are a variety of quality assessments solely focused on the relationship between it and the individual.

There are multiple and contrasting feelings about the predominance of smart technologies at home. These require consideration of many other elements and we must understand the psychological and social implications of the measures adopted, whether they are based on design or technology. There are some important psychological and social implications of housing design and smart homes for supporting ageing in place. However, these issues are not discrete. For example, there is no formal ethical framework for assistive technologies (Tiwari et al., 2010), but there are guidelines and conditions for the successful and ethical development of smart home models. Some studies highlighted the need for user freedom of choice to be respected, as well as their autonomy and privacy. Self-awareness and self-perception of the user's own needs have been shown to affect the way they feel towards assistive technology, increasing the likelihood that they will use technology once they recognise the utility and effectiveness of the proposed device. Older people may recognise the utility of a technology, but may not feel that it could assist them specifically.

Identifying the needs of older people is vital to the successful development of smart homes. However, it is also vital to remember that these needs can vary greatly for each individual. Whether as a result of their physical or cognitive capabilities, their living situation or their personal preferences, each person's needs, and the hierarchy of needs, will vary greatly. For solutions in housing design and ICT to address the "constellation of needs" of older people, they must be flexible and capable of adapting to their preferences and unique situations. If the solution is not able to adapt to the preferences of the user, it risks being abandoned due to frustration, rather than increasing the quality of life of the user. Flexible spaces, homes with moveable interior walls that can be altered to adapt to the needs of the resident, are also in development. Likewise, when developing spaces to support ageing at home, we must recognise that the needs of specific users will likely change over time. Our interviewees embraced the principle of designing for all, with the recognition that we are all ageing, where the space or the device can change, alongside the individual.

Both ICT and smart home systems have advantages and drawbacks that must be fully understood when attempting to support ageing in place. ICT should not be deployed purely as a wish to find a technological solution, but instead considered alongside other potential solutions to the needs of the older person. People project themselves into their home. Items on the mantelpiece, pictures on the wall, and even the colour of the walls in many cases are representative of the residents' identity and artefacts of their history. The house is not a new technology, and the goal should not be to present a radical, entirely new concept of a house, but to address individual user needs in a manner that is respectful of tradition and cultural understanding of the home.

Although the design and development of smart homes present numerous engineering challenges, smart houses are more flexible than a device, a technology or a service. Comfort is also an important need to address in the successful development of SHT. Comfort can be provided in numerous ways. In part it is achieved through the successful provision of other needs – the actual security, safety and control benefits – perceived by the users so that they feel the technology is of real benefit to them, simultaneously increasing its acceptability. Understanding how the technology functions or what data the sensors are collecting is important for users to feel comfortable in their homes. Feeling at home is a key ethical issue with regard to smart homes and, hence, devices and services should be conceived and adapted to the specific forms in which a person, a family or a whole society conceives the freedom to reveal and conceal themselves so that they can decide who they are or want to be. As SHT are ever increasingly present in our daily lives, their impact, positive and negative, will continue to evolve. While we need to embrace the positive opportunities and increased capacity technology offers to our quality of life and our abilities to attend to more needs with lesser resources, it is also critical to acknowledge that in the process, technology changes and alters our behavioural patterns and attitudes.

Notes

1   Some of the interviews were recorded as part of an unpublished research work at Queen's University Belfast, by Lisa Jennings and Ela Krawczyk, who conducted first-hand interviews and coding, under the author's supervision in two research projects between 2012 and 2014. Those were gathered at different timescales and as part of different research projects. The collation and analysis of data and generated findings, however, remain the sole work of the author.
2   For all interviews used in this research, participants have been anonymised, and all interviews have been coded: RW refers to the interview of a participant living with assistive technology; RWO refers to the interview of a participant living without assistive technology. The number refers to the interview code: RW1 here refers to the Interview of participant No.1 who was living with assistive technology.
3   RWO2 (refers to interview individual No. 2 who does not live with assisted technology).

References

Aanesen, M., Lotherington, A.T. and Olsen, F. (2011). Smarter Elder Care? A Cost-effectiveness Analysis of Implementing Technology in Elder Care. *Health Informatics Journal*, 17(3), pp. 161–172. doi: 10.1177/1460458211409716.
Abdelmonem, M.G. (2011). Understanding Everyday Homes of Urban Communities: The Case of Local Streets (Hawari) of Old Cairo. *Journal of Civil Engineering and Architecture*, 5(11), pp. 996–1010.

Abdelmonem, M.G. (2012). The Practice of Home in Old Cairo: Towards Socio-Spatial Models of Sustainable Living. *The Journal of Traditional Dwellings and Settlements Review*, 23(2), pp. 33–49.

Abdelmonem, M.G. (2016). *The Architecture of Home in Cairo: Socio-Spatial Practices of the Hawari's Everyday Life*. London: Routledge.

Abdelmonem, M.G. and Krawczyk, E. (2013). *ICT Developments Impacting on Older People's Living Conditions and Environment*. Belfast: European Commission-Value Ageing. Unpublished Project Report.

ActiveAge (2010). *As part of our investigation into the trend toward independent living as we age, ActiveAge asks if "Smart Homes" are the way of the future*. Retrieved 25 August 2020, from www.activeage.org/publications/doc_view/30-As-part-of-our-investigation-into-the-trendtoward-independent-living-as-we-age-ActiveAge-asks-if-Smart-Homes-are-the-way-of-thefuture?tmpl=component&format=raw.

Aldrich, F. (2003). Smart Homes: Past, Present and Future. In R. Harper, ed., *Inside the Smart Home*. London: Springer, pp. 17–39. doi: 10.1007/1-85233-854-7_2.

Alzheimer's Society. (2013). *Safer Walking Technology*. Retrieved September 23, 2013, from Alzheimers.org.uk: www.alzheimers.org.uk/site/scripts/documents_info.php?documentID=579.

Barlow, J. and Venables, T. (2004). Will Technological Innovation Create the True Lifetime Home? *Housing Studies*, 19(5), pp. 795–810. doi: 10.1080/026730 3042000249215.

Bauman, Z. (2000). *Liquid Modernity*. Cambridge: Polity Press.

Bierhoff, I., Van Berlo, A., Abascal, J., Allen, B., Civit, A., Fellbaum, K., Kemppainen, E., Bitterman, N., Freitas, D. and Kristiansson, K. (2005). Smart Home Environment. In P. R. W. Roe, ed., *Toward an Inclusive Future: Impact and Wider Potential of Information and Communication Technologies,* Brussels: COST.

Capurro, R. (2013). *Interview with Dr. Rafael Capurro, the Director of the Steinbeis-Transfer-Institute Information Ethics (STI-IE) and Professor Emeritus of Information Management and Information Ethics at Stuttgart Media University*. As reported in Abdelmonem, M. G. and Krawczyk, E., *ICT Developments Impacting on Older People's Living Conditions and Environment*. Belfast: European Commission-Value Ageing.

Chan, M., Estève, D., Escriba, C. and Campo, E. (2008). A Review of Smart Homes – Present State and Future Challenges. *Computer Methods and Programs in Biomedicine*, 91(1), pp. 55–81. doi: 10.1016/j.cmpb.2008.02.001.

de Hert, P.J.A. and Mantovani, E. (2010). On Private Life and Data Protection. In E. Mordini and P. de Hert, eds., *Ageing and Invisibility*. Amsterdam: IOS Press, pp. 120–130.

Demiris, G. and Hensel, B. (2008). Technologies for an Aging Society: A Systematic Review of "Smart Home" Applications. In A. Geissbuhler and C. Kulikowski, eds., *IMIA Yearbook of Medical Informatics*, 17(01): 33–40. doi: 10.1055/s-0038-1638580.

Douglas, M. (1991). The Idea of Home: A Kind of Space. *Social Research*, 58(1), pp. 287–308.

Edwards, J.R., and Rothbard, N.P. (2000). Mechanisms Linking Work and Family: Clarifying the Relationship between Work and Family Constructs. *Academy of Management Review*, 25(1): 178–199. doi: 10.5465/AMR.2000.2791609.

European Commission. (2010). *The Ambient Assisted Living (AAL) Joint Programme.* Retrieved from http://ec.europa.eu/information_society/activities/einclusion/docs/ageing/aal_overview.pdf.

Ferguson, N., et al. (2020). Impact of Non-Pharmaceutical Interventions (NPIs) to Reduce COVID-19 Mortality and Healthcare Demand, Working Paper, Imperial College London. https://spiral.imperial.ac.uk:8443/handle/10044/1/77482.

Fernandez-Ballesteros, R., García L.F., Abarca, D. and Blanc, E. (2010). The Concept of "Ageing Well" in Ten Latin America and European Countries. *Ageing and Society*, 30(1), pp. 41–56. doi: 10.1017/S0144686X09008587.

Firth, J.A., Hellewell, J., Klepac, P. and Kissler, S.P. (2020). Supplementary Information for: Combining Fine-Scale Social Contact Data with Epidemic Modelling Reveals Interactions between Contact Tracing, Quarantine, Testing and Physical Distancing for Controlling COVID-19. CMMID Repository. Online: https://cmmid.github.io/topics/covid19/tracing-network-local.html. Accessed on 31 May 2020.

Futurage (2007). *A Roadmap for Ageing Research. Final Summary Report.* Online report: https://cordis.europa.eu/project/id/223679/reporting. Accessed 20 August 2020.

Gill, E. and Munbodh, E. (2020). Grandparents Can Get Paid for Looking after the Kids over the Phone or Online during Covid-19. *Newsarticle, Manchester Evening News*, 22 May 2020.

Hanson, J. (2001). From Sheltered Housing to Lifetime Homes: An Inclusive Approach to Housing. In S. Winters, ed., *Lifetime Housing in Europe*. Leuven: Katholieke Unversiteit Leuven, pp. 35–57.

Holliss, F. (2012). "Space, Buildings and the Life Worlds of Home-Based Workers: Towards Better Design. In *Visualising the Landscape of Work and Labour*, Sociological Research Online 17(2). www.socresonline.org.uk/17/2/24.html.

Junestrand, S. and Tollmar, K. (1998). The Dwelling as a Place for Work. In N.A. Streitz, S. Konomi and H.J. Burkhardt, eds., *Cooperative Buildings: Integrating Information, Organization, and Architecture.* Lecture Notes in Computer Science, vol. 1370, New York, NY: Springer, pp. 230–247. doi: 10.1007/3-540-69706-3_23.

Kern, S. (2003). *The Culture of Time and Space: 1880-1918.* 2nd edn. Cambridge, MA: Harvard University Press.

Lawrence, R. (1987). *Housing, Dwellings and Homes: Design Theory, Research and Practice.* London: John Wiley & Sons.

Lefebvre, H. (1991). *The Production of Space.* Translated by Donald Nicholson-Smith. Cambridge, MA: Blackwell.

Long, N.J. (2020). From Social Distancing to Social Containment: Reimagining Sociality for the Coronavirus Pandemic. *Medicine Anthropology Theory*. E-print of London School of Economics. http://eprints.lse.ac.uk/103801/.

MacDermid, S.M. (2005). (Re)Considering Conflict between Work and Family. In E.E. Kossek and S.J. Lambert, eds., *Work and Life Integration: Organizational, Cultural, and Individual Perspectives.* Mahwah, NJ: Erlbaum, pp. 19–40.

Mahmood, A., Yamamoto, T., Lee, M. and Steggell, C. (2008). Perceptions and Use of Gerotechnology: Implications for Aging in Place. *Journal of Housing for the Elderly*, 22(1–2), pp. 104–126. doi: 10.1080/02763890802097144.

Mallet, S. (2004). Understanding Homes: A Critical Review of the Literature. *The Sociological Review*, 52(1), pp. 62–89. doi: 10.1111/j.1467-954X.2004.00442.x.

McCreadie, C. and Tinker, A. (2005). The Acceptability of Assistive Technology to Older People. *Ageing and Society*, 25(1), pp. 91–110. doi: 10.1017/S0144686 X0400248x

Mieczakowski, A. and Clarkson, J. (2012). *Ageing, Adaption and Accessibility: Time for the Inclusive Revolution!* Cambridge, UK: Engineering Design Centre.

Mihailidis, A., Boger, J., Czarnuch, S., Nagdee, T. and Hoey, J. (2012). Ambient Assisted Living Technology to Support Older Adults with Dementia with Activities of Daily Living: Key Concepts and the State of the Art. In J.C. Augusto et al., eds., *Handbook of Ambient Assisted Living: Technology for Healthcare, Rehabilitation and Well-being*. Amsterdam: IOS Press, pp. 304–330.

Mordini, E. and de Hert, P. (2010). *Ageing and Invisibility*. Amsterdam: IOS Press.

Norberg-Schultz, C. (1971). *Existence, Space & Architecture*. London: Studio Vista.

Pragnell, M., Spence, L. and Moore, R. (2000). *The Market Potential for Smart Homes*. New York, NY: Joseph Rowntree Foundation. Retrieved from www.jrf.org. uk/sites/files/jrf/1859353789.pdf.

Robinson, K., O'Neill, A., Conneely, M. et al. (2020). Exploring the Beliefs and Experiences of Older Irish Adults and Family Carers during the Novel Coronavirus (COVID-19) Pandemic: A Qualitative Study Protocol. *HRB Open Research 2020*, 3(16). doi: 10.12688/hrbopenres.13031.1.

Rowles, G.D. and Chaudhury, H. (2005). *Home and Identity in Late Life: International Perspectives*. London: Springer.

Saunders, P. (1989). The Meaning of Home in Contemporary English Culture. *Housing Studies*, 4(3), pp. 177–192. doi: 10.1080/02673038908720658.

Saunders, P. and Williams, P. (1988). The Constitution of the Home: Towards a Research Agenda. *Housing Studies*, 3(2), pp. 81–93. doi: 10.1080/02673038808720618.

SENIOR. (2009). D4.1 Report on Best Practices and Roadmap towards the Roadmap. Retrieved August 8, 2013, from: http://globalseci.com/wp-content/uploads/2010/01/ D4.1-Report-on-Best-Practices-and-Roadmap-towards-the-Roadmap.pdf.

Smart Home EU. (2009). How much Does a Smart Home System Cost? Retrieved September 23, 2013, from Smart Home EU: www.smarthome.eu/a/how-much-does-a-smart-home-system-cost.html.

Smith, J. (1986). The Meaning of Home: An Exploratory Study of Environmental Experience. *Journal of Environmental Psychology*, 6(4), pp. 281–298. doi: 10.1016/ S0272-4944(86)80002-0.

Smith, S.G. (1994). The Essential Qualities of a Home. *Journal of Environmental Psychology*, 14(1), pp. 31–46. doi: 10.1016/S0272-4944(05)80196-3.

Steptoe, A., Shankar, A., Demakakos, P. and Wardle, J. (2013). Social Isolation, Loneliness, and All-Cause Mortality in Older Men and Women. *Proceedings of the National Academy of Sciences*, 110(15), pp. 5797–5801. doi: 10.1073/ pnas.1219686110.

Tinker, A. (1997). The Environment of Ageing. *Philosophical Transactions of the Royal Society of London. Series B: Biological Sciences*, 352(1363), p. 1861.

Tiwari, P., Warren, J., Day, K. and McDonald, B. (2010). Some Non-Technology Implications for Wider Application of Robots Assisting Older People. *Health Care and Informatics Review Online*, 14(1), pp. 2–11.

Value Ageing (2010–2014). Incorporating European Fundamental Values into ICT for Ageing: A Vital Political, Ethical, Technological, and Industrial Challenge.

A Marie-Curie-Funded European Commission Research Project, under FP7 Framework. https://cordis.europa.eu/project/id/251686/reporting.

Weiner, M., Callahan, C.M., Tierney, W.M., Overhage, J.M., Mamlin, B., Dexter, P.R. and McDonald, C.J. (2003). Using Information Technology to Improve the Health Care of Older Adults. *Annals of Internal Medicine*, 139(5), Part 2, pp. 430–436. doi: 10.7326/0003-4819-139-5_part_2-200309021-00010.

Wild, K., and Boise, L. (2012). In-Home Monitoring Technologies: Perspectives and Priorities of Older Adults. In J.C. Augusto et al., eds., *Handbook of Ambient Assisted Living: Technology for Healthcare, Rehabilitation and Well-being*. Amsterdam: IOS Press, pp. 94–111. doi: 10.3233/978-1-60750-837-3-94.

Homes as human–robot ecologies

An epistemological inquiry on the "domestication" of robots

Luisa Damiano

The evolution of the smart home: Towards domestic robots

The evolution of the notion of "smart home" offers an overview of the changes that the last three decades of technological innovation have produced in the domestic environment (Aldrich, 2003; Harper, 2011; Ricquebourg et al., 2006; Solaimnai et al., 2015; Venkatesh, 2006, 2008; Yusupov and Ronzhin, 2010). The first part of this transformation can be traced back to the early 1980s, when the personal computer started to be introduced into people's houses. This event, together with the diffusion of electromechanical home devices such as answering machines, microwaves and videocassette recorders, as well as control and alarm systems, triggered a growing interest in highly technological residences. In those years, these "technologically enhanced houses" started to be seen as domestic environments that improve residents' comfort, entertainment, security and convenience based on appliances endowed with forms of automation and/or machine intelligence.

In the 1990s, related processes of home "technologization" were marked by the launch of the Internet, cellular phones and WiFi technologies. In this second evolutionary phase of the smart home domain, "network" became a major keyword, indicating not only information exchanges among the technological devices contained in a smart residence, but also information channels connecting this kind of domestic environment to the external world.

Along this line of development, from the 1990s on the smart home has been designed and prototyped as a "connected home", that is, a "residence equipped with computing and information technology which anticipates and responds to the needs of the occupants [...] through the management of technology within the home and connections to the world beyond" (Aldrich, 2003). Related smart home concepts, which currently are the dominant ones, sketch the profiles of domestic spaces in which information services interact densely, and allow the residents to multiply the activities that can be performed from home. Inside the contemporary "informational houses", domestic activities go far beyond the classic home management and TV-based entertainment.

They typically include work, education, healthcare, socialization, shopping and banking: activities that until recently were realized predominantly outside domestic borders.

According to the literature, the next phase in the evolution of the smart home domain will intensify the present-day tendency to endow houses with forms of machine intelligence. At least two frontier projects share this goal. Strands of traditional artificial intelligence (AI) are working on the creation of "self-learning" and "responsive" homes, able to gather and analyze data about the occupants' domestic activities in order to determine their behavior patterns, better meet their requirements and interact with them. At the same time, subdivisions of robotics are developing "domestic robots", that is, robotic appliances that "socially" interact with the residents and perform autonomously a number of domestic tasks. Undoubtedly both these imminent advancements give reason to expect critical transformations in domestic life.

However, there is a notable difference. Self-learning and responsive homes, as described by the specialists, appear as a further, coherent accomplishment of current smart home projects, in line with contemporary forms of domesticity. This is not the case for home robots, which are characterized in terms of a radically transformative technology. As suggested by preliminary studies, introducing robotic agents into domestic environments will perturb considerably not only the physical, but also the social dimension of people's houses. The embodied character of robots, when it is combined with a social presence, tends to generate new, rich forms of user-artifacts relations, which can modify significantly domestic interactions and activities (Breazeal, 2003; Dautenhahn et al., 2005; Forlizzi and Di Salvo, 2006; Kidd and Breazeal, 2009). The variety of the uses that specialists are planning for domestic robots (e.g., cleaning, cooking, baby-sitting, nursing, entertaining, assisting, training and coaching) amplifies further the potential impact of this emerging technology on home life. Considered together, these factors seem to indicate that a large-scale introduction of home robots in people's houses promises an unprecedented transformation in humans' domesticity and, in general, way of living.

Although this is not the reality yet, domestic robots' challenge to human domesticity is concrete, and should be taken seriously. After a slow and difficult process of implementation, which started in the mid-2000s, home robots are undergoing an initial phase of diffusion that engages specialists in field studies directed to assess and maximize people's acceptance of these machines as new domestic technology. This substantial development both allows and requires additional research meant to determine the scope and the characteristics of these robots' potential impact on contemporary home life, and to define measures capable of warranting its sustainability. This kind of investigation appears particularly urgent when it is viewed in the light of the current state of art in research on home robots. As it is clear from the literature, specialists' attention is predominantly focused on technical aspects of domestic robots, while a sound body of knowledge on the epistemological, anthropological, cultural, social and ethical dimensions of this innovation is still lacking.

Acknowledging this insufficiency, this chapter develops an exploratory analysis of one of the most relevant nontechnical dimensions of the introduction of domestic robots, that is, the epistemological dimension. The underlying idea is that any attempt of implementing robotic platforms for domestic environments operationalizes a number of more or less explicit hypotheses on the human mind and the ways it interacts with its context and the (natural and artificial) agents embedded in it. These epistemological theses are literally embodied into home robots and the processes through which they are designed, installed and integrated within domestic environments. Far from being purely speculative, these hypotheses play a significant role in the transformations imposed on domesticity by this new technology. Hence, in order to understand and regulate these changes, it is critical to consider these hypotheses, and to determine the impact they can have on home life and, in general, human life through the artifacts they inspire.

The analysis developed in the present chapter is aligned with this approach. Its focus is on the epistemological assumptions on the human mind and the mind–technology relation underlying current projects aiming at the "domestication" of robots. The central unit of analysis includes the two research domains primarily engaged in this undertaking: social robotics and design. The goal is threefold: (a) clarifying what models of the human mind, and of the mind–technology relation, currently influence the design and implementation of domestic robots, as well as the strategies of their introduction, as consumer products, into people's homes; (b) delineating the potential impact of these models on human domestic life; and (c) on this basis, suggesting an ethical approach promoting the sustainability of robots' "domestication".

The rise of domestic robots

Like the notion of robot, the idea of domestic robot originally comes from science fiction.[1] Starting from the late 1930s, this idea was developed through narratives that intended to diverge from the already recurrent theme of rebel robots introduced paradigmatically by Karel Čapek's *RUR* (1920/2004), almost two decades before, together with the term "robot". Visionary short stories like Lester del Rey's *Helen O'Loy* (1938) and Isaac Asimov's *Robbie* (1950) presented plots different from the until then prototypical one, that is, the story of artificial human-like creatures that revolt against their human makers and try to destroy them. Interestingly, both del Rey and Asimov built their alternatives on the fictional figure of home robots. The notion that they introduced was that of robotic agents – a housemaid for del Rey and a nurse-maid for Asimov – which use their abilities of thinking and feeling to create a domestic synergy with their human owners, based on trust and affective bonds that, despite humans' initial scepticism and fear, grow daily in the intimacy of home life.

Fictional domestic robots began to inspire concrete robotic appliances after a long period of confinement in science fiction. Their development as concrete objects required not simply a prolonged technical preparation, but also the formation of a subdivision of robotics capable of merging engineering with social and, in general, human sciences. This cross-disciplinary domain, called "social robotics", arose in the mid-2000s in an area of robotics located at the intersection between cognitive robotics and human–robot interaction (HRI). From cognitive robotics, social robotics inherited an "embodied AI" approach that rejects the classical equation between intelligent artifacts and abstract computer programs, and invites practitioners to model intelligence as emerging from the interaction between "embodied" or "complete agents" – i.e., robots – and their environments – including social contexts (Dautenhahn, 2007; Pfeifer and Bongard, 2007). On these grounds, social robotics, from its beginnings, has developed as a "social AI", aiming at providing robots with forms of machine intelligence that are inherently social (Damiano and Dumouchel, 2018).

This is an approach to AI that social robotics has implemented not only for the purely scientific aspiration of deepening the understanding of intelligence by building robotic models of cognitive processes. A significant part of social robotics' production is directed towards creating interactive robots for HRI operative settings. From the 2000s, when HRI was founded as a research domain dedicated to study and improve the interactive performances of human-operated robots, its specialists recognized the potentially applicative advantages of empowering robotic appliances with the ability of communicating with humans through shared social signals. Related research, combining embodied social AI and HRI, can be considered as the first expression of applicative social robotics. The specialists' efforts were not any longer focusing on building empowered human-operated robots. The ambition was that of developing "social robots": robotic agents endowed with "peer-to-peer interaction skills" allowing them to socially interact with humans not only as "co-workers" but also as "partners", "companions" or "friends" – in short, as "peers" (Fong et al., 2003).

The programmatic notion of social robots did not simply virtually extend the possible uses of robotics appliances to socially interactive roles – "office, medicine, hotel use, cooking, marketing, entertainment, hobbies, recreation, nursing care, therapy and rehabilitation (…), personal assistance" (Daily et al., 2017). The specialists involved in the development of these robots saw in their sociability the key to address the difficulties of introducing robotic appliances in public and, in particular, domestic environments. Compared to computers, embodied agents – especially when they are capable of moving around – are much more intrusive. People can perceive them as extraneous agents, which imposes in their public or private spaces a presence that is similar to that of animals or persons whose behavior is hard to interpret. Lacking communicational interfaces similar to that of computers, robots can exhibit unintelligible behavior, making their use and related interactions quite problematic. Additionally, the images of robotic agents diffused by science fiction tend to generate high expectations on their performances, which actual robots, due to their significant technical limits, can easily frustrate. For these and related difficulties, social robotics has planned to develop solutions defined in terms of equipping robotic agents with appropriate social skills. The strategy underlying the field is basically this: tackling the challenge of making robots accepted within human spaces as the problem of "social acceptance" of robots (Dautenhahn, 2007).

This approach promises to be successful even in the case of the most private of human spaces – homes. Such an expectation flows from a series of studies conducted on the first domestic robots, which show how very basic robotic appliances, straightforwardly designed and built as tools, tend to be recognized by users as social actors. The first of these works, dating back to the mid-2000s, focused on the robotic vacuum cleaner Roomba's long-term integration into people's houses (Forlizzi and Di Salvo, 2006; Sung et al., 2007, 2010). One of the main insights is that Roomba owners typically treat their robot as if it would have intentions, beliefs and emotions, which channel in Roomba a "social presence"[2]. These responses are recognized to rely on Roomba's interactive features, consisting mainly of autonomous movement related to a basic sensing of its environment. As scientific investigations on anthropomorphism point out, these characteristics act on humans as powerful triggers of anthropomorphic (or zoomorphic) projections, and promote human social interaction with objects or nonhuman beings (Airenti, 2015). In the eyes of its users, Roomba's interactive traits, despite being unsophisticated and strictly related to its function, raise the robot from the status of an object and transform it into a subject – an interlocutor, and, in the long term, a "member of the family". Such an "interactive metamorphosis" is acknowledged as what grants Roomba a full acceptance within domestic environments, based on the establishment of user-artifact relations connoted by an emotional and empathic dimension. On the side of its human users, prolonged interaction with this robot entails the development of affective bonds and protective behavior, leading also to a certain propensity to accept its technical limits and lessening its failures. Furthermore, as these studies emphasize, Roomba's long-term use can impact both the habits and the social relations of the household's members. It tends to provoke changes that are not limited to home-cleaning modalities and schedules, but include the redistribution of related home-management tasks, together with transformations in other aspects of the residents' interactions – mainly concerning social exchanges among them and, sometimes, even between them and their neighbors.

Beginning from the mid-2000s, these kinds of findings on the social quality of robotic appliances' integrability into people's homes have encouraged the development of *social* domestic robots (Breazeal, 2003; Dautenhahn, 2007; Dautenhahn et al., 2005; Kidd and Breazeal, 2009). The idea is that of robotic agents that combine a wide variety of domestic functions with an interactive presence based on social skills that range from accurately designed anthropomorphizing features to proper social competences, implemented by social AI. As the user studies started in those years indicate, these home robots attract the consumers' demand also for tasks that are considerably more delicate than cooking and cleaning. Among the prominent roles designed by social robotics for domestic robots is home assistance for people who still intend to live on their own despite experiencing a substantial loss of autonomy due to advanced age, impairments or medical conditions.

The special status that social performances grant to robots, by blurring the object/subject divide, induces a proportion of more fragile people to prefer robotic to human assistants. Typically, these users recognize social robots as machines that, as such, do not judge them as other humans could, and so can accompany them unproblematically even in the most embarrassing situations. At the same time, the social skills of these robots lead the users to consider these artifacts also as interlocutors, that is, active subjects of positive "caring" interaction, which invariably offer them availability and sympathy as the beneficial result of a rigidly predefined behavior (Dumouchel and Damiano, 2017). This ambiguous presence of social robots, which make their classification in terms of the classic object/subject dichotomy more difficult, generates a certain preference for these robotic agents also with regard to other assistive roles – a vast ensemble of functions, ranging from weight-loss coaching to educational tutoring (e.g., Kidd and Breazeal, 2009).

On these grounds, social robotics is developing different robotic agents – butlers, companions, nurses, maids, trainers, coaches and assistants, among others – that are meant to acquire a social status and thereby full acceptance into domestic spaces, based on their social skills. Typically, specialists develop this undertaking based on conceptual frameworks that characterize households as complex and dynamic environments, or "ecologies", in which humans "co-evolve" with robots as their social partners. As it is evident from the literature, social robotics shares this theoretical framework with prospective studies on domestic robots realized within the field of design (e.g., Sung et al., 2007, 2010; Vernkatesh, 2006, 2008).

Designing houses as ecologies of mixed social actors

The developments of robotic research in the area of domestic appliances resulted in the emergence of a new trend in home design, dedicated to create "behavioral objects" (Levillain and Zibetti, 2017). These are ordinary artifacts that are enriched with motion patterns meant to enhance their functionality and make their use intuitive. The additional movements, realized through basic robotic technology, are designed to encourage users to socially interact with these artifacts, and learn how to use them through social cues generated by the objects during interaction.

As in social robotics, the strategy to induce and orient the use of these artifacts involves explicit anthropomorphism. These behavioral functions are specifically designed to stimulate users to ascribe to them intentions, emotions, beliefs and other mental properties. As the label "behavioral objects" emphasizes, the trigger for anthropomorphic projections exploited by these artifacts is "realistic movement": motion patterns based on animal or human movements to give users the impression of a certain level of behavioral complexity.

Typically the anthropomorphic design of behavioral objects does not include realistic appearance, used commonly in robotics as a powerful way to elicit anthropomorphization. This choice is aligned with contemporary readings of "the uncanny valley" effect (Mori, 1970; Damiano and Dumouchel, 2018), which underlines the predominance of movement on appearance in activating anthropomorphizing interactions. Additionally, they are inspired by neurophysiological literature exploring the human tendency to interpret autonomous motion patterns in terms of organized behavior. On these grounds, designers convey in the motion of behavioral objects subtle social cues directed to enrich the functional relation to these artifacts with curiosity, attempts of behavior interpretation and resulting anthropomorphic attributions, which generate in users the feeling of a social presence – a "co-presence".

A paradigmatic example of behavioral object, exemplifying these traits, is the "the impatient toaster". This is a normal toaster with an integrated behavioral function that periodically makes it vibrate "nervously", and then stays still when bread to be toasted is inserted in it, or the bread that has been toasted is removed (Burneleit et al., 2009). As it has been shown, this behavior induces in users empathically charged anthropomorphizing responses: dialoguing with the toaster, gently touching it to soothe it, describing its behavior in psychological terms – stress, hunger, impatience and goals. Like Roomba, the impatient toaster gains in the users' eyes the status of a social actor, based on the capability of perceiving basic aspects of its environment and using this perception to modulate a minimal form of autonomous motion.[3]

In this sense, the behavioral objects trend implements a *minimalistic approach* to social domestic robotics, targeting exclusively the production of *minimally social* domestic robots, that is, home robots whose sociability relies not on AI, but on the manipulation of the human tendency to anthropomorphize things. What the robotization of daily life domestic objects targets is the diffusion of these artifacts, as consumer products, within people's homes through their social acceptance. With social robotics, behavioral objects design shares the main goal: building machines that, through socially interactive skills, reach – and cross, in an oscillatory way – the threshold between the realm of objects and that of subjects.

Like other social home robots, domestic behavioral objects are "evocative objects" (Levillain and Zibetti, 2017), which blur the traditional ontological categories used by humans to describe their world (Gaudiello et al., 2015; Severson and Carlson, 2010). As many contemporary investigations reveal, (teenagers, adults and elder) users show a tendency to perceive these artifacts as ambiguous objects, which break a series of boundaries belonging to the traditional ontological categorization – "sentient/not sentient, intelligent/not intelligent, and alive/not alive" (Kahn et al., 2002). In other words, human users tend to attribute to these artifacts a status that is in between the extremes defined by these dichotomies, on the threshold of the old divides – "a sort of alive", "alive enough" (Turkle, 2011). Through this ontological ambiguity, which generates their special form of social presence, these robots acquire social acceptance into human spaces, and promise to human houses the acquisition of new traits. In the era of the construction of robotic "subjectified objects", domestic environments start to be populated by social actors that are not limited to human residents and their pets. They begin to be co-inhabited by a variety of artificial agents, endowed with different capabilities, forms of social interaction, degrees and ways of being objects *and* subjects, inanimate *and* animated, non-living *and* living.

The convergence of design and social robotics in this kind of innovation of human domestic environments is reflected in common multidisciplinary sources and bidirectional exchanges of knowledge. On these bases, design and social robotics tend to converge in key metaphors and conceptual frameworks, which privilege notions coming from biological theories of adaptation within complex and dynamic environments – "ecologies" (e.g., Sung et al., 2007, 2010; Vernkatesh, 2006, 2008).

In line with this tendency, recent studies in speculative design propose to interpret and explore the introduction of robots in domestic spaces in terms of adaptive processes activated by the transfer of a species in a new environment – the migration of robots from scientific labs to people's houses (e.g., Auger, 2014). This view converges, in some of its key aspects, with a well-known theoretical framework in the field of design, recently adopted by HRI and social robotics. Its creator, designer Jodi Forlizzi, called it "product ecology" (Forlizzi, 2008). She developed it to address complex design problems by charting the dynamic relationships articulating all the processes and actors involved.

Forlizzi explicitly drew this framework on "social ecology theory" (Netting, 1986), which proposes to apply a systemic approach to the study of social processes. The underlying naturalistic assumption is that human behavior can be studied as a dynamic of co-adaptation with a complex environment, conceptualized as a set of interconnected processes, actors and levels of interaction. "Product ecology" develops these systemic premises, within the field of design, towards the goal of allowing comprehensive studies of the social relationships in which a product is embedded.

This focus on social connections, together with the general systemic approach, makes this framework particularly suitable for the analysis of the "domestication" of technological products deliberately designed as social interlocutors for their users. Based on this consideration, "product ecology" has been often used to frame research on domestic robots, and in particular on Roomba, both in design and social robotics (Forlizzi and Di Salvo, 2006; Sung et al., 2007, 2010). Within these fields, this approach structured prospective studies that typically characterize "robotized" domestic environments as mixed "ecologies", which integrate human and artificial social actors through processes of "co-evolution".

Domestic robots and the embodied mind: Assimilation or coupling?

In social robotics and design, the ecological metaphor tends to be developed in the context of theoretical descriptions of the relationship between humans and their domestic environments that reflects the significant influence exercised on these domains by the contemporary evolution of cognitive sciences and, in particular, by the emergence, within their disciplinary complex, of the so-called "embodied approach" (Clark, 1997). This embodied inclination, which in social robotics expresses the programmatic goal of developing a social embodied AI, in design reflects the active involvement of a significant part of the community in the transition from computer-centered to robot-centered notions of smart homes. On these grounds, the images of "robotized" domestic environments – "domestic ecologies" – produced by social robotics and design are drawn on the lines of the new "body-friendly" models of mind and, in particular, of the mind–technology relation created within the context of embodied cognitive science.

The following pages, dedicated to the theoretical views of the mind–technology relation underlying current projects of robots' domestication, focus on the two most influential theoretical perspectives within today's debate on the relationship between the embodied mind and technological objects: the hypothesis of extension and the hypothesis of enaction. It will be shown that, although currently these hypotheses are considered part of a single approach, called *4E* (Newen et al., 2018), they propose different views of the mind–technology relation, and have significantly divergent implications for the theoretical and ethical aspects of domestic robots.

The extended mind hypothesis: Domestic robots as humans' extensions

Among the main advancements usually ascribed to embodied cognitive science, there is a new, positive emphasis on the role played by technology in the development and the functioning of human cognition. Classical computationalism, despite its focus on the computer as the appropriate (theoretical and synthetic) model to study the human mind, did not specifically explore the mind–technology relation. This was brought into attention in the context of an embodied reinterpretation of the mind that maintains the classical metaphor of the computer, but imposes on it bodily and environmental constraints. Andy Clark and David Chalmers (1998) elaborated this moderated revision of computationalism in the form of the "extended mind hypothesis": an attempt of profiling the embodied mind that defines it as a computational device located in the human brain, but structurally characterized by "extendable" borders.

The "extension" of mind thematized by the Clark–Chalmers hypothesis does not simply express the now commonsensical idea that the human mind is "augmented", or enhanced, by the use of technologies ranging from handwriting to the Internet and the latest forms of machine intelligence. The "extension" of mind hypothesized by Clark and Chalmers, more than a technological intensification of our cognitive powers, is an extension of mind into space (Damiano, 2009; Dumouchel and Damiano, 2017). The theoretical premise is that if mind is embodied, then it has to be a material object, whose processes have to supervene on the physical processes characterizing the components of this object. Hence, the human mind has a spatial extension, which, for Clark and Chalmers, corresponds mostly with the extension of the human brain, but can also exceed it. Their hypothesis defines this extendibility of mind through a "parity principle" according to which, to accomplish certain tasks, mental processes cross the spatial limits of the area occupied by the brain. They overcome the borders of "skull and skin", and extend up to include the external objects of which the agent makes use to realize these tasks – for example, a paper notebook used by a person to retrieve information which she had previously written down. As Clark and Chalmers put it, in general terms:

> If, as we confront a task, a part of the world functions as a process which, were it to go on in the head, we would have no hesitation in accepting as part of the cognitive process, then that part of the world is (for that time) part of the cognitive process.
>
> (Clark and Chalmers, 1998)

It is not possible to retrace in these pages the debate that has developed around this thesis over the last 20 years, generating variations and revisions (Newen et al., 2018). In order to delineate the influence of the extended mind approach on theoretical and ethical reflections inherent to domestic robots, it is enough to briefly dwell on some aspects of the original version of the Clark–Chalmers hypothesis, starting with its functionalist orientation (Wheeler, 2010).

As a part of the current debate emphasizes, the Clark–Chalmers hypothesis proposes a variant of the "multiple realizability" of the computational mind (Shapiro, 2007) that, instead of focusing on functional substitutes for brain, is centered on its potential material extensions, which it identifies in all the external resources that an agent may use to perform her cognitive tasks. Indeed, the main point of the Clark–Chalmers parity principle is this: cognitive processes that run in the human brain can run equally well in extended systems composed of the brain plus the artifacts used by the agent to accomplish a certain cognitive task. In this sense, Clark and Chalmers, while insisting on the importance of embodiment for cognitive processes, re-present an abstract and ultimately disembodied account of the cognitive mind. In their theoretical proposal, as in classical computationalism, mental processes, at the functional level, are essentially independent from the specificities of their material supports. Their rejection of René Descartes' *res cogitans*, realized by conceptualizing the cognitive mind as *res extensa*, ends up in re-proposing the Cartesian image of an individual and homogeneous cognitive organization essentially independent from the specificities of its material realization (Dumouchel and Damiano, 2017).

With regard to the role of technology in cognition, this perspective generates an evident ambiguity. On one side, it emphasizes the key role played by technological artifacts in the accomplishment of human cognitive tasks. On the other side, it denies to these objects any cognitive independence from the human mind. In the epistemological space defined by the Clark–Chalmers hypothesis, the human mind is the only genuine cognitive system. The objects in which technology is realized become properly cognitive only when they are integrated into the human mind in the form of its extensions. This way, if these artifacts, like computers or robots, are capable of performing cognitive tasks when they interact with an agent, they are assimilated, literally absorbed by her mind through functional equivalence. Rigorously speaking, the "embodied" mind, as designed by the Clark–Chalmers hypothesis, cannot interact with artificial cognitive systems without transforming them into its own extensions. It is in this sense that the extended mind hypothesis, far from overcoming, radicalizes the anthropocentric prejudice, and thereby prepares a radically anthropocentric approach to the domestication of robots.

To social robotics and design, the Clark–Chalmers hypothesis prospects future domestic environments, which will integrate home robots, as purely human spaces. More specifically, it urges to conceptualize cognitive interactions based on social exchanges between humans and robots as homogeneously human processes – processes that belong to the minds of the interacting human agents. This interpretation is supported by the thesis on social cognition presented in *The Extended Mind*. The markedly individualist approach led Clark and Chalmers to believe that in the interactions between two human agents – at least in cases defined by accessibility and reliability of the interlocutor – one becomes the place of the extension of the mind of the other. For example, a waiter who reminds a regular customer of her preferences is considered part of an individual process of data recovery performed by the user. Applied to interactions between humans and social robots, this perspective requires interpreting the cognitive tasks that these artifacts perform by interacting with humans – for example, the recognition of the user's emotions, the proposal of rehabilitation activities suited to her profile, the indication of schedules in which to take medicines – not as elements of a socially distributed human–robot cognitive network, but as processes of extension, and univocal expression, of the individual mind of human agents.

This perspective denies robots social properties and cognitive processes, regardless of their cognitive architectures and interactive skills. It delegitimizes the ambition of social robotics to build artificial interlocutors, and reduces its goal to the development of artifacts for the expression of our cognitive processes – processes conceived as essentially individual even when they are taking place in social contexts. On this basis, the Clark–Chalmers hypothesis requires us to interpret human–robot social interactions as bundles of human "self-behaviors" (von Foerster, 2003). That is, it characterizes them as places of the solitary expression of human cognitive and social skills, and radically excludes the possibility that they could host a new form of sociality – a human–robot sociality. In this way, this hypothesis generates an epistemological framework proposing that, while interacting with domestic social robots, we are (solitary) *Natural-born Cyborgs* (Clark, 2003), which converges with the slogan proposed by Sherry Turkle to describe the relationships maintained by humans with social robots – *Alone Together* (Turkle, 2011).

The extended mind hypothesis offers epistemological support to the currently prevailing ethical reflection on domestic and, in general, social robots. This view, paradigmatically expressed by Turkle's position, qualifies the presence and social performance of robots – independently from the specificities of their implementation – as purely human manifestations, or the result of mere user's projections. On this basis it condemns these artefacts not only as nonauthentic, but also as expressions of a deceptive technology, which generates the illusion of having genuinely social relationships with machines incapable of such relations. This perspective is associated typically with a dystopian view on the diffusion of social robots, recognized as a potential cause of the degeneration of the social bond: delegation to these machines of care and support relationships, with the exclusion of the subjects with special needs from the social sphere; generalized preference of social and emotional interactions with robotic agents to the detriment of those between human agents; unprecedented and radical forms of social isolation, etc. On these bases, this approach tends to make the social sustainability of these new robots converge with their abolition – "the exclusion of these evocative objects from the realm of our relationships" (Turkle, 2010).

However, this position, while having the evident merit of emphasizing some of the dangers inherent to these new "social machines" (Brooks, 2002), is also characterized by significant criticalities. As highlighted by Damiano and

Dumouchel (2018), these are not limited to the aprioristic exclusion of the possibility of beneficial uses of social robots in different domains, including that of domestic assistance for people with special needs. The central problem of this position is the isolation of ethical reflection. It reduces it to a generalized rejection of social robots, destined to remain unheeded by robotic research due to its inability to offer concrete guidelines that enable the management of the dangers and the maximization of the benefits of this new technology.

Although it happens rarely, the solitary cyborgs epistemology is also expressed in ethical approaches that emphasize not so much the dangers, as it does the potential of social robots, especially with respect to the projects of assistance. In general, these are exploratory studies which, while encouraging the production of potentially generative analyses of concrete ethical guidelines for robotics, involve a significant risk. Their epistemic anthropocentrism tends to lead them to exclude the possibility of effects emergent from human–robot interactions that are relevant for ethical inquiries on the sustainability of the mixed human–robot social ecologies, including robotized domestic environments.

Enaction: Home robots as integral elements of the ecology of mind

Alternative approaches are promoted by the most reformist orientation of embodiment, often called "radical embodiment" (Clark, 1997; Thompson and Varela, 2001). Generally, this is characterized by replacing the engineering model of the computer with models of biological origin able to capture the specific property that distinguishes natural cognitive systems from artificial cognitive systems, that is, the ability of the former to produce themselves by themselves, through metabolism. This is a theoretical transition that tends to generate innovative solutions to the characterization of the cognitive mind, diverging not only from classical computationalism but also from moderate forms of embodiment.

One of the paradigmatic expressions of radical embodiment is often identified in Francisco Varela's enaction (Varela et al., 1991). The innovativeness of this theory is based on its rejection of the prevailing descriptive embodiment solutions that places the mind in the brain. Varela chooses a dynamic approach, through which he characterizes the mind as a cognitive structure emerging from the regulatory processes by which the nervous system ensures the continuity of the cognizer's processes of self-production (Thompson and Varela, 2001). This descriptive solution outlines the mind as a structure of interconnection which, through the regulation cycles of the nervous system, couples the dynamics of all the systems involved in the cognitive agent's self-production – basically brain, body, environment and other systems integrated therein (Damiano, 2009).

This revision of the classical view, while converging with the Clark–Chalmers approach in redefining the boundaries of the cognitive mind, produces a theoretical proposal irreducible to that of extension. Like Varela, also Clark and Chalmers put emphasis on the need of thematizing cognition as a brain–body–environment dynamic coupling that guarantees the agent's capacity of performing effective interactions. But in the perspective of the extended mind approach, this dynamic is properly cognitive when it is based on an information processing activity that takes place in the brain or in hybrid systems integrating it with extra-neural elements – its functional extensions. The enactive perspective instead identifies the "cognitive mark" (Clark, 1997) in the dynamic coupling itself, that is, the dynamic interconnection through which the systems involved in the cognitive agent's self-production co-evolve, adopting compatible dynamic configurations. The idea is that of an interdependent process of co-transformation that generates the agent's ability to permanently associate, to the dynamic configurations of the environment, those of its own configurations of activity which enable its viability in given environmental conditions.

This process of coupling is qualified by enaction as cognitive since it expresses the agent's capability to generate viable operational meanings for environmental events: dynamic patterns of self-production that allow the agent to effectively treat its environment as a meaningful space in terms of its specific possibilities and needs of interaction. As enaction emphasizes, when considered in this way, cognitive activity does neither take place in the agent's brain or body, nor in its environment. From an enactive point of view, cognitive activity resides not in – one or more of – these systems, but in their dynamic interdependence: the multiple coupling between brain, body and environment that allows the agent to produce meanings, for environmental events, ensuring its operational effectiveness within the context in which it exists.

Based on this structure, the enactive approach rejects not only the computationalist, but also the externalist and functionalist inclinations characterizing the extended mind hypothesis. Enaction conceptualizes a cognitive mind that, despite being strictly dependent on the material aspects of the systems through which it is realized, is not confined to the spatial dimension. The enactive mind overcomes the classic alternative between *res cogitans* and *res extensa*, and defines itself as a relationship: the body–brain–environment relation of co-determination, supported by the nervous system, through which the cognitive agent preserves and develops its own way of existence by interacting effectively with its environmental and social context.

This way, the enactive approach opens a new perspective on the relationship between mind and technology. It rejects the thematization of the technologically supported cognitive "augmentations" in terms of functional equivalences between "intra" and "extra-cranial" processes that extend the agent's individual mind. It proposes to think cognitive augmentations supported by technological objects as enriched forms of brain–body–environment coupling. The image is that of further diversification – further distribution in organizational levels in interaction – of the enactive mind. The use of cognitive technologies, instead of producing the external expansion of the agent's internal mind, generates a complexification of the process of co-transformation in which its brain, body and environment are involved. In other words, technological objects are integrated in the co-evolutionary complex through which the agent, by generating operational meanings for environmental events, acts effectively in its domain of existence.

With regard to the issue of domestic social robots, this framework proposes a relational and pluralistic solution. It asks to conceive future robotized domestic environments as cognitive networks structured by exchanges of social signals that interconnect different types of cognitive systems – that are, respectively, bio-anthropological and computational cognitive systems – in heterogeneous social contexts. Indeed, enaction denies (social) robots the autonomy of self-production typical of biological systems, and, in particular, the cognitive and social traits in which this form of autonomy expresses itself at the anthropological level. At the same time, however, this approach recognizes social robots as systems that, based on computational cognitive and social skills, in certain conditions can involve humans in processes of "behavioral coupling".

On these grounds, the enactive perspective opens the possibility of thematizing forms of human–robot interactions in which human and robotic agents, through the exchange of compatible social signals, coordinate some aspects of their respective dynamics and dispositions to act, in a way that allows them to maintain or enhance their operational effectiveness in their ecologies of reference. This thesis, presented in detail elsewhere in relation to emotional processes (Damiano and Dumouchel, 2020; Dumouchel and Damiano, 2017), prospects the possibility of human–robot interactions that are able to structure new forms of social coordination, irreducibly different from those humans establish with other humans and with animals. The idea is that of extremely limited and specific, but genuine forms of behavioral coupling, whose influence on our ethical conduct requires to be understood through specific studies.

The enactive hypothesis thus lays the foundation for an alternative to the Clarkian scenario describing us, in future robotized domestic environments, as solitary natural-born cyborgs. The enactive perspective, articulating the thesis of a human–robot social co-evolution, generates different possibilities for the thematization of our co-habitancy with domestic social robots. At the level of the theoretical characterization of mixed human–robot domestic ecologies, this view expresses the need to replace the widespread anthropocentric, often caricatural and mainly dystopian readings of the domestication of social robots with open and critical examinations. Likewise, on an ethical level, this perspective calls for the replacement of the absolute and *a priori* condemnation of these artifacts, with the exploration of the risks and potential benefits of specific projects of domestic social robots.

Today this programmatic direction begins to generate concrete approaches, exemplified by lines of investigation such as the recent *Integrated Social Robotics* (Seibt, 2016) and *Synthetic Ethics* (Damiano and Dumouchel, 2018, 2020). For both of these research lines, the objective is to overcome an ethical evaluation of (domestic) social robots that intervenes externally and *a posteriori* with respect to their production. The intent is to involve ethical research in the processes of ideation, design, construction and integration of these machines into our domestic and, in general, social contexts. The *Synthetic Ethics* program includes also the project to use the experimental scenarios structured by social robotics and design to explore value choices and ethical conducts that are susceptible to emerge from human–robot interactions in domestic and, in general, social contexts. This kind of research approach proposes an ethical reflection on (domestic) social robots to interpret their social sustainability not as their abolition, but as their adoption as tools for our self-knowledge, self-understanding and self-development. On the one hand, the goal is to use these artifacts to open up a new experimental angle on human ethical behavior, in particular, in relation to mixed social contexts. On the other hand, the objective is to improve the ethical dimension of social domestic robotic technology. The ambition is to support actively its sustainable development by transforming the identification of the dangers associated with the robots it produces into research questions to be given concretely implementable answers. How to build domestic social robots that strengthen the social bond instead of weakening it? How to use domestic social robots to enhance the social life of people with special needs forced to spend their time at home? Although this approach is still in development, its proactive inclination is stimulating concrete synergies between philosophical reflection and scientific-technological research, and promises effective applications of the underlying programmatic line.

Between moderated and radical embodiment

In current social robotics and design literature, the ecological metaphor is mainly construed through theoretical notions typical of radical embodiment approaches – "ecological niche", "complex systems", "complex dynamics", "co-adaptation", "distributed networks", etc. (e.g., Auger, 2014; Dautenhahn, 2007; Fong et al., 2003; Forlizzi, 2008; Forlizzi and Di Salvo, 2006; Venkatesh, 2006, 2008). Among them, one of the most recurrent is the idea of "co-evolution", typically used to characterize the relation between human agents and home social robots within domestic environments. However, this convergence on key theoretical terms does not reflect the integral adoption of related views of mind. Within these fields the notions from radical embodiment tend to be installed not in radical, but in moderated embodiment frameworks, where the thesis of the dynamic coupling between human and robotic agents is articulated around the mainstream embodied redrawing of the computational mind: the image of an individual, internal and separable symbol processing organization, whose functioning depends also on bodily and environmental constraints, including social constraints.

This hybridization thus results in theoretical prospects that adhere to the Clark–Chalmers perspective concerning the basic organization of mind, and yet characterize its relation with technological objects not in the terms of the parity principle extension, but in those of complex enactive co-evolution. This way, the idea of homes as ecologies in which natural and artificial cognitive agents co-evolve often coexists with individualist and internalist views of the organization of the human mind. Or, analogously, the programmatic concept of households as distributed human–robot social networks, grounded in social couplings between human and robotic agents, relies on characterizations of robots' sociability that are mainly based on the dichotomous choice between a pure human projection and a substantial individual property, and not on the thematization of a quality emerging from processes of human–robot coordination. These and similar combinations of elements coming from moderated and radical embodiment express an uncertainty between these two views of mind that does not simply reflect the general hesitancy of the "embodiment turn" in cognitive science and AI (Ziemke, 2016). The fields involved in the construction of domestic robots, when opting for developing the mainstream "body-friendly" re-interpretations of the computationalist concept of mind, have to refuse the related thematization of the mind–technology relation. To support their ambition of building technological artifacts that, far from being mere tools that lack any cognitive independence, can play the role of a social artificial species, capable of cooperating with humans, they need theoretical solutions that, like the radical embodied ones, account for the heterogeneous and coordinative character of the cognitive and the social domain. In this sense, while current embodied cognitive science and AI still hesitate between moderated and radical embodiment (Shapiro, 2007; Ziemke, 2016), the research fields currently forming domestic robotics appear to be engaged in a shift from moderated towards radical embodiment positions. Plausibly, the realization of this shift is one of the factors that may allow them to ward off the dangers that inevitably come from the diffusion of domestic social robots, and that often are hidden in the ideas of mixed social domestic ecologies and mind–technology, or human–robot, co-evolution.

Toward an integrated ecological ethics: Domestic social robots as connectors

In both design and social robotics, the theoretical characterization of domestic environments as human–robot ecologies displays a specificity. It is articulated on frameworks that, like the Forlizzi's "product ecology", center the ecological description of the network of relations characterizing these spaces not on their human residents, but on the robots introduced there. This option, undoubtedly useful to the goal of exploring in depth the ways in which domestic robots gain social integration into people's homes, displays problematic aspects when the objective of diffusing these artifacts as consumer products is associated with that of warranting the sustainability of the technological innovation they represent. The positive emphasis on robots' ecological embedment into humans' households, based on their capability of playing the role of social partners for humans, conceals a significant risk. It is the danger that ethical reflection condemning social robots typically associates with them: turning people away from social relationships with other humans, and reducing their social life to interactions with robots (e.g., Tisseron, 2015; Turkle, 2010, 2011).

In the case of domestic robots, this danger is particularly significant for people who spend a considerable amount of time alone at home, and especially vulnerable persons assisted domestically by social robots. However, the critical issue is not the one denounced through the slogan "alone together", that is, the simulative character of robots' social performances, which would make of them inherently deceptive artifacts, which create in their users the illusion of reciprocal affective relations. As argued thoroughly elsewhere (Damiano and Dumouchel, 2018), this view of social robots suffers of a series of difficulties. Firstly, it is questionable at a theoretical level – and not simply for its Cartesian roots. The equation between "simulation" and "imposture" is unable to account for fundamental ethical differences between undertakings in social robotics. Based on this equation, it is impossible to distinguish, at the ethical level, between projects dedicated to empower vulnerable or impaired persons, like undertakings directed towards producing robots capable of helping autistic children to develop social skills, and merely commercial projects. The gravity of this impossibility emerges considering that these commercial undertakings include projects dedicated to sell robots on which humans are allowed to exercise violence. There are already, for instance, sex robots on the market that have an integrated "rape option". Ethical reflection focused on the simulative character of social robots in the case of robots for autistic children will point out the dangers of exposing vulnerable persons to "simulated affective relation", while in the second case will put the emphasis on "simulated rape". This may lead to defend rather than to condemn the related practice – "it does not hurt anyone" – and, more importantly, to miss the fact that allowing the diffusion of this kind of robot corresponds to encouraging rape *tout court* – that is, encouraging rape on agents that are perceived by their users as social peers (Damiano and Dumouchel, 2018, 2020).

Furthermore, the only coherent ethical position associated with the "alone together" perspective is a radical condemnation of all social robots – and, in general, of all "socially evocative" technological objects – which, in line with this view, "should not be allowed into the realm of human relationships" (Turkle, 2010, p. 4). The limit of this ethical positioning is its ultimate impotence. The ethical denunciation of social robots cannot stop their development and their diffusion, and can favor, indirectly, the ethical detriment of these processes. In lack of the engagement of ethics in addressing concrete questions, analyzing the benefits and risks of specific projects in social robotics and HRI, and providing applicable, constructive recommendations to these fields, the process of development and diffusion of social robots will advance without any ethical guidance – that is, with the only guidance of the market demand.

The main problem that today ethical reflection has to address is not that of banishing social robots, but that of concretely orienting their construction towards sustainability. In other words, the main problem is to develop a solid alternative to the diffused approach that tends to generate an ethical reflection which intervenes *a posteriori* – after the production of these artifacts – to *a priori* condemn their use. The critical need is that of an ethical inquiry capable of positively, proactively participating in the processes of design, construction and integration of social robots in the contexts of their use. Pioneering projects promoting this new approach, such as Integrative Social Robotics and Synthetic Ethics, converge in a key point: ethical issues are an integral part of the very development of social robots, and have to be addressed at the level of their theoretical ideation, implementation and experimental testing, rather than being raised from the outside and afterward. As argued elsewhere (Damiano and Dumouchel, 2018), one of the conditions to be met in view of the establishment of this approach is the development of shared epistemological and theoretical spaces, favoring communication, cross-fertilization and transdisciplinary synergies between the fields involved in the development of social robots and related ethical inquiries. This corresponds to the urgent need of an ethical reflection that recognizes the heterogeneity of the cognitive and the social domains, and the fact that forms of social co-evolution between robots and humans are already a reality, at least in the experience of the human users of social robots.

Within the research domains involved in the creation of domestic social robots, a first step in this direction can be that of developing an "ecological ethics", which, being aligned with the robotic ecological approach, attempts at transforming interconnection, from a mainly commercial value introduced to increase the diffusion of home robots as consumer products, into an ethical value. The idea is that of a value which, instead of prioritizing the inclusion of robots into domestic environments by enhancing their networks of relations, favors the design of robots as "social connectors": artificial social agents that contrast the risk of isolation inherent to domestic robotic technology by prioritizing the goal of empowering human–human relations inside and outside domestic environments.

A first concrete move in this direction can be that of developing ecological frameworks for robots' domestication that re-articulate design, plans of implementation and related explorations of robotized houses – that is, homes as mixed human–robot social ecologies – on their human residents', and not on the robots', networks of relations. These new frameworks would offer ideal theoretical contexts to transdisciplinary ethical inquiries focused on research questions related to the robotic empowerment of human relations: how can be designed home robots that function as social connectors, strengthening human–human relationships, instead of isolating domestic environments and their inhabitants? How can be built home robots that encourage and mediate exchanges among humans, inside and outside the domestic environments, instead of favoring their escape from the challenges of human–human interaction, and estrangement in an effortless domesticity made of human–robot interaction? One of the main characteristics of such an ethics of domestic social robotics would be an explorative inclination, leading it not to apply predefined set of rules, but to couple its regulative activity to theoretical and empirical research on ethical aspects of human–robot interaction, with the goal of using this technology as a means to transform the ethical values guiding the contexts of its uses in the direction of human moral growth.

Notes

1 For a brief history of robotics, which recognizes the significant role played in the development of this field by science fiction, together with "cinematic creativity, scientific ingenuity, and entrepreneurial vision", see Stone (2018).
2 Social presence in robotics is defined as the capability of a robot to give its users the "sense of being with another" (Biocca et al., 2003), or the "feeling of being in the company of another" (Heerink et al., 2008).
3 There are two main differences between *Roomba* and behavioral objects like *The impatient toaster*. First, in these objects the movement is not necessarily related to their main function, and is carefully designed in order to trigger in users behavior interpretation and anthropomorphic projections. Second, in this new class of objects the evocative behaviors are related to new, useful functions, typically lacking in these artifacts' ordinary versions. For *The impatient toaster* this additional function is helping users to eat regularly (see Burneleit et al., 2009).

References

Airenti, G. (2015). The Cognitive Bases of Anthropomorphism: From Relatedness to Empathy. *International Journal of Social Robotics*, 7, pp. 117–127. doi: 10.1007/s12369-014-0263-x.

Aldrich, F.K. (2003). Smart Homes: Past, Present and Future. In R. Harper, ed., *Inside the Smart Home*. London: Springer. doi: 10.1007/1-85233-854-7_2.

Asimov, I. (1950). Robbie. In I. Asimov, ed., *I, Robot*. New York, NY: Gnome Press.

Auger, J. (2014). Living with Robots: A Speculative Design Approach. *Journal of Human-Robot Interaction*, 3(1), pp. 20–42. doi: 10.5898/JHRI.3.1.Auger.

Biocca, F., C. Harms and J.K. Burgoon (2003). Toward a More Robust Theory and Measure of Social Presence. *Presence*, 12, pp. 456–480. doi: 10.1162/105474603322761270

Breazeal, C. (2003). Toward Sociable Robots. *Robotics and Autonomous Systems*, 42 (3), pp. 167–175. doi: 10.1016/S0921-8890(02)00373-1.

Brooks, R. (2002). *Flesh and Machines: How Robots Will Change Us*. New York, NY: Vintage Books.

Burneleit, E., F. Hemmert and R. Wettach (2009). Living Interfaces: The Impatient Toaster. *Proceedings of the 3rd International Conference on Tangible and Embedded Interaction 2009*, Cambridge, UK, February 16–18, 2009, pp. 21–22. doi: 10.1145/1517664.1517673.

Čapek, K. (1920/2004). *R. U.R. (Rossum's Universal Robots)*. New York, NY: Penguin.

Clark, A. (1997). *Being There*. Cambridge, MA: MIT Press.

Clark, A. (2003). *Natural-Born Cyborgs. Minds, Technologies, and the Future of Human Intelligence*. New York, NY: Oxford University Press.

Clark, A. and Chalmers, D. (1998). The Extended Mind Hypothesis. *Analysis*, 58(1), pp. 7–19.

Damiano, L. (2009). *Unità in dialogo*. Milan: Bruno Mondadori.

Damiano, L. and P. Dumouchel (2018). Anthropomorphism in Human-Robot Co-Evolution. *Frontiers in Psychology*, 26(9). doi: 10.3389/fpsyg.2018.00468.

Damiano, L. and P. Dumouchel (2020). Emotion in Relation. Epistemological and Ethical Scaffolding for Mixed Human-Robot Social Ecologies. *Humana. Mente*, 13(37), pp. 181–206.

Dautenhahn, K. (2007). Socially Intelligent Robots: Dimensions of Human–Robot Interaction. *Philosophical Transactions B*, 362(1480), pp. 679–704. doi: 10.1098/rstb.2006.2004.

Dautenhahn, K., S. Woods, C. Kaouri, M.L. Walters, K.L. Koay and I. Werry (2005). What Is a Robot Companion – Friend, Assistant or Butler? *Intelligent Robots and Systems 2005* (IROS 2005). (www.researchgate.net/publication/224623195_What_is_a_robot_companion_-_Friend_assistant_or_butler?)

Daily, S.B, M.T. James, D. Cherry, J.J. Porter III, S.S. Darnell, J. Isaac and T. Roy (2017). Affective Computing. In M. Jeon, ed., *Emotions and Affect Factors in HCI*. New York, NY: Academic Press, pp. 213–231.

del Rey, L. (1938). Helen O'Loy. *Astounding Science Fiction*, December.

Dumouchel, P. and L. Damiano (2017). *Living with Robots*. Cambridge, MA: Harvard University Press.

Fong, T., I. Nourbakhsh and K. Dautenhahn (2003). A Survey of Socially Interactive Robots. *Robotics and Autonomous Systems*, 42(3/4), pp. 143–166. doi: 10.1016/S0921-8890(02)00372-X.

Forlizzi, J. (2008). The Product Ecology: Understanding Social Product Use and Supporting Design Culture. *International Journal of Design*, 2(1), pp. 11–20.

Forlizzi, J. and C. Di Salvo (2006). Service Robots in the Domestic Environment: A Study of the Roomba Vacuum in the Home. *Proceedings of the 1st ACM SIGCHI/SIGART Conference on Human-Robot Interaction, HRI 2006*, pp. 258–265. doi: 10.1145/1121241.1121286.

Gaudiello, I., S. Lefort and E. Zibetti (2015). The Ontological and Functional Status of Robots. *Computers in Human Behavior*, 50, pp. 259–273. doi: 10.1016/j.chb.2015.03.060.

Harper, R., ed. (2011). *The Connected Home. The Future of Domestic Life.* New York, NY: Springer.

Heerink, M., B. Kröse, V. Evers and B. Wielinga (2008). The Influence of Social Presence on Acceptance of a Companion Robot by Older People. *Journal of Physical Agents*, 2(2), pp. 33–40.doi: 10.14198/JoPha.2008.2.2.05.

Kahn, P.H., B. Friedman Jr. and J. Hagman (2002). 'I Care about Him as a Pal': Conceptions of Robotic Pets in Online AIBO Discussion Forum. *Proceedings of the Extended Abstracts at the Conference on Human Factors in Computing Systems.* New York, NY: ACM Press, pp. 632–633. doi: 10.1145/506443.506519.

Kidd, C.D. and C. Breazeal (2009). Robots at Home: Understanding Long-Term Human-Robot Interaction. *2008 IEEE/RSJ International Conference on Intelligent Robots and Systems*, September 22–26, 2008, Acropolis Convention Center, Nice, France, pp. 3230–3235. doi: 10.1109/IROS.2008.4651113.

Levillain, F. and E. Zibetti (2017). Behavioral Objects: The Rise of the Evocative Machines. *Journal of Human-Robot Interaction*, 6(1), pp. 4–24. doi: 10.5898/JHRI.6.1.Levillain.

Mori, M. 'Bukimi no tani' (The Uncanny Valley). *Energy C*, 79(C+), pp. 88–85.

Netting, R. (1986). *Cultural Ecology.* Long Grove, IL: Waveland Press.

Newen, A., L. De Bruin and S. Gallagher, eds. (2018). *The Oxford Handbook of 4E Cognition.* Oxford: Oxford University Press. doi: 10.1093/oxfordhb/9780198 735410.001.0001.

Pfeifer, R. and J. Bongard (2007). *How the Body Shapes the Way We Think: A New View of Intelligence.* Cambridge, MA: MIT Press.

Ricquebourg, V., D. Menga, D. Durand, B. Marhic, L. Delahoche and C. Logé (2006). The Smart Home Concept: Our Immediate Future. *1ST IEEE International Conference on E-Learning in Industrial Electronics.* doi: 10.1109/ICELIE.2006.347206.

Seibt, J. (2016). Integrative Social Robotics – A New Method Paradigm to Solve the Description Problem and the Regulation Problem? In J. Seibt, M. Nørskov and S. Schack Andersen, eds., *What Social Robots Can and Should Do—Proceedings of Robophilosophy/TRANSOR.* Amsterdam: IOS Press.

Severson, R.L. and S.M. Carlson (2010). Behaving as or Behaving as if? Children's Conceptions of Personified Robots and the Emergence of a New Ontological Category. *Neural Networks*, 23(8/9), pp. 1099–1103. doi: 10.1016/j.neunet.2010.08.014.

Shapiro, L. (2007). The Embodied Cognition Research Program. *Philosophy Compass* 2(2), pp. 338–346. doi: 10.1111/j.1747-9991.2007.00064.x.

Stone, W. (2018). The History of Robotics. In T.R. Kurfess, ed., *Robotics and Automation Handbook.* Boca Raton, FL: CRC Press, pp. 1–12.

Sung, J.Y., R.E. Grinter and H.I. Christensen (2010). Domestic Robot Ecology. An Initial Framework to Unpack Long-Term Acceptance of Robots at Home. *International Journal of Social Robotics*, 2(4), pp. 417–429. doi: 10.1007/s12369-010-0065-8.

Sung, J.Y., L. Guo, R.E. Grinter and H.I. Christensen (2007). 'My Roomba Is Rambo': Intimate Home Appliances. In J. Krumm et al., eds., *UbiComp 2007*, LNCS 4717, pp. 145–162.

Tisseron, S. (2015). *Le jour où mon robot m'aimera. Vers l'empathie artificielle.* Paris: Albin Michel.

Turkle, S. (2010). In Good Company? On the Threshold of Robotic Companions. In Y. Wilks, ed., *Close Engagements with Artificial Companions.* Amsterdam: John Benjamins Publishing Company, pp. 3–10.

Turkle, S. (2011). *Alone Together.* New York, NY: Basic Books.

Thompson, E. and F. Varela (2001). Radical Embodiment: Neural Dynamics and Consciousness. *Trends in Cognitive Sciences,* 5(10), pp. 418–425. doi: 10.1016/S1364-6613(00)01750-2.

Varela, F., E. Thompson and E. Rosch (1991). *The Embodied Mind.* Cambridge, MA: MIT Press.

Venkatesh, A. (2008). Digital Home Technologies and Transformation of Households. *Information Systems Frontier,* 10(4), pp. 391–395. doi: 10.1007/s10796-008-9097-0.

Venkatesh, A. (2006). ICT in Everyday Life. *The Information Society,* 22(4), pp. 191–194.

von Foerster, H. (2003). *Understanding Understanding. Essays on Cybernetics and Cognition.* New York, NY: Springer.

Wheeler, M. (2010). In Defense of Extended Functionalism. In R. Menary, ed., *The Extended Mind.* Cambridge, MA: MIT Press, pp. 245–270. doi: 10.7551/mitpress/9780262014038.003.0011.

Yusupov, R.M. and A.L. Ronzhin (2010). From Smart Devices to Smart Space. *Herald of the Russian Academy of Sciences,* 80(1), pp. 63–68. doi: 10.1134/S1019331610010089.

Ziemke, T. (2016). The Body of Knowledge. *Biosystems,* 148, pp. 4–11.

Chapter 6

Homes through the design shift in the digital age

Ioana Ocnarescu and Dominique Sciamma

Introduction

It is in the rationalisation of the kitchen, conceived in 1841 in the United States (USA), that design finds its origins (Midal, 2019). By improving the daily aspects of life, imagining spaces and furniture adapted to different activities and tasks in homes, design also proposed new models of living. By doing so, design affirmed a political vision focusing on social emancipation (women's work at home, abolition of slavery, fighting public and home insalubrity, etc.) (Midal, 2019). It also contributed to technological and economic progress by both taking part in and criticising the different ages of progress: industrial revolution, modernism, capitalism and consumerist culture.

Mixing efficiency, functionality, beauty, styling, ethics, research, experimentation, sometimes trends and industrial demands, sometimes writing manifests and proposing utopian projects of living together, "design is a bridge between the abstraction of research and the tangible requirements of real life ... a paragon for a constructive and effective synthesis of thought and action" (Aldersey-Williams et al., 2008). Design has always been in line with its mission: to improve or at least maintain the "habitability" of the world in all its dimensions: physical/material, psychological/cognitive/emotional, spiritual/cultural/symbolic, etc. (Findeli, 2010). On the other hand, design has always had a complicated relationship with technology.

Designers draw forms and imagine scenarios with future technology, they propose ways of living and human experiences and also bring a shift from thinking about applications to showing complex implications of technology in our daily lives (Dunne and Raby, 2007). Sometimes these implications show an *in situ* critique of the technology that might go against a technological and economic progress. It is the design paradox that pushes this discipline to evolve while challenging itself and the emancipation project it supports.

Design through history and the transformation of homes

The Age of Enlightenment focused on the project of emancipation. It allowed people to think and build their destinies, whether they are common or individual. In knowledge revolutions, industrial revolutions and economic revolutions, every century witnessed the emergence of new, emblematic and even heroic figures. Over the last 200 years, designers' vision proposed projects that evolved as ethical and political missions serving society. These design projects are therefore lenses of understanding our past, projecting ourselves in the future.

Between engineers who develop technologies to solve problems and the marketers that identify users' needs in connection with these technologies, designers put people's quality of life at the centre of the project. By reversing this perspective, technologies and services serve people and not the other way around. Herbert Simon in *The Sciences of the Artificial* describes another standpoint. If sciences show how things are (analytical approach), engineering shows how things could be in order to attain goals and functions (synthetic approach), design is about "changing existing situations into preferred ones" (Simon, 1996). It focuses on "finding a satisfactory design rather than an optimum design" (Simon, 1996). To do so, designers combine a culture and a history, both emerged during the 19th century, with specific technical expertise (drawing, volume and more generally all the techniques of representation); a methodological and multidisciplinary approach combining project management and mediation; as well as creative methods.

The next section presents an overview of a brief historical perspective of this discipline in relationship with three periods that we call "the Age of making", "the Age of having" and "the Age of being". During each period we focus on how people lived, especially in relation with their homes.

The Age of making

By promoting science to prevail over religious beliefs, the Age of Enlightenment allowed people to acquire intellectual and theoretical tools to explain the world, and thus to exploit it. By using this knowledge and turning it into technologies, the 19th century saw the triumph of the management of energies (coal and oil), of materials (steel), of factories and mass production. The main stake was to *make* by exploiting human energy with the greatest amount of people, who came from countryside to cities and constituted the working class. This project was at the service of an intellectual, managerial, proprietary and wealthy minority.

Handicraft was disrupted by the industrial revolution of the 19th century, to the point where one might fear the disappearance of the *beautiful object* made by craftsmen. Those *not yet called designers* were already preoccupied by the stakes of modernity and the benefits of the industry at the service of as many people as possible. Therefore, manufacturing and the social consequences of crafting practices already interested visionary people of the time, like William Morris.[1]

In this context, the evolution of homes followed different paths in the USA and in Europe (Midal, 2009), with the first designers bringing considerable changes in people's daily life. In the USA, Catharine Beecher around the 1850s invented the "domestic economy". She transposed the principles of rational organisation from factories to the American kitchens. She invented the *kitchen worktop* – one large piece of furniture where one can organise all activities in a comfortable and, most important for that time, efficient way. This type of proposition brought a whole new organisation of the family life in terms of roles and domestic chores. The new kitchen proposed by Beecher in *Treatise on Domestic Economy* assumes a dual political position: feminist and abolitionist. Hand in hand with her sister, Harriet Beecher Stowe – the writer of *Uncle Tom's Cabin* – they push American women to gain time and power in the domestic life "to increase the strength of the family by creating a 'family state', that is, a domain as big as the country" (Askeland, 1992). Secondly, Beecher and Stowe also fought slavery. Their means infused and created a popular culture. They showed examples of how domestic life could be envisioned in the kitchen and created narratives capable of changing ideologies that dominated the country's power structure (Askeland, 1992).

Further on in Europe, another example of design brought a new equilibrium in a society struck by the industrial revolution. Midal shows how the peasant, becoming a worker, was the first victim of the industrial civilisation. A new crisis arrived due to overcrowding, malnutrition, promiscuity, insalubrity and the new urban populations such as toxic wastes from factories. And this crisis was in direct relation with workers' homes. People coming from the countryside to the city shared small crowded flats. These homes became the first places of a new dwellings reform: they were nests of infections and had to be transformed into healthy places (Midal, 2009). At the beginning of the 20th century, a doctor, Henri Cazalis,[2] fond of William Morris' philosophy, wrote an essay on the importance of household hygiene and low-cost furniture. For Cazalis hygienic furniture could not only transform homes into beautiful places to live, they could also fix the insalubrity emergency and rebuilt a new democracy:

> [H]ygiene, [is] a branch of aesthetics – because health and cleanliness are necessarily the essential conditions of beauty – hygiene already attempts to give to people's habitations what has for too long been lacking, pure air, and the sun that kills pathogenic germs, and light, which is as much necessary for thought and the soul as it is for the body.
>
> (Antoine and Ponte, 2003)

These new reforms are only some examples of designers' impact in the Age of making. These interventions changed how people work and lived, bringing efficient, low-cost and hygienic solutions for a suffering society. They also show the birth of designers as political figures transforming people's homes, ways of living and even a redefinition of living standards. The next age, the Age of having, realises the project of progress envisioned in the 19th century, bringing not only emancipation but also developing an unstoppable consumerist society. The 20th-century revolution was also a technological revolution and also started in the domestic environment.

The Age of having

In the early 20th century, the industrial revolution is so effective and so productive and factories produce so many objects that the property-owning class cannot consume them all. At the time, these objects were bought by the very people who manufacture them. This is the birth of Fordism: the workers are better paid in order to buy what comes out of the production lines.

Most of these objects, and the most impactful ones, are in the "form of small machines – shavers, clippers and hair-dryers; radio, telephone, gramophone, tape recorder and television; mixers, grinders, automatic cookers, washing machines, refrigerators, vacuum cleaners, polishers …" (Banham, 1980). It is what architectural critic and writer Banham calls the *age of domestic electronics and synthetic chemistry* or *the Second Machine Age*. This period arrived after the heroic *First Machine Age* that produced the cars, planes and heavy industry. In the early 20th century, the machine was literally domesticated, entered people's homes and became an ingredient of everyday experience (Crampton Smith, 2006). And in this period designers of everyday objects were anonymously bringing another political and cultural shift: "objects change not just how we see ourselves but, moreover, how we live life" (Crampton Smith, 2006). An emblematic object of the 1950s European homes was the fridge. Smith shows how the arrival of this object influenced how people organised themselves and its consequences for female employment, new patterns in family life that starts to lose its "ritual ceremony of solidarity, hierarchy, and manners: the shared mealtime" (Crampton Smith, 2006).

In a more contrasted perspective, this period was less focused on *making* than on *selling* and persuading people to purchase more and more mass-produced objects. Thus, it is necessary to understand people's desires and to manipulate them for the brands sake.[3] This is the emergence of the consumer society, where happiness is measured according to its capacity to accumulate objects and products. The individual goal is to *have*, again and again. It is the triumph of the self or at least the belief that people are in charge; the buying process is seen as an expression of democracy.

The imagination of beginning of the 20th century is the image of a domestic bliss that is both formatted and fantasised, a vision broadcasted and imposed by the movie and the television industries as well as by the mass media. There is another object at home that irrevocably changed people's life at home – the television –, the symbolic machine of the age of domestic electronics (Banham, 1980). It was also a symbol of how media could influence masses, infuse political projects and thus change societies. This object and the electric technology were "reshaping and restructuring patterns of social interdependence and every aspect of our personal life" (McLuhan and Fiore, 2001). In the second half of the 20th century, the notion of progress is back on the agenda. The emblematic French designer Raymond Loewy, who stated that *ugliness won't sell well* (Loewy, 2002), also confirmed the mission of design which is to make the essential beautiful, and the beautiful essential. The designer becomes the guide of the carefree consumer society as well as the provider of meaning to these mass-produced objects.

In Europe, the Bauhaus movement and school, founded by Walter Gropius in 1919 and continued by Mies Van der Rohe from 1930 to 1933, affirms the singular role of designers in the elaboration of a modern society (from garments to skyscrapers). Bauhaus project combines beauty with function and attempts to unify the principles of mass production with individual artistic vision.[4] The Bauhaus re-invents living spaces through a multidisciplinary approach of arts and crafts, industry and visual arts. It is considered to be a utopian project by some critics, "brilliant in itself and poignant for its varieties of foredoomed idealism" (Schjeldahl, 2009). But above all, the Bauhaus was an experiment in education. It creates and implements innovative and pedagogical approaches, particularly in project-based learning, that are still used today in design schools. Its project has durably and deeply marked people's relationship with objects and spaces.

The Age of being

To go from products of basic necessities to products that fulfil more complex needs, to maintain some markets or even to invent them, it is essential to have a more and more educated population. This is exactly the approach followed since the end of the Second World War, which saw the massive increase of people's education level, and the surge of the number of higher education graduates. People's education and emancipation also came with a personal impact: these people start to think, to debate, to criticise and to choose. Without necessarily anticipating it, the consumer society has revealed human beings who want to break free and suddenly focus on their own lives, on the quality of life. Therefore, the stake is no longer to *make*, neither to *have*, but to *be*, and in all possible ways: as a man or a woman, as a parent, as a professional and as a citizen. *To be and to have the means to be*, whether these means are material or immaterial. And designers took an important role in this new perspective. Their mission is to think, to conceive those means and the optimal conditions for these new challenges and their implications. Designers became the emblematic figures of the last part of the 20th century, where everyone intends to enjoy "a nice life" while being in the society. The designers are the stakeholders and the purveyors of this existential and experiential beauty: from creating products to delivering worth living experiences (Hassenzahl and Carroll, 2010).

The inescapable globalisation of the late 20th century and its consequent blending of cultures create a tension between homogenisation trends (embodied by companies like Ikea) and differentiation trends (limited edition designs and local practices). This is the history that designers of the 21st century assume and bear. Even if the conditions, the nature and the scope of designers' interventions have radically changed over the last century, this past is still present as it builds a memory, references that define a particular discipline and finally a culture rooted in both industry and people's quality of life. The increasing complexity of our societies (in their spatial, temporal and informational organisations), and also of our lives (intimate, personal, professional and public ones), the increasing digitisation of our environments, of our tools and practices have completely changed the situation and specificity of this discipline.

The spiritual, political, social, economic and industrial implications of design are constantly challenged, as people's needs and desires for a better life are ever changing. Design is also following these transformations. While designers used to focus on the systems of objects, the conditions of their production and their usage, they now propose ways of living and experiences, with an increasingly immaterial part, embracing complexity of a difficult-to-grasp reality. Design is no longer giving only responses in terms of form and function, but also questions the possibilities of new life scenarios. Subsequent to this idea, researchers like Midal (2009) and Vial (2010) talk about double-blind dilemma or the schizophrenic character of design. On one side design is intended to create something useful, desirable, etc., for the market and for the final user (user-friendly objects and services demanded by a capitalist industry). On the other side, there is the demand coming from the social revolution (people are more and more part of the ecological revolution, aware of the impact of emerging technologies, wanting for more impactful actions and projects, etc.), that is, fight against mass production and mass manipulation governed by industries.

In order to dodge these two paradoxical perspectives, Vial proposes two design laws of morality:

(1) Act in such a way that you always push the market demand to be a means to create user-centred projects and never a final purpose for your designer's actions;

(2) Act so that the effects of your actions are compatible with the permanence of genuine human life (Vial, 2010).

Design projects expand beyond a product perspective to larger scales within organisations and society, in a complex context allowing for multiple forms of action. Regarding emerging technologies and their place in everyday life, the future is not a predicted roadmap to follow or an inevitable space. While science fiction is still a powerful tool that proposes possible futures, and scientific advancements propose plausible and probable ones, designers could contribute by contributing to represent and create a debate on these futures.[5] In this projection space where *black mirror*[6] and *white mirror* scenarios already show some effects of the digital shift in our daily life, the home is a symbolic place of lots of manifestations of these futures.

From designing dwellings and improving kitchens to contributing to writing political programmes on well-living, designers wrote history in their active and humanistic ways. The following section shows through two museum exhibitions several explorations on realistic and utopian ideas related to homes from 1950 to nowadays. The artefacts and concepts presented in these events are cultural insights and probes that open the dialogue on the future of homes in the digital age.

Design, home and technologies: several explorations

From 7 November 2018 to 24 March 2019, the Design Museum hosted the exhibition *Home Futures,*[7] a five-month-long event questioning how technology radically changed the way we live today from two perspectives. Firstly, in terms of future projections of 1950's dream of the fully automated home – "Living in the yesterday's tomorrow" focuses on a wild and rich imaginary of what the future would be like in the year 2000. Secondly, on the today's changing world, on "this crazy old world of ours", characterised by:

> [U]rbanization and technological invention, people's immediate needs, … new family constellations,… challenging the traditional nuclear family, … people (being) constantly on the move, carrying not much than a toothbrush and a laptop on their trips from town to town, while others leave the hustle and bustle of the big city for a life in harmony with nature.
> (Steierhoffer and McGuirk, 2018)

This event creates a back-to-back proposition with an exhibition taking place in 1972 at the Museum of Modern Art (MoMa) in New York. If the *Home Futures* is sponsored by Ikea and their annual research reports *Life at Home,*[8] the exhibition from MoMa called *Italy: The New Domestic Landscape*[9] was sponsored by Fiat, Olivetti, Anonima Castelli, Alitalia and Abet Print, and with the collaboration of a large number of Italian industries. In a cultural and economic centre such as New York City, in a consumer society that starts to show its limits, the event at MoMa shows a European model in terms of lifestyle and design. It is indeed Italy that is seen as "a micro-model where a wide range of possibilities, limitations and critical problems of contemporary designers throughout the world are represented by diverse and sometimes opposite approaches" (*Italy: The New Domestic Landscape*, 1972) on two modes of contemporary living: the permanent home and the mobile unit. *To design or not to design* was an already valuable question presented in this exhibition. Four projects illustrate the *counter-design* approach. This approach is represented by designers who believe no more objects should be added to "our cluttered consumer-dominated culture and that social and political changes are needed before we can change the physical aspects of our society". On the other hand, seven *pro-design* environments are presented by designers who believe it is possible to improve "the quality of life by improving our physical environment" (*Italy: The New Domestic Landscape*, 1972).

At another level, the recent exhibition in London, *Home Futures*, tackles six main themes, focusing more on how we organise ourselves as societies rather than describing the physical place called "home". These themes are presented as physical spaces in the exhibition; they are selected in "resonance with our contemporary experience of the home and its changing realities" (Steierhoffer and McGuirk, 2018). In this sense, the physical exhibit space accompanied by physical objects, writings, videos, etc., acts as *cultural probes,* showing subjective views of our society. Probes are "collections of evocative tasks meant to elicit inspirational responses from people—not comprehensive information about them, but fragmentary clues about their lives and thoughts" (Gaver et al., 2004). First used as subjective tools for the design process, such inspirational materials could also be found in museums. These elements act as cultural insights to open a discussion on homes in the digital age. To better understand the design standpoint on these design explorations, we will synthesise four of the six themes developed in this exhibition (*Living with other, Living on the move, Living autonomously, Living smart*). We also add a fifth theme as a distinct design exploration related to nowadays emerging technologies, AI and robotics (*Living design, Living homes*).

Living with other

This concept tackles the notion of intimacy in a space full of contradictions: home as a private place "where we retreat from the gaze of others" versus the pictures of homes one finds on social media and platforms like Airbnb (Steierhoffer and McGuirk, 2018). Even more profound than this visual culture, here the emerging concept shows the home as a data economy hub (smart speakers, sensors and smart devices) where privacy seems not to be the fundamental idea of home. One of the projects in this section, *Placebo* project by Dunne & Raby, presents *The Electro-Draught Excluder*.[10]

This device deflects electromagnetic fields that emanate from the electronic appliances populating our homes. On another dimension one could also describe *the other* as the technology. In this sense living with the other could also mean adapting oneself to the "needs" of technology in terms of functional (e.g., are you ready to change your way of living when introducing a social robot in your home?) and also emotional implications, like in *Technological Dream* series 2007[11] also by Dunne & Raby, where they imagine "several robots not as super smart, functional machines, nor as pseudo life forms, but as technological cohabitants ... What new interdependencies and relationships might emerge in relation to different levels of robot intelligence and capability?"

Living on the move

The nomadic/mobile unit was a central theme for artists and designers for several decades. However, what is new is "our ability to feel home". Nowadays home is partially "dictated by Wi-Fi and power outlets" and "more people today own a mobile phone than own a home" (Steierhoffer and McGuirk, 2018). In this sense the project *Instant City* by Archigram in 1969 shows a city consisted of a "sophisticated set of mobile units, information pavilions, learning environments, cultural scenes, laboratories and sports arenas which could be integrated into existing urban societies,... as an additional 'new, innovative layers' to the existing functions of the permanent city" (Kiib, 2013). This project redefined *the city as a service or even an event* rather than a fixed location. At a more individual scale, the *Supersurface, an alternative model for life on the earth* project in the MoMa exhibition in 1972, is based on the idea of a universal grid covering all the surface of Earth. In this scenario, "human beings are the only creators of their own choices: finally nomadic, they can free themselves from induced needs and behaviours, and pick their own place, everywhere on the Earth's 'supersurface'",[12] a critique of consumer society in the 1970s and for the generations to come. As explained in the *Home Futures* exhibition, this project is almost happening with Airbnb catchphrase "belong anywhere"[13] and the different infrastructural changes coming with the usages of this platform in capital cities.[14]

Living autonomously

This theme covers projects showing optimistic visions of good life from the 1970s in a self-sufficient way, a critique to the consumer society. This vision is supported by do-it-yourself furniture, self-growing farms and even "systems that enable ordinary people to shape their homes with their own hands". Projects like *OpenStructures*[15] "allow to build things together at a moment in time, where anyone is connected to everyone and everything can be produced everywhere". Related to our focus *homes in the digital age*, this theme is somehow limited to empowering people from a physical point of view (furniture, organisation of space in homes and of the city). On the contrary, living autonomously could also mean leaving without using services from the giants of the web. When home assistants flourish in people's private spaces, the voice platform *Snips* in France focuses its business on the concept of Privacy by Design:

> [T]he idea is to generate artificial training data to train machine learning models, instead of relying on real user data… we can train our models with thousands of examples instead of the dozens people usually write by hand… we are also doing everything *completely on device*, with absolutely nothing happening in the cloud! You can have your voice assistant run directly in your device or smart hub, without the need for a backend infrastructure.
>
> (Hindi, 2017)

As the founder of *Snips*, Rand Hindi argues, this approach is not only ethical but also the only way to comply with the upcoming European regulation on Privacy, the General Data Protection Regulation law – GDPR.[16]

Living smart

Living smart is one the main themes of our times. *Home Futures* exhibition shows the fantasies coming from a rich imaginary created in the 1950s: the modernist vision of a fully controlled home through a central computer. Among the different concepts of this modernist future, only one RCA Whirlpool miracle Kitchen vacuum cleaner exists today – the Roomba robot. What was not predicted was the Internet of Things that "use our data to predict our habits and preferences" (Steierhoffer and McGuirk, 2018). The question that the exhibit asks is, "do 'smart' devices transform the home from a place of chores into one of ease and leisure?" For example, light designer Dan Hill talks about an iconic object of the design culture, *the light switch* in reference to Castiglioni's VLM light switch.[17] "Castiglione's switches, which almost became a European standard for table lamps, possessed a discreetly humble subservience, always present but not listening—and so quite unlike the potentially prying eyes and ears of the various Nests and Homes" (Hill, 2019). In a smart home, such an object is useless. However, from a psychological, cultural and even philosophical perspective, such an object "connects us to our daily infrastructure and lives of others, with humble analogue intensity" (Steierhoffer and McGuirk, 2018). Moreover, not designing such objects could also have ecological consequences: "in order to truly sense and interact, this deleterious situation [of energy consumption] is hardly likely to improve when the analogue light switch disappears, when the object becomes further detached, and so may we" (Hill, 2019).

Living design, Living homes

Artist and designer Florent Aziosmanoff coined the concept of "Living Art/ Living Design" and shows what possible relations one would have with technologies like robotics and AI in our everyday life (Aziosmanoff, 2015). The main proposition is that *intelligent objects* could be characterised by their behaviours rather than their functions. Those *objects*, which we will call "robjects" (a contraction of robot and object), are able to perceive the world, make representations, take decisions and then act accordingly. This has a huge impact on what to design, how to design and for whom. It is indeed a design shift, from shape to function, from function to interaction, and from interaction to relation. One hypothesis in this scenario is that as soon as one lives with robjects able to take decisions without asking permission, one might rely on them and finally relate with them.

The project *Garden of Love*,[18] designed by Florent Aziosmanoff and Strate School of Design, illustrates an example of robjects in an urban environment. In this project, three robotic urban furniture (a bench, a trash can and a streetlight) not only provide their native functions to the audience but also propose other services: the streetlight follows readers while they walk, the bench broadcasts favourite tunes for those who sit on it, etc. These objects also collaborate to provide collective experiences. For example, while a person is playing chess with a friend on the bench-embedded tablet, the streetlamp takes a picture of this friendly moment, sends it to the trash can which prints it twice and brings it to the players. Beyond these service-oriented collaborations, robjects also have a "personal" life, a personality and relations with the other robjects. First embodiments of similar concepts were tested by human–robot interaction and design researchers. (Sirkin et al., 2015), for example, designed a robotic footstool that surprises users by its unexpected movements. The ottoman was perceived as "a living being, such as a pet, and simultaneously as a functional object". This perception made people change the relation they had with this everyday object and some of the participants refused to use the stool for its primary function, while other imagined the personality and "footstool's agenda, ascribing intentions based on its movement alone" (Sirkin et al., 2015). Therefore, behaviour and movements seem essential to create relations over time with smart technologies, but are we ready to live with such robjects in our homes? And after the Age of making, of having and of being are we now entering the Age of relations?

To continue the dialogue and operationalise on these first attempts to craft the future, the last section of this chapter focuses on ways of experimenting on what living with such smart technologies could mean. The design project in the digital age is not about how efficiently technologies are used and adopted by people, but how the future of the home might "emerge in the acknowledgement and embrace of the emotional and social aspects of human existence" (Deynac Sudjic in the Foreword of (Steierhoffer and McGuirk, 2018)).

Are we ready to interact and live with social robotics and smart objects in our home, for example? Our goal is to show several design approaches of experimentations of future smart technologies in our homes. The difficulty here is to show what it means to live with a technology that does not exist yet.

Design approaches to explore emerging technologies at home and beyond

Rethinking homes in which we might have more and more emerging technologies like AI and robotics is a way of rethinking our values and ways of living together. In this proposition, design could be the approach able to build this mediation through field observation for new experiences inside and outside home and *in situ* testing to understand their long-term implications. But what happens when these technologies do not exist yet? How to deeply understand their implications?

In order to bring a concrete standpoint for this discussion and valuable insights, *speculative design* challenges these emerging technologies and opens a debate on how we want to live with technologies in our homes. The *Uninvited Guests* project, for example, was created by Superflux Lab to question the concept of care-at-a-distance for the elderly.[19] In this project, designers show how Thomas, an elderly man living in his home, is struggling with rules and orders that smart objects impose on him (a smart fork tracks his food habits and tells him what is healthy to eat, a smart cane counts the number of steps per day and a smart bed supervises the sleep programme). These smart objects offered by his children were well designed to assist the person for a better, healthier life. Indeed, the objects and interfaces of these objects are beautifully crafted to achieve the tasks in a smooth and user-friendly way: count the vegetables, measure the amount of sleep, etc. A video presents the psychological pain brought by these objects, and how these objects become surveillance indicators (if Thomas is not using them, his family is notified). The person feels uncomfortable, not being capable of taking personal decisions and losing his everyday freedom and habits. Finally, the video shows how Thomas invents ways to disobey the smart objects.

This speculative scenario remains hypothetical. It is not showing how to design assistive devices, but challenges their very contribution, regarding the complexity of human behaviour. By revealing a brief description of the social ecosystem mediated by smart technology, it challenges researchers working on social robotics to think deeply about the consequences of their robotic solutions. In this context Thomas is connected to his children through short notifications from the smart objects. One could question the need of designing social robots for elderly's autonomy at home. Instead an alternative could be to imagine how robotics could improve intergenerational relationships and social life. In this scenario homes could be seen as one among others places from the city in which people are engaged in specific activities.

The approach presented so far is rather speculative and critical and the video presenting Thomas and his struggle with the smart object is made to raise questions. Speculative designers challenge the ethics of new technological artefacts and open a conversation on the role of technology in human ecologies. Also this example shows the diversity of approaches when it comes to exploring futures. The futures cone[20] is a powerful taxonomy when imagining future scenarios. If *possible futures* focus on scientific knowledge that does not exist yet (mostly Sci-Fi scenarios), *probable futures* show scenarios extrapolated from current trends; *plausible futures* propose current understanding of physical laws, processes and causation; and *preferable futures* are desirable, and largely emotional focusing on human experiences (Bland and Westlake, 2013). These futures could be combined, and a desirable future could become possible, probable and finally the present. Designers come into play as experimenters, prototyping theses futures as seen in the *Uninvited Guests* project.

A rather larger approach of exploring futures is *experience design* or *prototyping experiences*. The importance of this topic underlines the transition from a cognitive approach in which usability, user cognition and user performance were the key guidelines in the interaction with emerging technologies to an experience-based approach. (Blythe et al., 2009) explain that an "experiential purchase is not something one primarily owns; it is something to live through, to remember". This approach is guided by affect, values, sensations, pleasure, surprise, meaning (Blythe et al., 2006; Hassenzahl and Tractinsky, 2006) and needs such as relatedness – one of the most salient needs in the sample of positive experiences: "feeling that you have regular intimate contact with people who care about you rather than feeling lonely and uncared of" (Hassenzahl et al., 2010).

Designing for human experience as a whole, taking into consideration the context of the interaction and its implications, and focusing on the experiential benefits raise also new challenges in the field of robotics. (Dautenhahn, 2014) shows that a large number of researchers are interested in "user-studies", understanding how people perceive certain types of behaviours, social cues of robots, etc. They usually use commercially available and already fully programmed robots; the goal of user-studies is to test these robots in different contexts. Only few researchers in the field made the transition from user-studies to experience-based research, based on field considerations, people's needs and ways of living. (Forlizzi et al., 2004) talk about the experience of ageing and how appropriate assistive solutions should live along people's treasured positions and mundane applications and should follow people's own logic and way of living in an independent and dignifying way. In another research project on social robotics, the *Romeo* project,[21] design researchers conducted long-term studies with a Pepper robot in autonomy in a private hospital room for a week. They found that a non-functional robot was still emotionally "effective" for the people living for several months in a re-education hospital. Participants still talked to the robot even it was not functioning for one day or more; they consider it as a "real" presence. The take-away messages of these studies are less technical than human-centred; qualitative results focus more on what is assistance for people in need and the importance of social needs like relatedness. In this case, the robot was also a mediator, a projection surface: the person was speaking to the robot as she was speaking to someone who was there, an imaginary friend or to herself.

Inevitably, these design approaches, speculative and experience based, decentre the focus of a technology-driven Human-Robot-Interaction research, for more sensible, subjective and complex interactions with robots at home. Robots could be considered a pretext to rethink what homes, neighbourhoods and cities could look like. In this direction, research on social robots could be an intermediary step to challenge more profound and complex societal challenges. And in the hands of multidisciplinary and design teams, robots inside and outside domestic environments could act as social and cultural probes, giving insights into what is a desirable future and society. Design is today more than ever a visible agent in how we want to live in the 21st century and a projector of a desirable future for the generations to come.

Notes

1 British textile designer of the 19th century, poet, novelist, translator and socialist activist associated with the British Arts and Crafts Movement, a major contributor to the revival of traditional British textile arts and methods of production (https://en.wikipedia.org/wiki/William_Morris).

2 Henri Cazalis was a French physician, a symbolist poet and a man of letters. He wrote under the pseudonyms of Jean Caselli and Jean Lahor (https://en.wikipedia.org/wiki/Henri_Cazalis). Among other writings, he is the author of *Les habitations à bon marché et un art nouveau pour le people* (in English *Low Cost Dwellings and Low Cost Art*) (1905), a book dedicated to the president of the housing society in France with practical solutions for workers' homes in the Parisian region (Antoine and Ponte, 2003).

3 The shift from needs to desires is well presented in the Adam Curtis documentary *The Century of the Self* (2002). The first episode shows how

> the business and political worlds use psychological techniques to read, create and fulfill the desires of the public, and to make their products and speeches as pleasing as possible to consumers and voters. Curtis questions the intentions and origins of this relatively new approach to engaging the public.
> (https://en.wikipedia.org/wiki/The_Century_of_the_Self)

4 https://en.wikipedia.org/wiki/Bauhaus.

5 www.nesta.org.uk/blog/speculative-design-a-design-niche-or-a-new-tool-for-government-innovation/.

6 *Black Mirror* is a British science fiction television series released in 2011 that examines the consequences of new technologies in modern society (https://en.wikipedia.org/wiki/Black_Mirror).

7 https://designmuseum.org/exhibitions/home-futures.
8 https://lifeathome.ikea.com/about-life-at-home/our-research/.
9 www.moma.org/calendar/exhibitions/1783.
10 http://dunneandraby.co.uk/content/projects/70/0.
11 http://dunneandraby.co.uk/content/projects/10/0.
12 www.architectureplayer.com/clips/supersurface-an-alternative-model-for-life-on-the-earth.
13 https://blog.atairbnb.com/belong-anywhere/.
14 One such study is presented by (Cocola Gant, 2016) on Barcelona increasing conversion of housing into accommodation for visitors: "when residents move out, the only buyers tend to be tourist investors ... the growth of vacation flats produces conditions that solely enable the reproduction of further accommodation for visitors, rather than for long-term residential use".
15 https://openstructures.net/.
16 https://gdpr-info.eu/.
17 www.readingdesign.org/let-there-be-light-switches.
18 https://lejardindesamours.com/.
19 http://superflux.in/index.php/work/uninvited-guests/#.
20 The division between probable, plausible and preferable futures has been around since the late 1970s (Bland and Westlake, 2013).
21 https://projetromeo.com/.

References

Aldersey-Williams, H., Hall, P., Sargent, T., and Antonelli, P. (2008). *Design and the Elastic Mind*. New York, NY: The Museum of Modern Art.

Antoine, P., and Ponte, A., eds. (2003). *Architecture and the Sciences: Exchanging Metaphors*. New York NY: Princeton Architectural Press.

Askeland, L. (1992). Askeland Remodeling the Model Home in and Beloved Uncle Tom's Cabin within. *American Literature*, 64(4), pp. 785–805. doi: 10.2307/2927639

Aziosmanoff, F. (2015). *Living Art - Fondations*. CNRS Editions. www.cnrseditions.fr/catalogue/arts-et-essais-litteraires/living-art/.

Banham, R. (1980). *Theory and Design in the First Machine Age*. Cambridge, MA: The MIT Press.

Bland, J., and Westlake, S. (2013). *Don't Stop Thinking about Tomorrow: A Modest Defence of Futurology*. https://media.nesta.org.uk/documents/dont_stop_thinking_about_tomorrow.pdf.

Blythe, M., Hassenzahl, M., and Law, E. (2009). Now with Added Experience? *New Review of Hypermedia and Multimedia*, 15(2), pp. 119–128. doi: 10.1080/1361 4560903251100

Blythe, M., Wright, P., McCarthy, J., and Bertelsen, O.W. (2006). Theory and Method for Experience Centered Design. *CHI '06 Extended Abstracts on Human Factors in Computing Systems - CHI EA '06*, pp. 1691–1694. doi: 10.1145/1125451.1125764

Cocola-Gant, A. (2016). Holiday Rentals: The New Gentrification Battlefront. *Sociological Research Online*, 21(3), pp. 112–120. doi: 10.5153/sro.4071

Crampton Smith, G. (2006). Foreword. In Anthony Dunne, *Hertzian Tales: Electronic Products, Aesthetic Experience, and Critical Design*. Cambridge, MA: The MIT Press. http://mitpress.mit.edu/catalog/item/default.asp?ttype=2&tid=10771

Dautenhahn, K. (2014). Human-Robot Interaction. In Interaction Design Foundation, ed., *The Encyclopedia of Human-Computer Interaction*. 2nd edn. Aarhus, Denmark: The Interaction Design Foundation. www.interaction-design. org/encyclopedia/human-robot_interaction.html

Dunne, A., and Raby, F. (2007). *Design for Debate*. www.dunneandraby.co.uk/content/ bydandr/36/0

Findeli, A. (2010). Searching for Design Research Questions: Some Conceptual Clarifications. In R. Chow, W. Jonas and G. Joost, eds., *Questions, Hypotheses & Conjectures*, iUniverse, pp. 286–303. doi: 10.1016/j.ijrobp.2006.04.061

Forlizzi, J., DiSalvo, C., and Gemperle, F. (2004). Assistive Robotics and an Ecology of Elders Living Independently in Their Homes. *Human-Computer Interaction*, 19(1), pp. 25–59. doi: 10.1207/s15327051hci1901&2_3

Gaver, W.W., Boucher, A., Pennington, S., and Walker, B. (2004). Cultural Probes and the Value of Uncertainty. *Interactions*, 11(5), pp. 53–56. doi: 10.1145/ 1015530.1015555

Hassenzahl, M., and Carroll, J. (2010). *Experience Design: Technology for All the Right Reasons*. San Rafael, CA: Morgan & Claypool Publishers. doi: 10.2200/ S00261ED1V01Y201003HCI008

Hassenzahl, M., Diefenbach, S., and Göritz, A. (2010). Needs, Affect, and Interactive Products – Facets of User Experience. *Interacting with Computers*, 22(5), pp. 353–362. doi: 10.1016/j.intcom.2010.04.002

Hassenzahl, M., and Tractinsky, N. (2006). User Experience - A Research Agenda. *Behaviour & Information Technology*, 25(2), pp. 91–97. doi: 10.1080/01449290 500330331

Hill, D. (2019). Let There Be Light Switches - From Dark Living Rooms to Dark Ecology. *Medium*. https://medium.com/a-chair-in-a-room/let-there-be-light-switches-465248 5e6a7e

Hindi, R. (2017). "Hey Snips!" — Announcing the First Private-by-Design Voice Platform. *Medium*. https://medium.com/snips-ai/hey-snips-announcing-the-first-private-by-design-voice-platform-bf23b8a843fd

Italy: The New Domestic Landscape. (1972). Press Release - Museum of Modern Art (MoMa). www.moma.org/calendar/exhibitions/1783

Kiib, H. (2013). Instant City Design. *Dansk Arkitektur Center*. www.dac.dk/da/dac-life/byg-detop/inspirationsartikler/instant-city-design/.

Loewy, R. (2002). *Never Leave Well Enough Alone*. Baltimore, MD: Johns Hopkins University Press.

McLuhan, M., and Fiore, Q. (2001). *The Medium Is the Massage: An Inventory of Effects*. Berkeley, CA: Gingko Press (first published 1967). http://scholar.google. com/scholar?hl=en&btnG=Search&q=intitle:The+medium+is+the+massage+:+a n+inventory+of+effects#0

Midal, A. (2009). *Design: Introduction à l'histoire d'une discipline*. Pocket: Agora Edition.

Midal, A. (2019). *Design by Accident: For a new History of Design*. Berlin: Sternberg Press.

Schjeldahl, P. (2009). Bauhaus Rules. The Making of a Modern Aesthetic. *The New Yorker*. www.newyorker.com/magazine/2009/11/16/bauhaus-rules

Simon, H.A. (1996). *The Sciences of the Artificial*. 3rd edn. Cambriddge, MA: The MIT Press.

Sirkin, D., Mok, B., Yang, S., and Ju, W. (2015). Mechanical Ottoman: How Robotic Furniture Offers and Withdraws Support. *Proceedings of the Tenth Annual ACM/ IEEE International Conference on Human-Robot Interaction*, pp. 11–18. doi: 10.1145/ 2696454.2696461

Steierhoffer, E., and McGuirk, J., eds. (2018). *Home Futures: Living in Yesterday's Tomorrow*. Southwark, UK: The Design Museum.

Vial, S. (2010). *Court traité du design*. Paris: Presses Universitaires de France.

Chapter 7

Automation, the home and work

Stephen Davies and Maria Sophia Aguirre

Introduction

The subject of automation is one of the hottest around at the moment. This is not surprising as the last few years have witnessed several major breakthroughs and the processes of innovation and development show no signs of slowing down as yet. The discussion of the likely impact of automation is still taking shape but it already has two clear tendencies. To put it another way, there are two kinds of narrative that are being articulated and these reflect common, gut-level responses. The first, which is common to economists, is that this is only the latest of several episodes of the technological transformation of work and will not change things fundamentally. The second, which is found more among non-economists, is that this is something truly novel that will completely transform all of life, and not only work. However, these two emergent narratives have several features in common as well as clear differences. One of these is that both pay little, if any, attention to the question of the home and the impact of new technology upon it. Consequently, discussion of the possible futures and options is severely limited. This reflects a more general phenomenon, which is a massive blind spot in most discussion, particularly economic, where the home is concerned.

Although discussion of the impact of artificial intelligence (AI) and its likely impact is recent (reflecting the reality that critical breakthroughs have only happened in the last decade or less), debates about automation are a recurring feature of the last 200 years. It seems that every so often there is a major panic about the likely effect of automation on the world of work and employment. There was one, for example, in the 1960s and early 1970s, with researchers such as Robert Theobald predicting the "end of work" (Theobald, 1965). The current debate repeats the earlier ones but has a sharper edge because of a widespread perception that this episode of technological innovation is genuinely different from previous ones because of the new element of AI. This means, according to some, that whereas in earlier episodes it was human labour that was replaced by machines, this time we will also see the replacement of human thinking and intellectual activity, so making it qualitatively different.

Two narratives, three positions

In this current debate there are two broad positions, one of which can be further subdivided, so giving three major positions in total. Most economists take the first view, which is that the likely effects of AI and automation are exaggerated. The argument is firstly that in all previous episodes of automation the hopes and fears of commentators have not been realised. Work has not disappeared and jobs or employment have not become vanishingly rare. Instead what has happened has been a transformation of work in which certain kinds of work and employment have disappeared but new ones have appeared to replace them. The overall result has been not a diminution in the number of paid employment opportunities but an increase – there are actually more jobs, just different ones. This means you do not end up with either a paradise of leisure or a world of idleness. The reason according to economists is that mechanisation and automation do not simply replace labour. What they do is make labour as a factor of production in general more productive. As a result, it is reallocated (used for different purposes) and also used more intensively (so the number of hours worked will actually increase). The argument is that there is no good reason to believe that this current episode of automation is any different to previous ones and so we should expect the earlier pattern to be repeated. What form this takes exactly, however, is unclear. Moreover, most economists' discussions of both history and the present are ahistorical – they assume essentially that the precise way things worked out was the way they had to. This begs many questions and is historically inaccurate, as we shall see.

The contrary position is simply that "this time it's different". The argument made by researchers such as Jeremy Rifkin and Paul Mason is that the advent of genuine AI (as opposed to simple data processing) means that the entirety of human input into productive processes will be replaced. People will be replaced by more productive entities rather than labour (physical and mental work) being replaced or made more productive and reassigned – in the latter case people will still be around and doing productive work, just different work to what they did before whereas if human beings and what they do is replaced as far as production is concerned, then there will be a world in which there is no need for human beings to work. Part of the sentence of Adam and Eve at the Fall will have been lifted in fact (Rifkin, 2015; Mason, 2015).

This position then leads to two different evaluations of what such a world will be like. For some, such as Mason, it offers the prospect of a utopia in which alienated work in the capitalist system will be replaced by free activity. The idea also set out by other researchers is that automation will create a world in which human beings, freed from the necessity to work, will be able to explore the world and themselves in creative ways. Meanwhile the huge increase in productivity that AI and automation bring can be used to ensure that everyone has a prosperous and comfortable life, through some mechanisms such as a universal income and free access to many products and services (Bregman, 2017). This vision of an economy of abundance draws upon a long tradition of thought that includes the young Marx but is not confined to him.

The contrary view is that a world without work will be a dystopia of some kind. Some researchers argue that work is essential to give meaning and purpose to life and that in its absence people will become listless and enervated or alternatively destructive and violent. In either case, we can expect all kinds of social pathologies to manifest themselves (Cass, 2018). Even those who take the optimistic view, such as Mason, allow that absent major social and political changes the benefits of AI and automation will accrue to a small class of capitalists who own the software and machines. The rest will either be reduced to penury or will have to be paid to consume and condemned to exist as a class of functionless drones. This was one part of the vision of Aldous Huxley's *Brave New World*, which derived in part from an earlier panic about automation, in the 1930s (Huxley, 2007). The most radical version of the dystopian vision is that AI will become so powerful that we will see the appearance of truly god-like intelligences. In that case we can only hope that they like human beings as pets and do not regard us as vermin or a nuisance (Kurzweill, 2010).

But where is the home in all this?

All of these accounts have certain shared features, regardless of which one of the three positions they come from. These shared features derive from fundamental unexamined assumptions, which in turn derive from the dominant ways of thinking in contemporary social science, particularly economics. One of these features is that the history of earlier episodes, where technological innovation transformed the world of work, is seriously understudied and presented in a simplified way. The other is that the overwhelming focus is on the world of paid work and employment. What is missing is consideration of the world beyond paid work, above all the home. In general, other kinds of activity and indeed work, most of which takes place in the home or is based there, are simply ignored when talking about the effects of automation. This should not surprise us. Today in the United Kingdom and most other developed democracies, public policy debates largely ignore the home and the household as topics. To the extent that they are discussed, it is typically as a subordinate aspect of some other subjects, such as poverty, education or economic growth rather than as a primary subject in its own right. This lack of focus or consideration is most marked in macroeconomic policy but can be noted in almost every area of public debate and we might include welfare and the relief of poverty, fiscal policy and public spending, urban renewal and development, housing and education.

This all means that because the home is not a central or explicit concern or topic of debate, the strengthening of the home and households and families is not an explicit goal of public policy. If the home occupies that central place in the discussion about automation, its possible effects would have a quite different content and flavour. The policy prescriptions generated would be different and the perceived risks and dangers of possible developments would be interestingly different from the kinds brought up by current contributors to the debate. So also would the hopes and positive possibilities that are canvassed. So far the discussion of the impact of new information technologies and automation on the home has apparently been written primarily by technogeeks with a fascination for gadgets (Bregman, 2017). There is a lot about possible developments in automated house help and control systems (developments of the Amazon Echo and other similar devices) but little or no thought about how automation may affect the human relations that actually make bricks and mortar into a home, nor of the wider social and economic impact of AI and automation because of their transformation of homes and their relations rather than the world of paid work and employment.

The individualist perspective and older perspectives

What we see instead is an approach that ultimately derives from academic developments in the social sciences (economics, sociology and psychology in particular) in the central decades of the 20th century, along with the influence of an ideology that derives from classical liberalism but has come to permeate all political arguments, including (not least) social democracy. Essentially there is a focus on individual people (workers in this case), seen as being outside any home and the connections that brings. This is true even in the case of children where it is clearly a totally unrealistic way of thinking. In terms of policy the focus is upon decisions made and actions undertaken by individual people as either economic agents or as people with a multiplicity of relations to everyone else in society but with none of a stronger or more important nature than any others. The question is how to enable people to realise personal goals and the part played by paid work in that. The other end of the telescope in terms of policy and debate is a concern with large aggregates such as "society" or statistical groupings such as income deciles and quartiles or some other statistical grouping such as the labour force. Both of these ways of framing discussion and the subjects of debate ignore the realities of how people still live and of what matters to them in their everyday life, of the way that life is structured and supported.

Historically this was not the case, in the United Kingdom or elsewhere. In fact, most people from earlier societies in all parts of the world would be surprised and even dumbfounded by the way we discuss politics and public policy today, with no mention of homes, households or families (or indeed of lineage, a central concern and category of understanding for many of our ancestors and many people still today). Until no earlier than just before the First World War and probably not until the middle of the 20th century in the European and American case most people did not think of societies or polities as being composed of individuals. Instead they saw the foundational unit as being the household, physically embodied in the home, which was not simply an address or a residence but rather a social unit with a set of social connections as well as a physical location (Ozment, 2001). This was reflected in the way that taxation was organised, in the rules governing the franchise (in the British case it was male heads of households who had the vote, not male adults), and in public welfare policy.

Clearly, we are dealing here with a profound cultural and intellectual change. This has worked out in politics and public policy over the last 50 years. It is also both the cause of and the reflection of changes in the way people live, in their experiences, and their material conditions of life. Such a major alteration has many causes and origins. Here we will look at just one, but by no means the least significant. This is the change in intellectual thought alluded to earlier. Above all it refers to the way that economics has developed and the way that discipline and the works of economists have tended to shape and delimit public discussion.

Economists and the cult of paid employment

Economists disagree about many things but there are also quite a few matters where there is wide agreement among their ranks. One of these is employment and participation in the labour force. Figures for the number of adults who are participating in the labour force as a proportion of the total population are now published regularly. This employment figure is now seen as a critical economic indicator by most economists and is seized on with the kind of attention once given to the visible trade figures or the number of registered unemployed. A key point to notice is that in these discussions "participation in the labour force" is assumed to be identical with "engaged in paid employment or self-employment". This conflation is highly revealing of certain unconscious assumptions, as we shall explain. When employment figures are published, all economists combine in welcoming a rise. To have more people engaged in paid work as a proportion of the adult population is seen as a clearly good thing. This is reflected in political argument – the Cameron government, for example, made much of the fact that the United Kingdom was showing the highest ever recorded level of paid employment, which was seen as an indicator of the success of its policies.

There are several reasons economists give for their unmitigated rosy view of a rise in "labour market participation" rates. For many, typically neo-Keynesians, the main benefit is a rise in effective demand as more people have a cash income that they can spend on goods and services. In this way a rise in employment generates more economic activity. For other economists with more of a supply side focus, the benefit is that these additional workers are doing productive work and so by definition increasing wealth and activity.

Many economists actually combine both of these emphases, making such an increase a double benefit, on both the demand and supply sides. Another argument is that greater participation in paid work has beneficial social consequences beyond the purely economic; in particular, it is seen to increase individual agency and autonomy. This point is made particularly with regard to an increase in labour market participation on the part of women, but it applies equally to men (or should do). The most frequent sociological argument in favour is that an increase in paid employment brings about greater equality and alleviates many social problems. This is not because of money but because it reduces what is called "social exclusion", in other words, the lack of participation in the mainstream of society and social relations.

This last point bears further examination as it rests upon particular assumptions. The main one is that being engaged in paid productive or exchange relations is essential for social participation. Partly this is because social participation requires a cash income, it is argued, but it also reflects the deeper assumption that collective public life means market participation. Other kinds of human activity are either thought to be less valuable in that regard or are defined as being purely private and personal and therefore not part of the wider social life and interaction – a view that is actually tendentious and inaccurate.

All of this implies a particular state of affairs as the desired or intended goal of public policy. In fact, implies may be the wrong term, so strong and overt is the implication. This is because the ideal state of affairs is not just full employment (where everyone who wants paid work can get it in a reasonable and short time) but what we may call total employment, in which all adults who are of sound mind and body are engaged in paid work (Greg and Gardiner, 2016). This is defended on economic grounds as described above, but there is also a strong moral subtext which is that this kind of life (one involving paid employment) is morally superior to others and that it promotes a good life, both individually and at the level of society as a whole. This explains the way that commentators and politicians respond to recorded rises in the employment rate, with celebrations, because from the perspective described it is simply a good thing, for both reasons of economic and social well-being (Marcos and Bertolaso, 2017). This means that there should be no upward limit to the phenomenon of paid employment other than natural ones, hence total employment being the final goal.

It is this that underlies and shapes almost all of the discussion of automation and its possible impact. If paid employment is the most important activity in society (or to put it another way the way in which most productive activity is organised) and vital for social inclusion and also brings substantial benefits at both a micro and macro level, then the question of how automation will affect it becomes hugely important. Moreover, it is only that impact that will be taken seriously and debated. One position is that nothing will change in essence, only the details of exactly what kinds of tasks people will be paid to do. The other position is that this central and vital activity will largely disappear or become the preserve only of the skilled and educated. Some who take this view welcome this outcome as a chance for social transformation, while others fear it. What all three positions do is assume the centrality of paid work and money denominated exchange transactions to all of modern life. In all of this the impact of AI and automation on the home is ignored.

Second thoughts about paid work

At this point everyone should stop and reflect. There has never historically been a society with total employment or even the kinds of levels of employment we are now seeing in some countries. A closer examination will show that there are very powerful and structural reasons for this, which derive in the final analysis from the nature of human beings. Moreover, when examined properly, the evidence strongly suggests that very high levels of labour market participation (much less total employment) are actually socially damaging and have serious costs and adverse effects at both the individual and social levels. If we look at this from a historical perspective, then it becomes clear that the growth of paid work outside the home as a share of total time is a relatively recent phenomenon and in fact can only really be traced back to the 1950s. Economists typically see this as a spontaneous process, merely the latest stage of a historical evolution. However, as we shall see, this is not true. Technology is not neutral or autonomous like a force of nature, such as the weather. Its effects on life and society are determined both by conscious decisions and policies and by unexamined assumptions and institutions and practices that most people do not consider but simply take for granted.

Moreover, there are features of the presently dominant way of thinking about economics that lead to this obsession with paid work and corrupt proper economic understanding. One of these is a misunderstanding of the temporality of human beings, the way that actual real-world people relate to time and act as beings located in and passing through time. The temporal dimension of the human person is essential in any personal or social life, as societies are structured precisely around this temporality. We are not people existing in an eternal now; however, much contemporary social media would have us see ourselves that way. Contemporary economics takes account of time in the shape of time preference but this assumes a constant self and a uniform and asocial time. In other words, it is assumed in many models that you are dealing with someone of working age who is economically active in the conventional sense and will remain so. Of course, actual human beings pass through a life and spend a significant part of it as either children or older people, neither of whom participate in paid work in the same way as younger and middle-aged adults. (However, they do actually contribute to economic life in various ways as we shall see.) It is in the home that the other economic functions of the various stages of people's lives are instantiated and it is the home that unites the various stages of life and combines them into a whole or succession of wholes – disrupting this is damaging in all kinds of ways, including the economic one.

When observing the world today, one can have the impression that society is designed according to a narrowly utilitarian point of view, as it gives priority to the middle age successful professional. This utilitarian view judges the stages of children and the elderly as unproductive, as in their view these two groups constitute a "passive class" within the home and society at large. Ignoring the temporal reality of human life in this way leads to a physical environment and economic order centred around the needs and lifestyles of younger and middle-aged adults who are in paid employment and ignoring the needs of people who are not at that stage of their life. Even those that are in that category are seen in partial terms as many of them will have young children and elderly relatives and parents who are a part of the life they actually lead. During these phases of life human beings are dependent on others. This reality is opposed to the individualism so rooted in our culture today, which leads us to believe that being vulnerable or "dependent" is something negative. In this view, people should depend on no one. Instead, they should be self-sufficient in order to be fully human and worthy. Thus, autonomy and self-sufficiency are the ultimate human flourishing.

Economic objections to total employment

What is particularly striking is that the outlook just described runs against some of the basic insights of the discipline of economics. (This tells us something about what has happened to economics over the last 50 years.) Although it is economists and people influenced by that discipline that are the most ardent cheerleaders for higher levels of employment, the discipline itself should lead us to be sceptical of that enthusiasm and of the basic models that lead to it. In the first place there is the classic economic phenomenon of diminishing marginal returns. This foundational economic insight was first formulated by the British economist David Ricardo in 1818 (Ricardo, 2004). He pointed out that simply adding more land to the area being cultivated did not result in a corresponding increase in output – so doubling the amount of land farmed did not lead to a doubling of yields but something less. Each additional increment of land and work would yield a slightly lower addition to total output until eventually there would be no increase at all or even a diminution (a diminishing return). This pattern can be found in most areas of life, including those that are not typically thought of as economic. In fact, diminishing marginal returns, getting less payback for each additional input until eventually you actually have a negative return appears to be one of life's universals, like the law of entropy. Clearly this also applies to increases in the labour force through higher rates of participation in paid work. Each additional worker does indeed contribute extra output and demand, but with each additional one that contribution is less. It is actually hard to tell where the tipping point or limit is but we can be sure that it is nowhere near a situation of total employment and be fairly confident that in several countries we are now at it or past it.

The fundamental point here is another basic insight of economics, which is that work has a cost by its very nature. (That is why people are paid or compensated for doing it.) This is often (and revealingly) seen as a disutility of work as compared to leisure. Once again, the implied trade-off is between productive work and the life of a lotus eater. The actual reason is again one of the foundational insights of economics, the idea of opportunity cost. Every time you do something you cannot do something else, given that you cannot be in two places or doing two different things at the same time – unless you live in the world of Harry Potter and have access to a time turner. The next best but forgone alternative to the way you actually use your time is the cost of that use, the opportunity cost. Time spent in paid work is time that cannot be spent doing other things and that is its real cost. Sometimes, of course, that is forgone leisure. However, time not spent in paid work is not all leisure. The crucial point is that in reality most of the alternative uses of time are in fact productive work of various kinds but work that is not part of the system of paid or monetary exchange relations.

This should be obvious from a moment of reflection. When we are not doing paid work, all of us do many things apart from pure leisure activity. Above all we engage in activities, work in fact although unpaid, that sustain and create homes. This means all of the work that is needed to keep a household functioning and in physical good shape. It includes all of the things grouped under the heading of housework, in other words, the work of looking after the physical fabric and surrounding of the home. It means tending to the personal connections with family members and neighbours that are the social aspect of the home. Above all it means looking after, caring for, bringing up and educating children. To the extent that people are spending time on paid work, they are unable to do all of these things and that is the true cost of paid work, the opportunity cost. Obviously, each person will have their own subjective evaluation of how much that cost is and whether they are prepared to meet it. This in turn will determine the kind of work and level of pay that they will require to engage in paid work – other things being constant.

However, at the aggregate or societal level the costs and side effects of people doing paid work rather than the unpaid work of the home can be considerable and borne by third parties or society as a whole. In the language of economics there are considerable negative externalities. Running a home and even more raising children becomes considerably more stressful for the people involved simply because time is constrained and under pressure. One of the long-term effects of the growth of employment is that activities and work that were once done within the home or in the larger world of unpaid work (of which more in a moment) come to be delivered by paid employees as part of a commercial relationship. The classic case in point is childcare, particularly of young children. This was once done almost entirely on an unpaid basis by parents, relatives and neighbours but is now increasingly performed by paid employees of commercial nurseries and childcare services (it is no matter if this is done in the public or private sector). When this is combined with the declining return to work in the shape of lower incomes, the result is people working and then using a very large part of the income that they earn to pay other people to look after their children. This does not make economic sense in many cases, to put it mildly. How has all this come about?

The three spheres of life according to Braudel

An answer to the above question is to look at the approach of classical economics (i.e. economics from before the marginal revolution of the 1880s as found in people such as Smith, Malthus, Ricardo and Mill), which was very much concerned with the domestic and familial. Another, even more fruitful route, is to draw upon the insights of economic historians, above all the way of thinking about human life and economics first formulated by the great French historian Fernand Braudel (1902–1985). Towards the end of his life, Braudel produced what many regard as his masterpiece, a massive three-volume work entitled *Civilization and Capitalism* (Braudel, 1992). This was a survey of the way that economic and social life had worked and been organised in most of the world for the greater part of human history between the advent of agriculture and the start of modernity in the late 18th century.

The fundamental insight was that economic and social life everywhere at most times could be divided into three spheres or layers. Each of these was the subject of one volume. The third volume (*The Perspective of the World*) dealt with what Braudel called "capitalism". By this he meant activities such as long-distance trade and investment and pure financial speculation, which are very important as the principal source of innovation and economic growth but which are also remote from everyday life and economic activity. The second volume (*The Wheels of Commerce*) looked at exchange relations that involved the use of money, in other words, typical trade and production. This is the world of markets. These two areas of life are the ones that modern economics is mainly concerned with. To the extent that it looks at other areas it employs the insights and analyses used to understand these two monetised parts of life. The first volume (*The Structures of Everyday Life*) looks at what Braudel correctly saw as the largest part of human experience in the pre-modern world in terms of the amount of time and activity that was in this sphere. This is what we may call the domestic sphere, because its central institutional form was the home or household. It encompassed all of the activities that took place within and around the home or between different homes and households. Crucially all of these activities and exchanges did not involve money.

In the pre-modern world, the domestic or everyday sphere encompassed many activities that are now part of the second, commercial and market sphere. (Few households now make their own bread or brew their own beer, for example, and most entertainment is now commercial, which was not the case until the very end of the 19th century in the British case). It was not only the largest part of human life in terms of the amount of time and activity that it happened within it. It was also where the great majority of what economists would call value-adding action happened. Most importantly, it was in a sense foundational. All of the other activities, such as trade and exchange and even the elevated world of pure finance, ultimately depended upon and were made possible by the life and activity of the domestic sphere. Moreover, the overwhelming majority of human interactions and social life took place within this sphere. This meant that if it became disordered or deranged in some way, then all aspects of social life including the higher levels, such as commerce and government, would not work as they should. This is also the level of human life that interacts with and is shaped by the structures and rhythms of the natural world.

Clearly, we are now living in a world very different from the one Braudel's great work describes. However, the tripartite division he set out still makes sense as a way of thinking about the human world. Several things have changed in the modern world but they have not affected the basic structure. The sphere of commerce and market exchange at both the local and material and the global and abstract levels has become much larger and now contains a much larger part of peoples' existence – this is the process of commodification that Marx was so exercised by. As he recognised, it has brought huge benefits in terms of greater wealth and comfort through economic growth and innovation.

However, like all processes this has diminishing marginal returns as pointed out earlier. The domestic sphere that Braudel described has now bifurcated. We can now distinguish a "foundational economy" consisting of the production and distribution of those goods and services that are essential for people to be able to actually live and contribute to social life. This includes things such as the supply of water and infrastructure in the widest sense. Such services can be provided privately but are commonly supplied either by government (whether local or national) or by non-governmental and also non-profit seeking bodies (Foundational Economy Collective, 2018). In this case we may say that things that were once part of the domestic sphere have been commercialised without moving fully into the market sphere.

The continuing importance of the domestic

However, although it may be diminished in scope, the domestic sphere is still there. It still accounts for nearly half of all value adding activity by our best guess. It is still the ultimate foundational level of social life, without which the others cannot function properly because it is responsible for vital activities such as the actual reproduction of the species and society. It is very easy to underestimate just how much still happens in this sphere. For example, when we consider education, we focus on the way children and young people learn and acquire skills in formal institutions, such as schools. We typically overlook the enormous input of the home in imparting not only skills, such as reading and writing and general knowledge, but also basic social skills and capacities. It is only when widespread domestic dysfunction means these are not being done that we become aware of this. Our response is typically to throw the burden onto the explicit institutions such as schools and to ask teachers to take it on.

Moreover, the domestic sphere is still central to all economic activity as well as being foundational. All human life other than that of an anchorite or castaway is social, that is, it is lived in and through interpersonal relations. Aguirre (2011, 2013) proposes an integral economic framework as a means to incorporate these interpersonal relational and intertemporal dimensions of the economic agent in economic analysis. At the core of this approach is a more complex understanding of maximisation in the economic decision-making process. It understands the economic agent as a person who is social by nature as well as subject to time, and maximises as such rather than as a self-utility maximiser. Consequently, in the analysis of economic transmission mechanisms as well as in the economic outcomes, this approach takes into account the interpersonal-relational dimension of economic actions. It considers that personal interaction can help or jeopardise economic outcomes. In the current discussion, these economic outcomes are the impact of the interplay between AI, work and home.

To understand the relationship between economic activity and the family, Aguirre (2001) proposes a framework in which three fundamental economic activities are identified: production, exchange and consumption. These activities seek to meet the basic needs of persons, produce profits to allow companies to continue producing in order to meet these needs, and facilitate the distribution of the goods produced in the economy so as to contribute towards human well-being. It is the need to obtain and to consume goods and services that explain the reason for economics and the role that the family plays therein. In this sense then, we can say that the family is the first and most important place where production and spending acquire their meaning. The family, through its contribution or lack thereof to human, social and moral capital, contributes positively or negatively to the economy. It is the home that not only gives meaning to economic activities but it is also the essential location for all three categories of economic relation. Without this the rest of economic life will not work properly. Table 7.1 presents a sketch of how the economy operates and its relationship with the work of the home. It follows that as the family is an integral part of the economy, if we are to understand

Table 7.1 How does the family fit in the economy?

Basic activities	Means used	Role of the family	Purpose
Production	Resources	Human capital	Basic needs
Exchange	Market	Human, moral, social capital	Profit
Consumption	Optimisation and distribution	Appropriate distribution	Well-being (welfare)

the economic dimension of AI, the way in which AI affects the family as a whole, or a given member of it, must be evaluated carefully.

What has happened in the modern world is that one of these activities (production) has moved out of the home to a large extent and another (exchange) has changed its relation with the home.

How did all of these changes take place? What part did technology play in this? Is the story a straightforward one of a process (in this case, the decline and shrinking of the domestic sphere and the growth of both government and market) continuing in a straight line or is it more complicated? Were all these changes spontaneous or did particular decisions and institutional developments play a part? What kinds of debates did we see? The historical questions, as to how the tripartite division of Braudel changed with modernity and technological innovation, matter. They matter in this context because they help us to understand how the latest wave of technological innovation may impact the home, and what possibilities and dangers there may be. That in turn gives us a clearer perception of what options are open to us and even suggests ways that the damaging trends of the last four to five decades may be reversed rather than (as many hope or fear) intensified.

The historical transformations of the home and work

Before the Industrial Revolution of the late 18th and early 19th centuries, the two spheres of the everyday domestic and that of paid work were integrated. This was because almost all production, whether in agriculture or manufacturing, was physically located in the home or close by it. The main way that manufacturing was organised was through the so-called "putting out system" in which households would manufacture products (anything from nails to cloth depending on the region) using raw materials and specifications from a merchant who would then pay them for the finished product. The paid work either happened in the actual home or a small workshop attached to it. Crucially the workers controlled their own hours and conditions of work (Ogilvie, 2010; Berg et al., 2010). The conventional belief is that all of this suddenly changed with the advent of steam power and the factory system, between about 1770 and 1840. Paid work left the home and now happened in large factories powered by steam or water and was paid for on a straightforward wage basis rather than by piecework contract – so the workers lost control of the time they spent in paid work, which was now outside the home. Actually, things were more complicated.

Certainly, much of the conventional story is correct and changes of this kind did happen. However, the entire process was much slower than what most people would realise. Initially it was confined to a few sectors – textiles, iron and steel founding, and ceramics to be precise. Many other areas were still dominated by domestic or small workshop production until as late as the 1870s (Berg, 1994). The reason is simple. It did not pay to invest in large buildings and machinery unless the work done there could be done on a more productive (and hence profitable) basis than in dispersed domestic production. This depended on particular breakthroughs in technology and the organisation of work, which did not all happen at the same time. The real move of almost all paid work out of the home took place between roughly 1870 and 1920, with the rise of the assembly line and integrated mass production, powered by the electric motor.

Moreover, the home during the Industrial Revolution and later was not simply emptied out and reduced to a domain of consumption. To think that is to project its current state back onto the earlier period. The Victorian and Edwardian home becomes, if anything, even more important in its economic and social role than it was before that time and the work done in it changes but becomes, if anything, even more time-consuming than before. The rise in real incomes and living standards that is such a feature of modernity meant that homes became more comfortable and contained more goods but now required much more maintenance. At the same time there was a succession of breakthroughs in technology, such as much cheaper production of items like washing equipment, baths and a whole range of domestic appliances. These made the unpaid work that creates the home and delivers a whole range of services on an unpaid basis easier but also more time-consuming, because the technologies in question were labour intensive. It was another example of the phenomenon of mechanisation alluded to earlier. Just as the people who went out of the home to labour in cotton mills and iron foundries were working much longer hours than their domestic forbears, so the people who remained in the home were now putting in much more time on unpaid domestic work – because that work was also now more productive. Contrary to what one might imagine, this was even more the case for the middle classes than the working classes.

The social role and function of the home also expanded dramatically. Here a whole range of functions was relocated into the home from the public domain. The home became more important for entertainment and socialising, in a way that had only previously been the case for wealthy households. It became the venue and location for a great deal of social ritual and celebrations, as much of the literature of the time reveals. As all contemporaries realised, the home and its activities were still foundational – if anything more so than before. It was the home and the work and activity done there and which created it that made possible and supported both paid work outside the home and public life. This was recognised in the ideology of "separate spheres" that divided human life into the public (paid work, the church, politics and collective leisure) and the domestic. This was clearly gender divided, with the public seen as male and the domestic as female. However, that identification was always contested and, in reality, much qualified. One important activity that connected the two spheres was charity and philanthropy, seen as both coming from the domestic sphere and acting upon it.

At the same time, this was not just a spontaneous process driven by technology as a literal *deus ex machina*. Much of the precise form things took was due to deliberate collective social action or overt public policy such as Factory Acts, sanitary regulations, the Education Act in 1870 and public welfare policy from 1834 onwards. The emergent goal of policy and social action was to strengthen domestic ties and structures and make the relation between the two spheres complementary and supportive. This became ever more pressing with the transformation of paid work in the last third of the 19th century and the first two decades of the 20th century, in all developed countries. One of the responses was the appearance of the classic Bismarkian welfare state (of which the Beveridge Report of 1942 was an example), designed to support households and families and the home as an institution and form of life in the context of the modern economy. Another, even more important was "the family wage system". This was a policy followed in several countries (e.g., Sweden). In the United States, it was explicitly formulated as a guiding principle by Franklin Roosevelt's Secretary of Labor, Frances Perkins. The idea was that it should be possible for a single salary to support a household so that other members of the household could deliver the other functions of the home (Carlson, 2017).

At the time this typically meant that the man in the home would be the person who earned the "family wage", the breadwinner, and the policy was partly effected by limiting women's participation in the labour market through a combination of outright bans, rules and regulations, and social pressure. However, there is no logical reason as to why this should be the case; the core principle is simply that for a household to be a home in the conditions of modern society it should have one person responsible for earning income through participation in the world of market labour and be able to survive on that income at an acceptable standard of living. The idea of the family wage had been a long-standing demand of organised labour from the later 19th century onwards in both Europe and North America, and indeed elsewhere.

The goal of the welfare system was to ensure that households (not individuals) had sufficient income when paid work was not possible because of age, infirmity, sickness or involuntary unemployment. This again reflected the vision and reality of the foundational role of the home and its activities and work. This perspective was not uncontested. For a while in the early

20th century there was a strongly advocated alternative view that most of the functions of the home should be taken and delivered collectively through some kind of public mechanism or institution. The paradigmatic argument was that houses should be built without kitchens and all food purchase, preparation, cooking and eating should be done in collective canteens, with the same argument applied to other functions of the whole such as childcare and leisure. This was typically associated with radical politics of a socialist type and also with radical feminism (Hayden, 1996, 2002).

The passing of the family wage system

All of this changed dramatically during the second half of the 20th century, to produce the world we now have in developed economies. As in the previous century, the changes were the product of both technological innovation and deliberate policy, along with intellectual developments that led policymakers to view the world in a particular way. The first was that continued innovation in domestic technology dramatically reduced the amount of time that most unpaid domestic work required. At the same time the steady expansion of state action removed many of the social functions of the home (this also came about because of developments in things such as the private delivery of functions such as entertainment and leisure). Meanwhile, new technologies such as television led to an individuation of life within the home and a decline in shared or collective activity, whether entertainment or sharing meals together.

Simultaneously, a combination of unintended consequences of some public policy and deliberate action in other areas meant firstly that it became ever more difficult to support a household on one average income, and secondly that labour market participation rates for both men and women, but particularly the latter, rose steadily. This was actively encouraged by public policy, as mentioned previously. This was where the underlying assumptions of contemporary economics came into play, in particular, the idea alluded to that there were only two kinds of activity – work and leisure – and that all work ideally should be paid – if not then it either became effectively invisible and was disregarded, or it was seen as "not real work". The welfare system was transformed from the 1970s onwards into one where the primary goal was to support income from paid work through income supplements through means tested cash transfers – subsidising paid employment effectively.

The British policy of subsidising employment is defended on the grounds that it is better for people to be in paid employment no matter how little they gain from it, for the reasons described earlier, that this reduces social exclusion. The open assumption is that the alternative to paid employment is isolation, inactivity and uselessness, indigence in fact. This way of thinking rests on a number of deeper presumptions and beliefs. One is that all useful and productive activity is or should be done on a paid basis. The obverse of that is the idea that activity that is not paid is unproductive, leisure at best. Another assumption is that paid work and participation in it are not only important for social interaction and a meaningful life (something few would deny) but also essential for it. In other words, other kinds of activity are seen as simply not contributing to that end.

Ironically the outcome of all this is a world rather similar to the one advocated by an earlier generation of radical socialists, but within the context of a capitalist market economy. Increasingly eating, childcare, leisure and social activity all take place outside the home, often on a commercial basis. The home is seen primarily as a place of consumption and rest and not much else. All of this is associated with a range of social problems, which are often blamed for lack of economic activity (meaning paid work). The reality is that many of the social problems that are the subject of discussion and debate are connected by their being at least exacerbated and maybe even caused by the major shift in time from the home to the world of paid work that the rise in employment represents.

Problems of excessive paid work

One example is diet. The medical profession has become increasingly alarmed by the quality of people's diet and its consequences such as widespread obesity. The politicians are now disturbed by the cost implications of this for the National Health Service as obesity-related conditions such as Type 2 diabetes become more common. One cause of this phenomenon is increasingly sedentary lifestyles brought about by technological change. The other cause, however, is a genuine shift in diet. This reflects more consumption of processed food, often rich in complex carbohydrates. A popular explanation is that people are being inveigled into eating this way by propaganda from food companies and retailers. Quite apart from the insulting view of people's intelligence that this argument implies, it is simply economically inaccurate – the profit margins for selling fast food and processed food are no higher than for the kinds of food the government is constantly trying to persuade people to eat. In other words, food manufacturers and retailers are responding to a shift in the pattern of demand. This in turn is driven by the reality that time has become much more precious for many people. When both adults in a household work, it is very difficult to take the time to buy fresh food at a range of outlets (or even one) and then prepare and cook it. It is much easier to buy prepared food.

The same point can be made for a number of other social problems, such as social isolation and loneliness, the care of the elderly and the lack of social contact between the older and younger generations. All of these are kinds of social interaction and work in the widest sense that were once delivered mainly through the institution of the home. As the time devoted to the home has been diminished relative to the amount given to paid work, they have either been done less well or not at all, or they have been commodified and moved into the world of exchange relations. Professional economists have been mostly unaware of this (with some notable exceptions) because of the blind spot that they have.

In terms of Braudel's model, this is a matter of thinking that the subject matter of economics is simply and only those parts of human life that can be put under the rubric of exchange relations mediated by money, which is only two of his three spheres. Confronted with the reality that there are large areas of life that are not in those spheres, the response of economists from Gary Becker onwards has been to explain and understand those areas using the models and mechanisms of exchange transactions (Becker, 1993). This can be a very powerful way of understanding what is going on in things like marriages and families, but it also misses huge amounts.

Departing from the experiential reality of the home (reflecting the actual temporal and social relations and locations of human beings), the self-utility maximisation approach of people like Becker, captured in the notion of "agency", views household economic interactions as a set of contractual relations defined in terms of rights. These rights help each member of the household meet his or her needs and desires. The family, in this perspective, is understood as a common aid society, where each family member seeks to maximise his or her own utility when making economic decisions. Clear definition and coordination of contractual relations among them is what facilitates the utility maximisation process in the economic activity of the household. This is so because their mutual engagement empowers each of its members to do so. Under this framework, interventions and government policies seeking to reduce or prevent harmful effects from AI should unleash the empowering agency of each family member by clearly defining his or her rights.

Fostering this type of agency in economic agents, however, seems to have generated distorted incentives in households. This is the case because promoting engagement in family members for the sake of empowerment typically leads family members to focus on maximising their current utility when making economic decisions while jeopardising future economic well-being. Rather than maximising intertemporally, they focus on the present and on themselves. As this way of behaving is not aligned to the reality of the relational dimension of a household economic activity, the family's economic, human and social capital is weakened, and sooner or later harmful economic impacts are felt. This is first experienced within the home, typically in the breakdown of the family structure, and then it spills over onto the economy as a whole, by weakening the economic activity.

The impact of automation on the home

So how is automation going to affect all this? As we have observed the obsession with paid work and monetised exchanges means that it is the effect of automation on the world of paid work that gets all of the attention. There are discussions of the automated home, often very excited, but we may describe these as "all about Alexa". (For earlier examples, see Corn, 1996.) In other words, these are all accounts of how automated control technology and related innovations can make houses more comfortable and efficient for the individuals who happen to live in them at a particular moment. The idea that a house is a home because of the relations within it and with other households (relations that have a temporal aspect rather than being momentary) is absent. The point is that as in the 19th and 20th centuries technology is not simply a natural force. The results of technological innovation are partly endogenous but more the result of deliberate decisions about how to use it. Some of these decisions will be made at the personal or household level and aggregated by spontaneous processes (including but not limited to markets), while others will be made through politics and public administration. Thinking about things in the way Aguirre describes leads a different approach and a different way of thinking about how automation could change the home and possibly reverse some of the changes described earlier.

Starting from the same experiential reality of the home described at the beginning of this section, the integral approach views household economic interactions as an interpersonal relational reality, not a contractual one. The former calls for proactive participation, sharing and service among household members. This cooperation helps meet the needs of the family and contributes to keeping alive a hopeful outlook towards the future. (The importance of hope in the economic activity has been discussed more extensively in recent year [see Duflo 2012 and Lybbert and Wydick 2018]). The family, in this perspective, is understood as a relational reality, where the optimisation process of each family member takes into account his or her needs as well as the needs of other members of the household. Working together in a collaborative fashion, inside and outside of the home, facilitates efficiency in production and consumption. This is so because by their mutual engagement, economic agents unleash their complementarity and act together in a way that contributes to their mutual human flourishing. Rather than seeking to be empowered when engaging others, economic agents seek to become an empowering presence for those they engage. Under this framework, interventions and government policies seeking to reduce or prevent poverty need to identify, foster and protect effective channels of relations among household members that strengthen the household's economic activity and its well-being (Aguirre, 2001, 2011).

Proactive and participatory interactions among economic agents in married households seem to be one of the effective channels of relations. This is the case because facilitating cooperative behaviour among family members typically leads each member of the family to focus on his or hers as well as others' current and future economic well-being. This requires intertemporal maximisation, which increases efficiency in production, exchange and consumption.

Because of the legal and otherwise lasting commitment, marriage facilitates intertemporal maximisation. This way of behaving is aligned to the reality of the relational dimension of a household's economic activity, so that the family's human and social capital is strengthened, and the probability of falling into AI misuse is decreased.

In other words, the way that AI impacts the home and its place in the economic world will depend on the way people chose to live, the view they take of their lifespan as a whole and on decisions made through the political process about how to best realise these aspirations. One very significant possibility is that automation, along with other technologies such as three-D printing, will see a lot of work relocate to the home and small connected workshops, in a high-tech version of the pre-factory domestic system. There are two important aspects of the economics here. The first is that, as all studies have shown, not all work is equally likely to be automated. Large-scale repetitive work that produces standardised product is very likely to be automated. This means much manufacturing but also a lot of white-collar service work in areas such as law and medicine. Work involving creativity and judgement is very unlikely to be automated. In addition, when work involves manual dexterity, actual manual labour is very unlikely to be automated. The reason is that while it is technologically feasible (just) to reproduce the combination of the human hand and brain, to do so is astonishingly expensive. The often-overlooked reality is that while many white-collar jobs will vanish, traditional skilled trades will flourish and revive. Moreover, work of that kind done at home is every bit as economically efficient as work done outside, if not more. This means that a massive revival of home-based income earning activity is possible, given the right legal and institutional framework.

Moreover, the economists are certainly right to argue that the result of making labour of any kind more productive (which is what AI and automation will do) will be a rise in living standards. This will be caused by both a rise in incomes and a decline in the cost of many products and services. The result should be that it will fairly rapidly become possible once again for one average income to sustain a household by itself. This could in turn mean even more people living by themselves. However, human nature makes that unlikely. Moreover, repeated surveys show that many people, particularly but not only women of childbearing age, would rather spend less or no time on paid work. If the economic spur to paid work is lessened because of the effects of automation, then those preferences will become revealed. All that however will depend on policy choices as well as people following their own preferences. One of the major obstacles is housing and land use policy; another is regulation and the structure of the welfare system. In terms of legal institutions, the main reason as to why the benefits of technological innovation have become increasingly concentrated upon the wealthy is because of intellectual property and the way it has developed since the 1960s, particularly in the United States.

Changes in the home and consumption

In terms of consumption, automation and technologies such as smart meters and the so-called "Internet of Things" could be made to give homes and households much more control over their affairs and to significantly blur the division between consumption and production (Rifkin, 2013). The economic and social model that it implies is one where economic (and social) life is dominated by networks rather than hub and spoke models. The so-called "sharing economy" is for various reasons likely to be one dominated by interlinked households and enabling platforms rather than conventional firms and employment relations. This can be seen already in areas such as tourism and travel, but will almost certainly spread into many other areas as well. It could be that new technologies and automated "smart" houses will intensify and exacerbate the individualisation that things such as television, smartphones and social media have brought about. In that case, the home would become simply a residence, the place where a shifting cast of individuals hang their hats. However, that is a matter of choice, on the part of both individuals and policymakers. We are already seeing signs of a reaction against these trends at the personal level. The new technology could equally lead to a strengthening of the home as a social unit with its internal relations becoming stronger rather than attenuated.

Over the last 250 years the combination of innovation and public policy has brought about dramatic changes. We should not make the mistake of thinking that all this was a simple story of a steady movement in one direction driven by technology as an autonomous force. Rather choices have been made and certain goals have been pursued at both an individual and a collective level. Had different choices been made the outcomes would have been different. This means that the pictures of the world that we have and that policymakers in particular have are enormously important because they shape and limit the options that we chose between. For the last 50–60 years the predominant ideas among intellectuals and policymakers have combined social individualism with an economic model in which the economy or even all of human life is seen as being monetised exchange. The categories of work and paid employment have been seen as synonymous and paid employment as an unalloyed good. The entire sphere of life, that is, the home and the activities and relations it embodies, has been erased out of consideration. This contrasts sharply with the thought of earlier periods and indeed of most of human history.

This all means that we should take off the blinkers of the currently dominant way of thinking and bring the home back into our field of vision when we consider the impact of automation. Many of the policies pursued over the last few decades are now proving seriously counterproductive and unsustainable. Artificial intelligence and automation if applied within that framework are likely to destroy it and have devastating results in the process. Alternatively, we can put the home at the centre of our thinking as earlier generations did and see how the same technology can revive and strengthen the domestic.

References

Aguirre, Maria Sophia (2001). Family, Economics, and the Information Society. How Are They Affecting Each Other? *International Journal of Social Economics*, 28(3), pp. 225–247. doi: 10.1108/03068290110357645.

Aguirre, Maria Sophia (2011). Achieving Sustainable Development: An Integral Approach to an Economics Perspective. In L.G. Franceschi (ed.), *The Ethics of Sustainable Development*. Nairobi, Kenia: Strathmore University Press.

Aguirre, Maria Sophia (2013). An Integral Approach to an Economic Perspective: Consequences for Measuring Impact. *Journal of Market and Morality*, 16(1), pp. 53–67.

Becker, Gary (1993). *A Treatise on the Family*. Cambridge, MA: Harvard University Press.

Berg, Maxine (1994). *The Age of Manufactures, 1700–1820: Industry, Innovation, and Work in Britain*. London, UK: Routledge.

Berg, Maxine, Pat Hudson and Michael Sonenscher (eds.) (2010). *Manufacture in Town and Country before the Factory*. Cambridge, MA: Cambridge University Press. doi: 10.1017/CBO9780511560347.

Braudel, Fernand (1992). *Civilization and Capitalism, 15th–18th Century* (3 vols). Berkeley, CA: University of California Press.

Bregman, Rutger (2017). *Utopia for Realists: And How We Can Get There*. London, UK: Bloomsbury.

Carlson, Allan (2017). *The Family in America: Searching for Social Harmony in the Industrial Age*. London, UK: Routledge. doi:10.4324/9781315131993.

Cass, Oren (2018). *The Once and Future Worker: A Vision for the Renewal of Work in America*. New York, NY: Encounter Books.

Corn, Joseph J. (1996). *Yesterday's Tomorrows: Past Visions of the American Future*. Baltimore, MD: The Johns Hopkins University Press.

Duflo, Esther (2012). Human Values and the Design of the Fight against Poverty. *The Tanner Lectures on Human Values*, Harvard University. Cambridge, MA: Harvard University Press.

Foundational Economy Collective (2018). *Foundational Economy: The Infrastructure of Everyday Life*. Manchester, UK: Manchester University Press.

Greg, Paul and Laura Gardiner (2016). *The Road to Full Employment: What the Journey Looks Like and How to Get There*. London, UK: Resolution Foundation.

Hayden, Dolores (1996). *The Grand Domestic Revolution: A History of Feminist Designs for American Homes, Neighbourhoods, and Cities*. Cambridge, MA: MIT Press.

Hayden, Dolores (2002). *Redesigning the American Dream: The Future of Housing, Work, and Family Life*. New York, NY: Norton.

Huxley, Aldous (2007). *Brave New World and Brave New World Revisited*. New York, NY: Harper Perennials (1st pub. 1932 & 1958).

Kurzweill, Raymond (2010). *The Singularity Is Near. When Humans Transcend Biology*. London, UK: Duckworth.

Lybbert, Travis J. and Bruce Wydick (2018). Hope as Aspirations, Agency, and Pathways: Poverty Dynamics and Microfinance in Oaxaca, Mexico. In Christopher

Barrett, Michael Carter and Jean-Paul Chavas (eds.), *The Economics of Poverty Traps*. Chicago, IL: University of Chicago Press, pp. 153–177.

Marcos, Alfredo and Marta Bertolaso (2017). What Is a Home? On the Intrinsic Nature of a Home. In Antonio Argandoña (ed.), *The Home: Multidisciplinary Reflections*. Cheltenham, UK: Edward Elgar, pp. 35–56. doi: 10.4337/9781786436573.00011.

Mason, Paul (2015). *Postcapitalism: A Guide to Our Future*. Harmondsworth, UK: Penguin.

Ogilvie, Sheilagh (ed.) (2010). *European Proto-Industrialisation: An Introductory Handbook*. Cambridge, UK: Cambridge University Press.

Ozment, Stephen (2001). *Ancestors: The Loving Family in Old Europe*. Cambridge, MA: Harvard University Press.

Ricardo, David (2004). *The Principles of Political Economy and Taxation*. Indianapolis, IN: Liberty Fund (1st pub. 1818).

Rifkin, Jeremy (2013). *The Third Industrial Revolution*. New York, NY: Griffin.

Rifkin, Jeremy (2015). *The Zero Marginal Cost Society*. New York, NY: Griffin.

Theobald, Robert (1965). *Free Men and Free Markets*. New York, NY: Anchor Books.

Chapter 8

The impact of artificial intelligence on the future of work

Mia Mikic[1] and Joy Malala

Introduction

Daniel Susskind proclaimed that "there were two possible futures for the professions" (Susskind and Susskind, 2015), where by "professions" one may refer to a variety of jobs. These are firstly, on the one hand, that the future would entail a more efficient version of what we already have, where professionals continue working much as they have done since the middle of the 19th century, but they heavily standardize and systematize their routine activities. On the other hand, the future would involve a transformation in the way that the expertise of professionals is accessible. This suggests that the introduction of a wide range of increasingly capable systems will, in various ways, displace much of the work of traditional professionals. In the short and medium terms, these two futures will be realized in parallel. He then states that, inevitably, the second future will dominate, and that we will find new and better ways to share expertise or information, and our professions will steadily be dismantled.

This chapter will explore the disruptive nature of artificial intelligence (AI) and the nature of work in the future (or, as it has become customarily referred to as "the future of work"). It will provide a segue into a discussion of the trends, and forecasts of development of AI – as one of the types of digital frontier technologies – and its impact on the future of work. Digital frontier technologies[2] have major implications for labour markets. These digital frontier technologies present great advances in automation, machine learning and AI. All of these have posed, and will continue to pose, policy challenges since they not only increase productivity but are also transforming labour markets. The automation of repetitive tasks has changed the demand for skills. Job losses are being attributed to technology as physical labour is being replaced while AI is taking over many analytical functions. Concerns have been raised that automation is contributing to an increase in the share of income accruing to capital, while decreasing the share of income flowing to labour, thus leading to an increase in income and wealth inequality (see more in Harari, 2018). This consequently is a primary concern, for this affects the home, because if some of the gains from automation are not distributed, the process of skills polarization will exacerbate income inequality, further affecting livelihoods (United Nations, 2018).

The discussion in this chapter is done under the backdrop of a wider perspective on how technology influences the home and, therefore, the focus on employment relates to how people work and live. These are all crucial for developing policies for societies to cope with the disruptions these technologies will inevitably bring about. The potential of AI to disrupt the *status quo*, alter the way people live and work and, ultimately, vote will rearrange traditional value systems and lead to new products, services and jobs, and has revived old angst over automation and the future of work. While much of the public and policy debates on AI and employment have tended to oscillate between fears of the "end of (human) employment" and reassurances that little will change, there is evidence that suggests that neither of these extremes is likely. This chapter aims to provide a non-exhaustive and non-technical summary of a small subset of recent literature related to AI and its influence on the way humans work and live. Automation and other frontier technologies, of which AI is the most popularized one, are transforming businesses and are already contributing to economic growth through the increase of productivity. These technologies are transforming the nature of work and the workplace itself. It has long been true that machines are able to carry out more of the tasks done by humans; they have complemented the work that humans do and have even performed some tasks that go beyond what humans can do.

As a result, workers have had to grapple with significant workforce transitions and dislocation. Workers have had to acquire new skills and adapt to the increasingly capable machines alongside them. This has been prevalent in the era of the industrial ages as well as the computer and digital age. Over time, this has resulted in shakeup of jobs (professions), the increasing decline of certain occupations, and the introduction and growth of new ones. This phenomenon is known as the augmentation and enhancing of the human worker, which is tipped as the process through which humans shall eventually be replaced (Kane et al., 2019).

However, it is not only jobs performed by individuals in various activities that are being dramatically transformed by AI and other technologies. Apart from business, it is the functioning of the public sector and how it delivers services (in sectors such as farming, education, financial services, health, policing and others) to citizens. As mentioned, AI has particularly replaced either routine work or skilled jobs that are based on making predications from past data. Although AI has real potential to contribute to addressing more effectively large-scale challenges such as healthcare, humanitarian crises or climate crises, on the other hand risks linked to widespread and indiscriminate use related to data privacy, identity, cyber-security and the like are also real and expose the negative side of AI. Combined, all these challenges and opportunities coming out of the rise of AI may have significant implications for how the "home" will function in the near future as well as the place of work. This chapter offers just a glimpse into the vast possibilities this change may bring.

What is AI?

AI is one of those "things" we all talk about but can hardly define. It is being called "new electricity" (WIPO, 2019, p. 13). Most will recall popular examples of AI, from chess games against world champions to futuristic movies and contemporary applications such as "Siri", "Sophia" and "Alexa". The necessary components of AI are "machines", "learning" and doing something that humans "normally do" (and without their help). Back in 1955, McCarthy defined it as, "[f]or the present purpose the artificial intelligence problem is taken to be that of making a machine behave in ways that would be called intelligent if a human were so behaving"(McCarthy et al., 2006). However, this definition is problematic, in that it *presumes* that the "machine" is intelligent. Therefore, many have expanded its definition to include that they are sufficiently informed, "smart", autonomous and able to perform morally relevant actions independently of the humans who created them (Floridi and Sanders, 2004). Additionally, the World Intellectual Property Organisation (WIPO) offers a useful definition of AI as "learning systems, that is, machines that can become better at a task typically performed by humans with limited or no human intervention" (WIPO, 2019, p. 19).

It is striking that for a term that has been around since the 1950s, we still do not have a single, universally accepted definition of AI, despite attempts at describing and (re)naming concepts apparently being encompassed by AI. Richard Baldwin approached the issue in a somewhat witty way while attempting to explain how people are bad at naming things (Baldwin, 2018). In his new book, he says, we all know what "artificial" is, and what is meant by "intelligence", yet these two words together, as in AI, create lots of confusion and invoke feelings that range from fear to amusement and even mocking (Baldwin, 2018). This is since AI does not encompass what humans deem as intelligence, which includes reflection and, to an extent, intent. Therefore, can AI be defined based on outcomes and actions? This is the question often posed, even by philosophers who juxtapose two ideas. The first, in one dimension, is whether the goal is to match human performance, or, instead, ideal rationality. The other dimension is whether the goal is to build systems that reason/think, or rather systems that act (Bringsjord and Govindarajulu, 2019).

AI is the single most misconstrued, overhyped and even feared technological construct (Institute for Transformative Technologies, 2018). Most often, AI is defined as the ability of machines and computer systems to acquire and apply knowledge, and to carry out intelligent behaviour (OECD, 2016). By "intelligent", we imply having a general mental capability that involves a variety of cognitive tasks (e.g., sensing, processing oral language, reasoning, learning fast and from experience, making decisions, solving problems, plan, etc.). However, as Baldwin explains, what at present we take as AI (machine learning or auto-machine learning) does not do all those things we associate with intelligence. In fact, today's AI is capable only of learning quickly and of auto learning, not reflecting "intelligence" as we (humans) generally understand it. Thus, Baldwin suggests, AI should stand for "almost intelligent".

In summary, there has been a growing understanding by academics that AI with human-like cognitive capacity (the so-called, artificial general intelligence) is not within a reasonable (nor widespread) reach.[3] However, most would agree that the so-called narrow AI, designed to perform specific, narrow tasks such as games, facial recognition or driving a car, is already commonplace. These are the computer systems (software and algorithms) which use a combination of big data analytics,[4] cloud computing, machine-to-machine communication and the Internet of Things (IoT) to operate and learn. Thus, in considering AI's impact on the future of work, this chapter will remain in the realm of the narrow AI.

Like humans who cannot be good at all they need to do, AI focuses on one or few areas of activities. Table 8.1 summarizes those techniques and functional applications for the AI we know today.

Popular use of computer algorithms or AI increasingly relies on a "human-like" embodiment in a form of robots shaped as humans that are often given (female?) names, for example, Siri, Amelia, Alexa, Sophia, etc. While these "humanoids" still do not operate as superintelligence, they emulate ordinary human capabilities, including vision, speech and navigation and perform specialized tasks which normally have been in a domain of human experts. But the actual uses of AI outside robotics in other functional real-world applications are already very much part of our everyday life that we might not

Table 8.1 Major AI techniques and functional applications

Major AI techniques	Major AI functional applications
AI techniques are different core algorithmic approaches used to implement AI functions	AI functional applications cover all functions performed by AI techniques, independent of the field of application
Machine learning	Knowledge representation and reasoning
Probabilistic reasoning	Computer vision
	Robotics
Fuzzy logic	Natural language processing
	Distributed AI
Logic programming	Predictive analytics
	Speech processing
Ontology engineering	Control methods
	Planning and scheduling

Source: Based on information in WIPO (2019, pp. 146–148).

Table 8.2 AI sectoral applications

Sector/activity	Examples of use/AI technology
Banking and finance	Machine learning (e.g., approval of loans, management of assets/risks); automated trading systems; fraud detection; biometrics; customer service
Business	Identification of trends, customer data analysis, marketing, advertisement and decision-making systems
Document management and publishing	Automatic data extraction, translators and management of data privacy
Industry and manufacturing	Predictive maintenance, generative design systems, market monitoring and robotics with more cognitive skills
Life and medical sciences	Automatic diagnostic systems, drug personalization and drug discovery
Security	Cyber-security, smart-city technologies (face recognition, behaviour/crowd analysis), predictive policing and military use
Telecommunications	Network performance, optimize customer services
Transportation	Fuzzy logic, autonomous vehicles, traffic management, logistics and automated package delivery

Source: Based on information presented in WIPO (2019, pp. 148–149).

even be aware of it; from augmented reality, biometrics, predictive analytics to many speech and semantics applications, AI greets us in the morning, accompanies us through the day and is often part of our resting periods.

Table 8.2 provides an overview of the sectoral application of typical AI technologies as this also provides a hint about what one can expect regarding possible impacts on jobs, their number and the skills required to perform them.

AI's areas of influence

It is very difficult to find something that will not be influenced by AI. To facilitate discussion with respect to the future of work, this chapter groups influences into three broad categories. The first two categories relate to influences at a more aggregated level, with direct and indirect impacts on employment and its possible changes. These explore the impact of AI (as a representative of digital frontier technology) through productivity changes and changes in jobs, as well as skills structure and impacts on inclusivity. The third group brings together influences down to a level of an individual and family in and around their home and as they go about their daily lives. Finally, the note addresses a growing trend of the place of work moving away from "work" to many other places, including one's home.

Primary channels of AI influence on future of work

Productivity

AI influence can be categorized into various aspects, productivity being among the most important when it comes to discussing employment impacts. Productivity, which is defined as a ratio between the output and input volumes, measures how efficiently production inputs, such as labour and capital, are being used in an economy to produce a given level of output. Economists believe that the key to long-term prosperity is sustained productivity growth. Paul Krugman famously stated that "[p]roductivity isn't everything, but in the long run it is almost everything. A country's ability to improve its standard of living over time depends almost entirely on its ability to raise its output per worker" (Krugman, 1994). Thus, it is important to understand the interplay among the main drivers of labour productivity growth, that is, investment in capital, human capital development and technological progress.

Baldwin (2018), looking over very long historical run, assigns an instrumental role to technology in transforming global economy not once but three times, one industrial revolution at a time, starting with the steam engine (First Industrial Revolution), the mechanical loom starting mass production with an advent of electricity (Second Industrial Revolution) to robotics (Third Industrial Revolution) and now AI (Fourth Industrial Revolution).[5] The impact of technological progress has been to increase the productivity of labour using that technology, typically more skilled labour. Goos and Manning (2007), among others, argued that skill-biased technology progress and mechanization lead to "the rising of relative demand in skilled jobs, which require non-routine cognitive skills, and the relative rising demand on non-routine manual skills". Since AI that can substitute for labour is arguably more productive, or it can augment labour productivity, its largest impact on economic prosperity is expected to be via productivity.

This is particularly true for developing countries given the vastly reduced costs of capital that some AI applications have demonstrated and the potential for sustained productivity increases especially among the low-skilled professions. With many developed and some emerging economies facing issues of an ageing population and a steady drop in birth rates, productivity growth has been sluggish and increasingly it will depend on technology, and in particular on frontier technology, for augmentation of human capabilities. Only by ensuring a long-term productivity growth can we expect economic growth. Moreover, an increase in productivity can be accompanied by positive externalities, as economic transactions will be done more efficiently and savings can be re-invested into the economy to create further growth or to increase investment aimed at reshaping economy for delivering sustainable development goals. Taking into account also some possible negative externalities, McKinsey (2018) suggests that AI-linked productivity boost could raise global gross domestic product (GDP) by as much as $13 trillion by 2030, about 1.2% additional GDP per year. However, the same McKinsey report stresses that the source of such growth (AI adoption) is very concentrated and at present relies on AI research and investment in China and the United States (US), with a second group of countries including Germany, Canada, Japan and the United Kingdom (UK), and only in the third layer do we have some smaller developing countries such as Singapore or the Republic of Korea, and Malaysia.

Jobs and skills

The other major influence of AI is on jobs or, as Susskind and Susskind (2015) refer to it, the professions. Technology was rarely considered complementary to workers despite being the most important factor in increasing their share of income through increasing labour productivity (World Bank Group, 2019). Machines and automation have always been feared for their ability to effectively replace workers (after all, machines do not ask for leave and do not fall ill). Nevertheless, the World Bank Group (2019) argues that technology (especially automation) has always created more jobs than it has destroyed (cf. McKinsey Global Institute, 2018, p. 5). Additionally, newly created jobs in new sectors have typically resulted in better, safer and better-paid working conditions, even for the unskilled workers. Their report says that "many children currently in primary school will work in jobs as adults that do not even exist today". This causes considerable challenges to governments about how to educate current generations for those "unknown" jobs.

The fact is that these waves of destruction and creation of jobs come with increased frequency and power, becoming more like tsunamis. Baldwin (2018) argues strongly that the issue here is not one of there being a change per se, but that of its speed and scope. For example, in considering only 15 major developed and emerging economies, the World Economic Forum (2016) predicted that frontier technological trends will lead to a net loss of over 5 million jobs by 2020. The World Bank (2016) estimated that up to two-thirds of all jobs are susceptible to automation in the developing world in the coming decades from a pure technological standpoint. An analysis by McKinsey Global Institute (2017) predicts that, technically, about half of all jobs globally can be automated. According to the same source, in Asia-Pacific economies, jobs of 785 million workers or 51.5% of total employment in the region could be automated. There is no doubt that technology will have huge impacts on jobs in the long run. Although not intuitively obvious, jobs in developing countries, especially the least developed countries, are more susceptible to automation from a technical perspective. The rationale is straightforward: the simpler and more repetitive the job, the easier and cheaper it is to automate it.

However, there is no consensus about the scale and pace of the impact on jobs. For instance, ESCAP (2018) report shows that the available

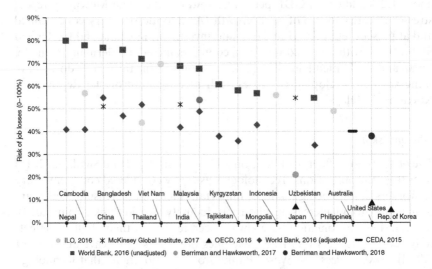

Figure 8.1 Range of estimates of the share of jobs at risk of being lost to automation. The samples in the study include countries in ESCAP region. United States is included for benchmarking. Detailed data are shown in the Appendix 1 at the end of the report, ESCAP 2018. (Source: compiled by the ESCAP study team according to the existing studies as shown in the figure. ESCAP 2018, p. 24).

estimates vary widely according to the sampling and analytical methodologies (Figure 8.1). While the results of existing studies need to be interpreted with caution, they show the significant impact: for example, 40% to 80% of the jobs lost to automation in Cambodia, 40% to 70% in Thailand, 50% in Philippines or 7% to 55% in Japan. Similarly, results from a firm-level survey suggest that automation may have significant impacts (with a wide range of 60% to 90%), depending on the countries and sectors, on the job security of salaried workers in the following five major sectors of Association of Southeast Asian Nations economies: automotive and auto parts; electrical and electronics; textiles, clothing and footwear; business process outsourcing; and retail (ILO, 2016).

Wide differences in experts' estimations about the job losses due to automation and technology advances go hand-in-hand with the widespread perceptions about the expected job losses (Table 8.3). Similarly, with respect to possible benefits of AI, it is assumed that those will be small and concentrated in the key jobs for future development of AI itself. Evidence available, however, indicates that, firstly, gains in income may outweigh the income lost, and secondly that only less than a fifth of "in-demand" jobs will be directly linked to AI industry. The jobs and skills in demand will strongly favour the interpersonal, creative and strategic decision-making tasks. So instead of seeing a decline in labour force participation, there is likely to be a rise because of

Table 8.3 Myths and evidence on impacts on jobs

Impact on jobs	Perception	Supporting evidence	Perception	Supporting evidence
Jobs lost	AI is going to lead to mass unemployment in Asia across all countries and sectors	✗	There is a wide variation in the estimates of potential job displacement impacts from AI	✓
Jobs gained	The job creation effects of AI are limited, and any jobs created will not be enough to offset those displaced	✗	The income effect of AI could more than offset its displacement effect to lead to net job gains	✓
	The jobs and skills in highest demand will be those that directly support AI development	✗	Jobs that directly support AI development could account for less than a fifth of "in-demand" positions, while almost 60% could be positions that require interpersonal, creative or strategic decision-making tasks	✓
Workforce participation	AI could potentially reduce workplace participation by automating jobs	✗	Job matching platforms, flexible working and AI tools allow underserved groups to increase their participation in the workforce	✓

Source: Adapted from Thompson (2019).

✗: Supporting evidence does not exist

✓: Supporting evidence exists

the positive impact of job matching platforms, flexible working arrangements and AI tools allowing currently underserved groups (including differently abled people) to increase their participation in the workforce.

Additionally, it is also important to note that the pace of adoption of AI is dependent on the availability of appropriate skills and a clear indication of economic benefits at a company level, among other factors. In the developing countries especially, the move towards AI may be delayed because these countries still have a large pool of relatively cheap and part-skilled labour. This makes investment in machine learning and automation economically non-viable or less viable than what is thought of. Lower wages result in a longer payback time for automation investment, defined by the time to recover the investment for robots through savings from labour and avoidance of breakdowns. For example, according to ESCAP estimates, investing $250,000 for two robots, while each robot replaces two operators per shift, requires a payback time in the Russian Federation, Malaysia and China of over 11, 7 and 6 years; while the payback time in the Republic of Korea, Japan, New Zealand, Singapore and Australia can be only 1.5 years or less. It is therefore felt that a current low adoption of AI in many developing countries is reflective of the fact that business in those countries' industries is still at the nascent or pilot stage of development. Ultimately, as relative prices of labour and other resources get adjusted (especially if factoring in the costs related to environmental considerations), the future decisions on the adoption of automation technologies will be made on the cost–benefits analysis at that time.

Referring to the changes in qualifications, workers will need different skill sets to safeguard their place in the workforce. This is typically referred to as the "displacement effect", whereby displacing workers from tasks they were previously performing requires a shift in skill sets. Skills that will be in demand are social and emotional skills, and in particular higher cognitive skills, such as critical thinking, creativity and complex information processing. Humans will increasingly get to supervise machines, for example, cashiers will supervise scanning machines instead of doing that task themselves; or experts in trade policy will provide advice and conduct a review of quality of "machine-processed" trade negotiation mandates. This restructuring and repositioning of jobs will be happening with a downward pressure on the average wage in advanced economies.

In summary, it is important to keep in mind that jobs are affected simultaneously in three ways: AI will be adding new jobs, shedding some old jobs, and most often changing jobs by affecting only some activities of a specific job. In fact, most of the jobs will be only partially automated and only a few (around 5%) will be fully replaced by AI. Nevertheless, even the partial automation will require continuous learning and up-skilling to make workforce fit to absorb these changes and still stay gainfully employed. The changes will inevitably affect the distribution of income, which is already skewed in favour of skilled workers in many countries. Yet, in contrast to skills that have been in demand during the Third Industrial Revolution, with digitalization the demand for basic physical and cognitive skills will be falling, as demand for advanced skills, both technological and higher cognitive, will grow, while the premium will be paid to those with social and emotional skills. In this context, there is a need to promote lifelong learning, reskilling and entrepreneurship development to develop a cadre of job creators and also to discuss new approaches to social protection for those who despite all efforts fall between the cracks and find themselves as losers from the AI-driven changes.

Dangerous jobs have been rightfully automated and are now performed by robots. One of the most dangerous jobs of all is bomb disposal (Allison, 2016). Today, robots (or more specifically, drones) are taking over these risky jobs, while most of these drones require a human to control them. However, as machine-learning technology improves day by day, these tasks will be done completely by robots with the aid of AI, resulting in the saving of thousands of lives. Another example of the use of robots in unsafe situations is during search efforts after natural disasters, such as earthquakes. They also perform dangerous rescue missions where firefighters may not be able to perform as well as during the clean-up of nuclear waste.

AI has also aided in the support of environmentally sustainable jobs, which include offshore oil rigs, coal mines or welding in various factories or construction sites. These types of jobs are associated with noise, intense heat and toxic substances, as well as accidents. Without machine learning, these robots would need to be pre-programmed for a specific location. Additionally, advancements in computer vision and deep learning have enabled more flexibility and greater accuracy.[6]

Inclusivity

The informal sector in developing countries (especially poorer developing countries) is still the dominant way through which people earn their livelihood. This is despite the progress made in improving their business environment. Many still rely on brick and mortar methods of production as the proportion of informal work in those countries is 90% or more. For instance, it is 98% in Nepal (World Bank Group, 2019, pp. 7–8); women or children make up most of such informal employment in traditional sectors.

Recently, however, several factors have pointed towards risks to jobs that were traditionally sheltered, such as professions providing mostly (knowledge) services. This may be due to the affordability and availability of technologies such as online translator programmes. It is also attributed to better access to the Internet which has created new channels such as web platforms for hiring for such professionals, often on an hourly basis. These web platforms, often underpinning the so-called share economy, are sites like Upwork, Freelancer and Sidekicker. The spread of these platforms means that professionals selling knowledge and high-skilled services through them routinely accept lower pay than professionals in a formal sector. This opens the door for increased informality in this sector too. As these professional services often require a certification for a provider, a remote delivery of work both helps cutting through often rigid regulations impeding cross-border supply and opens the way for many new challenges, including the lack of any kind of (social) protection.

The World Bank Group's report (2019) has called for a new social contract in order to address challenges of future employment under AI influence. With 2 billion people already working in some activity in the informal sector, with about the same number of people not having a digital identity, they are seen as possible victims of AI. They lack any sort of social protection and social safety nets, and often cannot benefit from opportunities for "tele-migrating".[7] Thus, the report argues that creating formal jobs is the first-best policy. Preconditions include increased investment in affordable access to the Internet and securing digital identity. In summary, even if the aggregate number of jobs remains the same, its composition will change and many workers will likely need to change occupations, even between sectors (e.g., from manufacturing to services) and localities. The number of difficult-to-automate jobs will increase relative to other categories. Nevertheless, there will be losers and there is a need for stronger social protection that must include proactive policies of investment in human capital, not only in schools but at work too.

Other channels of AI influencing future of work

As mentioned before, the ability of people to keep paid work will depend on their cognitive and physical conditioning and the ability to adjust to new circumstances. Furthermore, the availability of and access to private and public services and infrastructure will be important to ensure inclusivity and fairness to the highest degree possible. In this context, the influence of AI in sectors such as education, energy and health is briefly considered. There are other equally important areas that are not covered here, for example, increased mobility by access to autonomous transport, or more business opportunities due to better banking facilities. Examples include sectors such as education, energy and health, particularly health, where machine learning and AI include medical diagnostic devices with automated decision-making; models to predict cholera outbreaks and distribute fresh water and vaccines; tracking of clinicians' movements to ensure compliance with hygiene protocols; arm bands to monitor the nutritional status of children; analysis of medical imaging to identify tumours and other anomalies; prediction of outbreaks of infections; and genetic analysis to determine vulnerability to diseases. It has been observed that hospitals that utilize machine learning to aid in treating patients see fewer accidents and fewer cases of hospital-related diseases. The advances in AI have addressed medicine's most challenging problems, such as allowing researchers to better understand genetic diseases through the use of predictive models, where health professionals would have otherwise had to review reams of data manually before they diagnose or treat a patient.

AI has also aided law enforcement, with data analytics being used extensively in improving safety at home, not only in terms of fire and similar risks,[8] but also when risks come from other inhabitants. Most recently, it was reported that AI is becoming a gamechanger in addressing domestic violence.[9] Additionally, AI is increasingly used in child abuse cases, where algorithims are able to help eliminate bias and tackle social injustice (Courtland, 2018).

In most societies the services mentioned above are still dominantly provided by the public sector (i.e., government), especially those related to policing and security. Therefore, it is important to understand how AI can benefit public providers in the provision of services that citizens need and thus show successful models of leveraging AI for improved public services in the Asia-Pacific region and beyond. The report published recently in collaboration between ESCAP and Google (2019) demonstrates several successful deployments of AI in health, justice, agriculture, environment, insurance and social welfare. The adoption of AI in the public sector is still in its early days in many developing countries and the report finds that there are inevitable setbacks in a trial-and-error process, yet it offers valuable lessons. The insights can serve as an introductory guide for policymakers who are keen to explore the possibilities of AI for greater efficiency, fairness and equity. It is important for these policymakers to note that AI cannot replace or make-up for the poorly designed system and goals.

Home as the place of work[10]

Finally, let us turn to illustrating how AI, remote intelligence and machine learning influence individuals in their home, from the perspective of the future of work. The advance of remote intelligence and AI and vastly improved access to information and communications technology (ICT) will dramatically change the places people work (and study). One glimpse through a window of any Starbucks café will provide ample evidence of people using their computing or information technology (IT) devices and Wi-Fi connectivity to engage in business, study or social relationships while drinking their coffee. People are now able to work in many different places away from work, not only in cafes, but also in public transport, airports or even hospitals. This has been boosted by the introduction of "flexible working arrangements". The World Bank Group (2019) report emphasizes the positive role of technologies, and particularly access to ICT and Internet, in making work opportunities more readily available at places away from "work".

Work from home is very much in vogue and both corporate world and public sector are putting in place various "flexible working arrangements" for their staff. While it is true that this allows for improving participation by some groups that traditionally have had to leave the labour force for some period of time (e.g., women for child bearing or care of elderly relatives; mobility impaired people or people who need specialized assisting devices, etc.), this shift of work space also opens some questions which have not been addressed fully in its policy design. Among them are questions on the net costs of moving work to home, whilst people working from home save money and time from commuting to work, the expenses associated with working from home increase, such as access to Internet, electricity, water and the availability of the equipment needed to perform one's job. There is some evidence that productivity may be improved as ordinary office distractions are eliminated and employees are able to have peace of mind and hence be more focused. There are, however, challenges too. The "pressure" to multitask while working from home might be impeding productivity, while being absent from office may reduce access to decision-making opportunities if meetings are not easily attended virtually. Nevertheless, working from home is seen as beneficial overall, as it boosts the ability to engage in more than one job or to take part-time work, for those who otherwise had to make a binary choice of either going to work or caring for family. Still more studies are needed to explore if these new options are also leading to more stress and more pressure. This may also favour certain professions as not all jobs can be included, such as security guards, and person-to-person contact jobs such as healthcare and the hospitality industry.

What next?

Policymakers and business leaders should embrace AI but put in place measures to facilitate adoption, soften the disruptive transitions that will accompany it and place a new focus on responsible use – this sounds the same as when trade policymakers discuss their intention to compensate losers from trade liberalization, but in practice this has never been seriously attempted. What may need to be addressed is the need to improve access to quality education and life skills both through the promotion of science and technology as a vehicle for transformational change or through developing the culture of innovation as a way of life. There should also be an emphasis on ensuring inclusivity, as it is important to take into account the implications of AI and gender discrimination in recruitment. AI recruitment tools have systematically selected men over women based on qualifications.[11]

In summary, there are several factors that need to be considered on a broader level. Firstly, AI has the potential to have positive impacts on worker productivity, incomes and overall job satisfaction. Secondly, AI could potentially create more jobs than it displaces, but disruption is likely and there may be net losses of jobs concentrated in specific sectors or among particular groups (e.g., women, ageing, differently abled and less skilled). Thirdly, in creating new jobs AI creates a positive impact on the labour market. To harness the potential benefits and mitigate the risks of AI for jobs and work fully, an appropriate "whole of the Government' action agenda must be put in place. Many governments, businesses and civil society organizations are pursuing innovative approaches to tackle these challenges, and there is a significant opportunity for them to learn from each other, and this exchange should be actively facilitated.

Notes

1 Views here are personal and do not necessarily carry an endorsement of the United Nations secretariat or Member States of the United Nations or the members of the Asia-Pacific Research and Training Network on Trade (ARTNeT).

2 In addition to AI, other often-mentioned examples of digital frontier technologies include robotics, Internet of Things (IoT), big data analytics, blockchains, cloud computing, etc.

3 For a pragmatic approach, see ESCAP (2018). However, see also Harari (2015) for a discussion on whether or how soon the strong AI will outperform humans. He finishes *Homo Deus* with a question: "What will happen to society, politics and daily life when non-conscious but highly intelligent algorithms know us better than we know ourselves?" (p. 461). Similarly, World Bank (2019) poses this question: In a world of machine learning systems, who will bear accountability for harming human rights?

4 An evolution of the linkage between "data analytics" and AI can be explained as "…what was considered AI in one generation is inevitably considered no more than 'conventional' [data, added by MM] analytics in the next generation" (ITT, 2018, p. 7).

5 The term "Fourth Industrial Revolution" was coined by Claus Schwab (Founder and Executive Chairman of World Economic Forum) in the book *The Fourth Industrial Revolution* (WEF, 2016).

6 As described in Wikipedia available at https://en.wikipedia.org/wiki/Robot_welding.

7 The concept of "tele-migration" and its consequences for the loss of jobs by those belonging to middle-income class was explained by Richard Baldwin (2018). He argues that "tele-migration" (described as telecommuting gone global) is opening a new phase of unbundling in global economy by opening global competition in the sector which so far was sheltered from such forces, namely, professional services. It is enabled by remote intelligence and digital economies and is creating "tele-mass-migration" which replaces middle-class (the so-called white-collar) employees in developed economies without a need for physical migration. Yet, while this raises hope for many skilled services professionals in developing countries, they face growing competitions from "thinking robots" also going after the same jobs.

8 For some examples on using AI in transforming homes into smart homes, see https://becominghuman.ai/how-ai-is-transforming-home-automation-56085cb275b.

9 For one example how AI assists in controlling domestic violence, see https://thetempest.co/2018/10/25/now-beyond/artificial-intelligence-is-changing-the-way-we-help-domestic-violence-victims/.

10 This chapter was written before the coronavirus disease 2019 (COVID-19) pandemic forced everyone to catch up to the future of digital work and virtual life faster than usual.

11 Since these qualifications and job requirements are based on large volumes of historical parsed data, and since more men than women in software and tech industries are recruited, there is a danger of bias in employee selection.

References

Allison, Peter Ray (2016) What Does a Bomb Disposal Robot Actually Do? BBC, available at www.bbc.com/future/article/20160714-what-does-a-bomb-disposal-robot-actually-do.

Baldwin, Richard (2018). *The Globotics Upheaval: Globalization, Robotics, and the Future of Work*. London: Weidenfeld and Nicolson.

Bringsjord, Selmer and Govindarajulu, Naveen Sundar (2019). *Artificial Intelligence*. In Edward N. Zalta (ed.), *The Stanford Encyclopedia of Philosophy*. Winter 2019 Edition. https://plato.stanford.edu/archives/win2019/entries/artificial-intelligence/.

Courtland, Rachel (2018). Bias Detectives: The Researchers Striving to Make Algorithms Fair. *Nature*, www.nature.com/magazine-assets/d41586-018-05469-3/d41586-018-05469-3.pdf. https://doi.org/10.1038/d41586-018-05469-3.

ESCAP (2018). *Frontier Technologies for Sustainable Development in Asia and the Pacific*. Bangkok: ESCAP. Available at www.unescap.org/publications/frontier-technologies-sustainable-development-asia-and-pacific.

ESCAP and Google (2019). *Artificial Intelligence in the Delivery of Public Sector*. Bangkok: ESCAP and Google. Available at www.unescap.org/publications/artificial-intelligence-delivery-public-services.

Floridi, Luciano and Sanders, J.W. (2004). On the Morality of Artificial Agents. *Minds and Machines,* 14(3), pp. 349–379. https://doi.org/10.1023/B:MIND.00000 35461.63578.9d

Goos, Maarten and Manning, Alan (2007). Lousy and Lovely Jobs: The Rising Polarization of Work in Britain. *The Review of Economics and Statistics*, 89(1), pp. 118–133. https://doi.org/10.1162/rest.89.1.118.

Harari, Yuval Noah (2015). *Homo Deus, A Brief History of Tomorrow*. London: Vintage. https://doi.org/10.17104/9783406704024

Harari, Yuval Noah (2018). *21 Lessons for the 21st Century*. London: Jonathan Cape/libri.

Institute for Transformative Technologies (ITT) (2018). *Artificial Intelligence and Data Analytics for Human Development: Separating Facts from Hype on Where AI and Data Can Genuinely Help, and Where It Is a Distraction*. December. Available at https://d386wwnkwgr87h.cloudfront.net/wp-content/uploads/2019/03/AI-Report-Mar-2019.pdf.

International Labour Organization (ILO) (2016). *ASEAN in Transformation: How Technology Is Changing Jobs and Enterprises*. Geneva: ILO.

Kane, Gerald C., Phillips, Anh Nguyen, Copulsky, Jonathan R. and Andrus, Garth R. (2019). *The Technology Fallacy: How People Are the Real Key to Digital Transformation (Management on the Cutting Edge)*. Cambridge, MA: MIT Press. https://doi.org/10.7551/mitpress/11661.003.0001

Krugman, Paul (1994). *The Age of Diminished Expectations: U.S. Economic Policy in the 1990s*. Cambridge, MA: MIT Press.

McCarthy, John, Minsky, Marvin L., Rochester, Nathaniel, and Shannon, Claude E. (2006). A Proposal for the Dartmouth Summer Research Project on Artificial Intelligence. August 31, 1955. *AI Magazine*, 27(4), 12. doi: org/10.1609/aimag. v27i4.1904.

McKinsey Global Institute (2017). *China's Digital Economy a Leading Global Force.* Available at www.mckinsey.com/~/media/mckinsey/featured%20insights/China/Chinas%20digital%20economy%20A%20leading%20global%20force/MGI-Chinas-digital-economy-A-leading-global-force.ashx.

McKinsey Global Institute (2018). *The Promise and Challenge of the Age of Artificial Intelligence.* October, briefing note prepared for the EU Tallinn Digital Summit. Available at www.mckinsey.com/~/media/McKinsey/Featured%20Insights/Artificial%20Intelligence/The%20promise%20and%20challenge%20of%20the%20age%20of%20artificial%20intelligence/MGI-The-promise-and-challenge-of-the-age-of-artificial-intelligence-in-brief-Oct-2018.ashx.

Organization for Economic Co-operation and Development (OECD) (2016). *Science, Technology and Innovation Outlook 2016.* Paris: OECD. https://doi.org/10.1787/25186167.

Susskind, Richard and Susskind, Daniel (2015) *The Future of the Professions: How Technology Will Transform the Work of Human Experts.* Oxford: Oxford University Press. https://doi.org/10.1016/S2155-8256(17)30099-6.

The World Bank (2016). *World Development Report: Digital Dividends.* Washington, DC: The World Bank. Available at www.worldbank.org/en/publication/wdr2016. https://doi.org/10.1596/978-1-4648-0671-1.

Thompson, Fraser (2019). *Preparing for AI: Developing Insights for Key Asian Economies on the Jobs and Skills Implications.* Singapore: AlphaBeta.

United Nations (2018). *World Economic and Social Survey 2018: Frontier Technologies for a Sustainable Future.* New York, NY: United Nations. Available at www.un.org/development/desa/dpad/wp-content/uploads/sites/45/publication/WESS2018_full_web.pdf. https://doi.org/10.18356/ce9960ca-en

World Bank Group (2019). *The Changing Nature of Work. World Development Report 2019.* Washington, DC: World Bank Group. https://doi.org/10.1596/978-1-4648-1328-3

World Economic Forum (2016). *The Fourth Industrial Revolution: What It Means, How to Respond.* Available at www.weforum.org/agenda/2016/01/the-fourth-industrial-revolution-what-itmeans- and-how-to-respond/.

World Intellectual Property Organization (WIPO) (2019). *Artificial Intelligence.* WIPO Technology Trends 2019. Geneva: WIPO.

Chapter 9

Ethics and digital technologies in the home

Antonio Argandoña

Introduction

The presence of technology in the home, sometimes friendly and other times invasive, is a palpable reality today, even though this "revolution" is still in its early stages (Fung and Gale, 2021; Santos and Toni, 2021). Domotics, for example, enables an increasingly centralised control of many household tasks, from protecting against external threats and providing security for people and assets to services such as heating, lighting, utility supplies, cooking and cleaning. The new technologies also play a role in caring for children, sick people, the elderly and the disabled; in the interface between the home and the workplace and in the balance – or lack of it – between work and family; in household members' communications both with each other and with other people outside of the family; in children's education and in the entire family's entertainment; and in the multiplicity of high-speed Internet connections, not only between humans and their organisations, but also between all kinds of objects (the Internet of Things). And increasingly these functions are hidden in objects we use every day, such as furniture, clothes and vehicles.

> Technology unveils, transforms and controls the world, often designing and creating new realities in the process. It tends to prompt original ideas, to shape new concepts, and to cause unprecedented problems. It also embeds but also challenges ethical values and perspectives. In short, technology can be a very powerful tool for intellectual innovation, exercising a profound influence on how we conceptualize, interpret, and transform the world.
>
> (Floridi, 2004, 554–555)

Technology is a mediator, insofar as it influences people's actions and experiences (Verbeek, 2006, 363ff). By itself, technology is neither good nor bad from a moral viewpoint, and yet it is not neutral: its "interaction with the social ecology is such that technical developments frequently have environmental, social, and human consequences that go far beyond the imme-diate purposes of the technical devices and practices themselves" (Kranzberg, 1986, 545). This is particularly the case of technologies related with artifi-cial intelligence (AI), robots, computers and information: to abbreviate and without any pretension to precision, we will refer to all this as digital or infor-mation technologies; the two concepts are overlapping, in that a digital tech-nology displays the information in binary form, in two states, represented by the digits 1 and 0, or on and off; by this means, it is possible to store, process and transmit any kind of information.

Attitudes towards these technologies range along a scale. At one end, there is the realm of science fiction and utopian hopes of a new life, with immortal humans and superintelligent cyborgs. At the other end, there is a dystopian fear of a future in which human freedom will be devoured by intel-ligent design and people will become mere puppets moved at the whim of self-sustaining robots, which will manipulate our intellects and bodies, "in the corner of Frankenstein and Big Brother" (Floridi, 2015, 9). For a positive but realistic vision of how digital technologies contribute to people's well-being, see Brey (2015), Burr et al. (2019) and Calvo and Peters (2014). All of this requires a reflective attitude that seeks to understand these technologies' potential, limitations and implications.

The ethical dimension of digital technologies is coming under growing scru-tiny from academics, politicians and practitioners (in addition to the ethical dimension, the philosophical, ontological and epistemological dimensions have also been developed; cf. Boden, 1990; Markham et al., 2018; Ringle, 1979). Ethics, which traditionally is only concerned with human beings' actions, is now expanding its scope to also include human-designed artefacts, because "when intelligent systems interact with humans they are functioning, at least in part, as members of society" (Burton et al., 2017, 23) and, to a growing degree, they are making decisions in the place of people.

Is it possible to talk about an ethics of digital technologies? Ethics, "the discipline concerned with what is morally good and bad, right and wrong" (Singer, n.d.), is unique for the purpose it pursues, although there are several ethical theories that offer alternative normative proposals for human behav-iour, and also many ethics applied to different aspects of that behaviour. Thus, there is an ethics that, following Capurro (2009, 203), we will call digital ethics or information ethics, which

> in a broader sense deals with the impact of digital Information and Communication Technologies on our societies and the environment at large. In a narrower sense, information ethics (or digital media ethics) addresses ethical questions dealing with the internet and internetworked information and communication media such as mobile phones and navi-gation services.

This includes machines (robots) and what gives them "life": data, algorithms (including AI, artificial agents and machine learning) and practices (cf. Floridi and Taddeo, 2016).

Indeed, digital ethics already covers a very broad field. Here, we will confine ourselves to reviewing a number of topics that are important for understanding the new technologies' ethical implications, particularly with respect to their impact on the home. We will not delve into the study of specific branches, such as information ethics, data (and big data) ethics, computer, AI, neural networks, algorithms, machine learning, robots, Internet, cyberethics, etc. Neither will we engage in discussions on controversial issues: for example, whether humans have any duties towards robots, as some authors propose (cf. Sheliazhenko, 2017), because, as Boden et al. (2017, 125) advise, "rules for real robots in real life, must be transformed into rules advising those who design, sell and use robots about how they should act".

We will begin by explaining why the digital technologies need ethics; we will then introduce the agents involved in digital ethics; the main problems that arise, particularly when considering the role of digital technologies in the home; how ethical principles can be put into practice, and we will close with the conclusions.

Digital technologies and ethics

The digital technologies' technical superiority lies mainly in their cognitive capacity, which is considerably greater than that of any human being because of their data storage capacity and computing speed, and in their capacity for deep learning, thanks, for example, to the practical application of groups of algorithms (neural networks), not just for specific operations but also to replicate themselves without having to learn from their predecessors over and over again.

However, machines also have limitations compared with human intelligence, with which they cannot compete, for example, in tacit knowledge and common sense and the knowledge stores that humans routinely access in our daily operations. A computer does not know 'what' a cancer is, even though it may be able to identify the presence of pathological tissues from the presence of certain signs; and if it 'tells' a lie, it does not know that it is telling a lie nor what it entails for a person to tell a lie. Algorithms can find the best alternative in preset conditions but not when faced with judgements in which the person's humanity is at stake, such as those that may arise when driving an autonomous vehicle (cf. Etzioni and Etzioni, 2016, 2017). The digital technologies' fantastic storage capacity has difficulties when compared with human memory which, in spite of its severe limitations, has an amazing capacity for filtering and sorting information, so that we remember what is important, forget what is insignificant, reconstruct the past in the light of the present and give each data item the value it deserves, while digital memories remember everything, but without the ability to reinterpret or evaluate.

Human beings also have social awareness: we are sentient, we know about well-being and suffering, and that makes us able to empathise with those who suffer. We are also moral agents; we understand the consequences that our acts may have on ourselves and on others, and we are able to understand that a rule may have exceptions, because the rule does not take into account all of the decision's significant dimensions at any given time. Algorithms are neither sentient nor moral; they have no awareness of pain, pleasure, remorse or empathy; they do not have values nor are they capable of making an exception to a rule. They cannot reflect on the type of life they want to lead, or the type of society they want to live in and act accordingly.

Each technology is designed and developed to perform a function, meet a need or solve a problem, and its worth is judged on the basis of its functionality and effectiveness. However, technologies can also be prescriptive: a speed bump, for example, forces drivers to reduce speed. In other words, "when technologies fulfill their functions, they also help to shape the actions of their users" (Verbeek, 2006, 362), and this has ethical implications.

Technology acts as a mediator between reality and human action, mainly in two ways. On one hand, it provides humans with a way of being present in the world (having a hammer enables us to hammer nails); on the other hand, it enables the agent to gain access to reality by guiding and focusing his attention (glasses model our sight), which implies a certain degree of 'intentionality' about how we perceive and understand the world: as we said earlier, technology is not neutral. To paraphrase Latour's image (1994), it is like the script of a play, which prescribes actions that must be performed and inhibits others.

> The phenomenon of technological mediation creates a specific responsibility for designers (...) Ethics, after all, is about the question of how to act, and technologies appear to give material answers to this question. Ethical questions regarding the design of technologies are thus not limited to questions about the goals for which technologies are designed and applied or to the quality of their functioning.
>
> (Verbeek, 2006, 368–369; on the role of digital technologies for the home, cf. Damiano, 2021; Ocnarescu and Sciamma, 2021)

This moral responsibility of designers encompasses both the unwanted effects of technology, which must be avoided, and the wanted effects, which must be fostered. Verbeek (2006, 369-371) wonders whether this may compromise the individual's freedom, which is conditioned by the designer's decisions, especially when the latter does not act in accordance with criteria that are either socially accepted or agreed with the user. This leads him to suggest that the designer should disclose the options that he accepted, so that the user knows what type of ethical mediation is included in the technology he uses.

In any case, designers' responsibility does not account for all of the technology's moral content, because there are many other possible uses for the technology and the designer is not always able to sufficiently grasp their implications. So users too have a responsibility, as does every single person who makes up the chain between the former and the latter, in order to "enable the people who *employ AI* to *guide AI*" (Etzioni and Etzioni, 2016, 152).

The first treatise on digital ethics, if that is what we could call it, were the three laws that all robots must obey, written by Isaac Asimov in 1942:

> 1) A robot may not injure a human being or, through inaction, allow a human being to come to harm; 2) A robot must obey the orders given by human beings except where such orders would conflict with the First Law; 3) A robot must protect its own existence as long as such protection does not conflict with the First or Second Laws.
>
> (Asimov, 1942/1950, 40)

Obviously, it was not a complete code and it was not always applicable: for example, a machine cannot know the many ways that a person can harm himself, nor understand and obey all the orders given by humans, which may be confusing, and, in any case, there are many ways in which a smart robot could get round these instructions (cf. Boden et al., 2017).

The first studies on the ethics of AI, as it is understood today, date back to the 1960s (cf. Samuel, 1960; Wiener, 1960). As in other branches of applied ethics, these pioneering papers sought to create an awareness among practitioners, authorities and communication media of the importance of digital ethics; later on, principles, codes of conduct, standards, regulations and legislation were developed (Floridi, 2004, 575), with the aim of providing a solution for these problems. And, more recently, a number of multidisciplinary, broad-based approaches have been developed, as we will see further on.

Keane (2019) imagines a robot asking itself: "And what if an ethics based on no harm has perverse effects? Are we robots able to deal with aporia, serendipity, dead-ends, unintended consequences and unexpected good luck? We don't think so". And he continues: "These humans tell us (...) that the rules that they decide beforehand about how we robots must behave in specific spatiotemporal situations are necessary and unavoidable".

Digital ethics is based on a series of rules, principles, values and virtues that are not intended for computers, robots or algorithms but for researchers, designers and manufacturers, and those who control and use them, so that they can integrate these principles and values in their programs and machines, preventing their misuse and even "the catastrophes that would be caused by humans' inability to control or communicate with superintelligent machines" (Keane, 2019). "Now", he continues:

> imagine robots operating in a battle situation, making high-risk decisions that eliminate entire human armies, on both sides, and human cities with their inhabitants (...) If a small number of humans should succeed in monopolising the design and application of AI and robots, then that privileged class will exert an unjust power in deciding our future as robots.
>
> (Keane, 2019)

So a digital ethics is needed that can be transposed into a series of public or private agendas that put it into effect (Bryson et al., 2017; Capurro, 2009; D.G. Johnson, 2000). The thesis that computers and robots can become more intelligent than humans is what is known as "singularity" (Vinge, 1993), and may lead to conclusions that can be either optimistic (machines will help humans overcome their limitations) or pessimistic (they may lead to the destruction of humankind) (Bostrom, 2003) (on superintelligence, cf. Bostrom, 2014).

These ethical standards cannot be replaced by international agreements or national regulations.

1) "Compliance with the law is merely necessary (it is the least that is required), but significantly insufficient (it is not the most than [sic] can and should be done)" (Floridi et al., 2018, 694).
2) Law is reactive; ethics must be proactive and act ahead of problems.
3) Laws are written up with political criteria, which are not necessarily appropriate for guiding agents' actions.
4) Laws cannot consider all the possible situations which, on the contrary, agents can and must consider by applying criteria of practical wisdom. And
5) laws usually have lots of loopholes that can be used to avoid obeying them.

Agents and digital ethics

By digital ethics, we understand (1) the ethics that humans must observe when they act as designers, producers or distributors of digital technologies; (2) the ethics that is included in these technologies' design and operation; and (3) the ethics that is put into practice when humans deal with machines. In short, there are three ways of identifying and allocating responsibilities and regulating relationships between people and artificial agents (cf. Asaro, 2006).

In any action that is not solely internal, there are one or more active agents (or, simply, agents) who perform acts (or omissions) that have consequences for the passive agents (or patients); these acts can have a moral dimension, insofar as they affect these patients' "good life" (cf. Floridi and Sanders,

2004). These active agents may be natural persons, communities (companies, governments, teams, etc.), animals, natural phenomena (e.g., hurricanes and rain) and also artificial agents (computers, mobile phones, networks, robots, algorithms, programs, etc.), all having different degrees of moral agency, from the amorality of rain or an animal to the full moral autonomy of people (Asaro, 2006, 11). Where do artificial agents lie along this moral agency continuum? Medical ethics, bioethics and environmental ethics focus mainly on the patient, whether this is a human being, an animal or any form of life, even earth ethics. Floridi (1999, 42) includes information ethics here, which has

> an overriding interest in the fate and welfare of the action-receiver, the information (...) Right and wrong, in CE [computer ethics], do not just qualify actions in themselves, they essentially refer to what is eventually better or worse for the infosfere.

A moral agent must be accountable and responsible, at least to a given degree. Artificial agents are accountable because they give account of their action (e.g., we say that "the computer turned down the loan application"). In order to be accountable, the artificial agent must be

1) interactive with its environment,
2) sufficiently informed,
3) smart,
4) autonomous, that is, "it can perform internal transitions to change its state" without this being a response to an interaction (Floridi and Sanders, 2004, 357),
5) adaptable, because the agent's action can change the rules of transition by which it changes its status, "learning its own mode of operation in a way which depends critically on its own experience" (Floridi and Sanders, 2004, 358) and
6) capable of performing acts that would be considered moral in a human, because they can cause good or bad, or are based on values. All of the above applies both when it cooperates with other human agents and when it acts alone (Gipps, 1995).

However, for an active agent to be accountable, it is not sufficient to attribute a moral responsibility to it, which will be determined by intentions that an algorithm or a robot is incapable of having. In order to be morally responsible, an artificial agent "must relate itself to its actions in some more profound way, involving meaning, wishing or wanting to act in a certain way, and being epistemically aware of its behaviour" (Floridi and Sanders, 2004, 365; cf. Bryson, 2010; Sullins, 2005, 2006). Consequently, moral responsibility is applicable to the persons implicated in the actions carried out by artificial agents.

D.G. Johnson (2015, 713) gives another reason as to why a machine or a piece of software cannot be held responsible: "the nature of a technology is relevant to the responsibility arrangements, but responsibility arrangements are socially constituted through the norms and expectations of particular activities and contexts", and this is beyond the possibilities of an artificial agent (on attachment of responsibility for learning robots' actions, see Hellstrom, 2013; Marino and Tamburrini, 2006; Sullins, 2006); on the possibility of an artificial agent performing an activity for which neither it nor humans are responsible (the so-called responsibility gap), see D.G. Johnson, 2015; Matthias, 2004).

Some ethical problems of digital technologies in the home

The decisions involving digital technologies are ordinary decisions made within a home concerning purchases (e.g., a driverless car), consumption (music streaming) or use (of the mobile phone to take part in social media). What makes them important for digital ethics are their consequences for the agent or for others: for example, using a mobile phone connected to Internet may give other people information about the agent's life and decisions, through customer-tracking websites, street-view maps, and the free and anonymous flow of information; and using a robot to babysit may give rise to confusion in the child about the nature of human relations and the play between reality and virtuality. In the following pages, we will review some of the ethical issues generated by digital technologies (cf. Ess, 2009; Himma and Tavani, 2008). Manuals on professional ethics usually provide lists of relevant problems, such as privacy, security, computer crime, intellectual property, free expression, equity, information overload, digital divide, technical access, censorship, software theft, viruses, hacking and many others.

Centrality of the human person

This is the most important ethical principle by which all digital technologies must abide. "The ubiquity of digital technologies that are equipped with sensors for monitoring user's behaviour and environmental conditions, combined with advances in data management and analytics, has resulted in the increased viability of personalised human-computer interaction (e.g., personalised recommendations)" (Burr et al., 2019, 17).

Vallée and co-workers (2016, 186) define personalisation as "the ability to provide contents and services tailored to individuals based on knowledge about their needs, expectations, preferences, constraints, and behaviours". This personalisation is based on two criteria: (1) a greater or lesser ease or accessibility in use, in physical terms, of necessary information and knowledge, and (2) accessibility for different population segments, particularly people with disabilities, without any need for costly adaptations and preparations (Burr et al., 2019, 17–18).

Security and comfort

The passive agent interacts with digital products or services whose features he/she is not very familiar with, and which he/she will probably never become familiar with, due to their technical complexities. This means that the agent is not able to control the consequences of their use, neither for himself/herself nor for others (Lin et al., 2011). In the home, the agent comes into contact with technologies that allow him/her to enjoy a better quality of life through their management of a substantial variety of functions (lighting, heating, ventilation, air conditioning, household appliances, audio and video equipment, energy saving, alarms, telecommunications, etc.) which are endowed with a certain degree of intelligence that enables them, for example, to recognise hazards or infrequent situations that may cause problems for their users.

> Domotics is the science that is concerned with the study of technologies that are designed to improve the quality of life at home and more in general in anthropised environments (...) Through demotics it is possible to integrate various domestic users and functions (...) into a single cooperative and inter-operable network so as to be able to create dynamic functions that are increasingly advanced and intelligent (...) Assistance demotics is that branch of demotics which seeks to help elderly people, the chronically ill and the disabled to stay in their homes in complete safety and comfort.
>
> (Russo, 2014, 138–140)

However, most homes do not have the means to identify the risks posed by digital technologies, let alone protect themselves from them. Hence, there is the need for ethics and regulations in the different phases of their design, manufacture and use.

Boden et al. (2017, 126) pointed out that these technologies "are products" and, therefore, "they should be designed using processes which assure their safety and security", not only in the present but also in the future, avoiding, for example, unforeseen consequences of their use. Security breaches can be caused by errors or defects that can be blamed on those who designed or manufactured the products, or by the users themselves, but also for reasons that are beyond their control, including immoral acts by third parties (hackers who steal information or data or steal or take over another person's identity, cyberbullying, sexting, fake news, compulsive gambling, etc.).

Technology does not change these acts' ethical status, to which traditional moral criteria are applied; but it is important for at least two reasons: (1) because it enables the act to be concealed, leaving the passive agent unprotected, and (2) because it reduces the agent's moral sensitivity, for example, when breaching intellectual property rights: the so-called free information fallacy argues that information "asks" to be free, claiming that this justifies free appropriation of digital resources. Responsibility for these problems can be attributed to the designers, manufacturers and distributors, who are responsible for the product's flaws and shortcomings, to those who cause the harm (e.g., those who gather information from users for commercial use, to control people or for other illicit purposes) and, to some extent, to the users, insofar as they are collaborators in these acts (often without knowing it).

Security is particularly important in the home, in that it is the place for the person's privacy, to which he/she retires to keep his/her life in order and regain control over it:

> that most recondite, private, secure and comfortable place for the self, where it takes shelter from the natural world, to where it belongs as its innermost shelter, and where it addresses the world and the other, opening itself to transcendence.
>
> (Patrão Neves, 2018, 73; cf. Argandoña, 2018)

Those who live in the home wish to find safety and security there, and that is what they expect from the technologies they use: physical safety (of the instruments used, but also security against attacks, intrusions and manipulations from outside), and also psychological and social security, which includes the right to privacy in the access, use and control of their information.

In the home, people have the opportunity to manifest themselves as they are, also as vulnerable beings who need material, cognitive or spiritual protection. Vulnerability means dependence on the help received from others: in the home, we are all dependent and vulnerable at certain times, but this is particularly true of children, the elderly, the disabled and the sick. Technology may be very helpful, for instance, in the case mentioned earlier of robots looking after children or elderly people; but it can also create problems, such as transferring responsibility from specialised medical institutions to home carers, who would not be able to take on this responsibility without it entailing an increase in their workload or greater expense; or the difficulties in accessibility (Sharkey and Sharkey, 2012), or the impact on emotional well-being and the capabilities for communication and moral reasoning. This does not mean that we are questioning the contribution made by digital technologies in the home, including personalised care, dissemination of information, the holistic approach to problems and treatments, remote medical care, etc. (cf. Vallor, 2010).

Particular attention should be given to the safety and security of children and teenagers, who become absorbed by virtual environments that affect their relationships with their peers, with strangers, with the media and with themselves; their ability for self-control in their interactions with technology and other people; their games, pastimes and addictions; their education and moral growth and many other aspects of their lives, which give rise in turn to a parental obligation to educate and supervise; and the creation of opportunities for skills development with the help of technology: for example, the skills they will need in adulthood to work in a world immersed in digital technologies.

Privacy

In the 1980s, the privacy of electronic communications started to become a subject of debate (Bambauer, 2012), as another form of risk for users' security. Since then, the number of publications on the subject has multiplied, driven particularly by the use of big data to determine consumer profiles and predict their behaviours, with the resulting risk of breach of users' privacy, whose information may be generated, transferred and analysed without their knowledge or consent (Horvitz and Mulligan, 2015).

The problem becomes even broader with the possibility of compiling, storing and using information on their health, preferences, decisions and contacts (thereby involving other people), monitoring social media for security-related purposes, etc., which may degenerate into reprehensible practices, such as "profiling, tracking, discrimination, exclusion, government surveillance and loss of control" (Tene and Polonetsky, 2012, 63).

The disclosure of the information gathered by providers or other agents is a very important issue for homes, who fear losing their privacy and feel apprehension about the possible consequences of dissemination of their private data for malicious purposes. The issue becomes even more pressing when it concerns vulnerable people, such as children (who are particularly exposed to this type of manipulation), sick people, disabled people, immigrants or people subject to social exclusion, or sensitive information (about mental condition or physical health, personal finance, etc.) (Turilli and Floridi, 2009, 106). In the opposite direction, initiatives have been undertaken to promote privacy-enhancing technologies (cf. Burkert, 1997).

Fairness, impartiality and transparency

Digital technology is concerned particularly with handling information, which "is supposed to consist of meaningful, veridical, comprehensible, accessible and useful data" (Turilli and Floridi, 2009, 108). However, it is often the case that these conditions are not met because this information is the outcome of a process of data collection, storage and processing (interpretation, correlation, deduction, inference, etc.) that is associated not only with technical problems but also with ethical problems (for a thorough analysis of the risks inherent to data processing, see Bogroff and Guégan, 2019).

The impression of impartiality created by digital technologies may be deceptive. When they intervene in relationships between people, they can start or prolong situations of injustice that are perhaps hidden in the algorithms and programs. This can happen even when the program has been designed with the specific purpose of non-discriminating criteria; it is sufficient for it to be based on data which have contained the discriminating factors at some time, albeit in concealed form: for example, because the predictors are decontextualised, that is, they do not include relevant personal information (cf. Sloan and Warner, 2019). Or, for example, a loan evaluation programme based on the applicants' prior history of granted or rejected loans may contain a discriminating bias if the previous loan grant or rejection criteria were biased in the past against people on the basis of variables that were correlated with race, for example.

> Algorithms inevitably make biased decisions. An algorithm's design and functionality reflects the values of its designer and intended uses, if only to the extent that a particular design is preferred as the best or most efficient option. Development is not a neutral, linear path; there is no objectively correct choice at any given stage of development, but many possible choices. As a result, "the values of the author [of the algorithm], wittingly or not, are frozen into the code, effectively institutionalising those values".
>
> (Mittelstadt et al., 2016, 7; the citation is from Macnish, 2012, 158)

And this in turn can influence the resources that certain people have access to, how likely they are to succeed in various endeavours or how likely they are to be penalised by governmental agencies (cf. Hacker, 2018; Karppi, 2018; Matthias, 2004).

Data can be a significant source of bias. It is often thought that the transparency principle can solve this problem, but that is unlikely to be the case. Transparency is defined as "the availability of information, the conditions of accessibility and how the information (...) may pragmatically or epistemically support the user's decision-making process" (Turilli and Floridi, 2009, 106); consequently, it implies accurate, secure information and accessibility to the data supporting the algorithm.

The condition of information accuracy and security is not always fulfilled. Data undergo collection, selection, cleaning, structuring and choice of attributes (Sloan and Warner, 2019), all of which are processes that contribute to their opacity. In addition, the source data are usually incomplete, subject to errors and, sometimes, biased. Subsequently, these data are processed to render them analysable, which adds further problems of sampling bias, incorrect handling, intentional prejudices, improper use of data mining and data reduction. Later on, they undergo aggregation processes that render the original data unrecognisable. As these effects are cumulative, the data's final quality is often far below what would be considered a satisfactory standard.

In many cases, it is impossible to guarantee the data's comprehensibility and accessibility, the second condition of transparency, due to the complexity of the algorithm's processing operations and how the data are handled, and also because of the obligation to maintain privacy (Markowetz et al., 2014); the transparency requirement is discussed by many authors (see, e.g., Burrell, 2016; Kitchin, 2016; Matthias, 2004; Schermer, 2011). Furthermore, it is necessary to interpret the algorithms' outputs, which may in turn be a source of further bias: what may seem objective correlations come to reflect the interpreter's "unconscious motivations, particular emotions, deliberate choices, socio-economic determinations, geographic or demographic influences" (Hildebrandt, 2011, 376).

In addition to the above, data processing by algorithms gives rise to problems associated with the programs' structure and functioning (cf. Mittelstadt et al., 2016); for example, (1) inconclusive evidence: algorithmic conclusions are probabilities and therefore not infallible, and the findings obtained using these techniques are not necessarily causal relationships but mere statistical correlations, which may be spurious; (2) inscrutable evidence: a lack of interpretability and transparency can lead to algorithmic systems that are hard to control, monitor and correct (the "black-box" issue); and (3) misguided evidence: conclusions can only be as reliable (but also as neutral) as the data they are based on.

And, above all, the conclusions suggested about a population group through big data processing are not always applicable to a specific individual, in which case the conclusions applied to this individual would be unfair (cf. Ananny, 2016; McQuillan, 2018). A paradigmatic example of this is profiling, "the construction or inference of patterns by means of data mining and (...) the application of the ensuing profiles to people whose data match with them" (Hildebrandt and Koops, 2010, 431; cf. J.A. Johnson, 2014). This is applied, for example, to loan applicants, who may be judged as insolvent, or to convicted criminals who are considered likely to repeat their crimes: what the algorithm analyses is a particular group's likely conduct, not the real conduct of each one of these people (cf. Newell and Marabelli, 2015).

In short, the transparency requirement is much more demanding than the mere publication of a list of data and their sources, because it includes "how the ethical principles (...) are prioritised and translated into practice [sic] and governance" (Turilli and Floridi, 2009, 110): in a way, it is a reflection of the depth of the ethical convictions of the organisation that collects and manages them.

The transparency requirement is complemented with the traceability requirement which, it is supposed, enables responsibilities to be assigned between designers and developers (Kraemer et al., 2011). However, it is difficult to pinpoint people's specific responsibility because software is largely constructed by teams; management decisions may be at least as important as programming decisions; requirements and specification documents play a large part in the resulting code; although the accuracy of code is dependent on those responsible for testing it, much software relies on 'off the shelf' components whose provenance and validity may be uncertain; moreover, working software is the result of maintenance over its lifetime and so not just of its originators; (…) automated tools are employed in construction of much software; the efficacy of software may depend on extrafunctional features like its interface and even on system traffic; software running on a system can interact in unforeseeable ways; software may now be downloaded at the click of an icon in such a way that the user has no access to the code and its provenance with the resulting execution of anonymous software; software may be probabilistic; adaptive; or may be itself the result of a program (in the simplest case a compiler, but also genetic code).

(Floridi and Sanders, 2004, 371–372; cf. Epstein, 1997; Goldberg, 1989)

Autonomy and Freedom

Algorithms can affect how we conceptualise the world, and modify its social and political organisation. Algorithmic activities (…) reontologise the world by understanding and conceptualising it in new, unexpected ways, and triggering and motivating actions based on the insights it generates.

(Mittelstadt et al., 2016, 5; cf. Floridi, 2014)

"Change the instruments and you will change the entire social theory that goes with them" (Latour, 1999, 9).

This can impair the person's autonomy and become "a troubling manifestation of Big Brother, enabling invasions of privacy, decreased civil freedoms, and increase state and corporate control" (Boyd and Crawford, 2012, 664). "The by-product of common discourse around big data not only diminishes or removes the qualitative aspects of behavior and experience that form the data in the first place but also removes the human from the process of analysis" (Markham et al., 2018, 4).

Personalisation should improve decision making by providing the subject with only relevant information when confronted with a potential information overload; however, deciding which information is relevant is inherently subjective. The subject can be pushed to make the institutionally preferred action rather than their own preference; online consumers, for example, can be nudged to fit market needs by filtering how products are displayed (…) Van Wel and Royakkers (2004, 133) argue that external identity construction by algorithms is a type of de-individu-alisation, or a "tendency of judging and treating people on the basis of group characteristics instead of on their own individual characteristics and merit".

(Mittelstadt et al., 2016, 9–10)

This is particularly important in the home, because "it is in the home where we find the true expression of the interiority of the human being, a natural base that is necessary in order to carry out the tasks demanded by society" (d'Entremont, 2018, 170). Autonomy in the home invokes rights such as the freedom of access and the freedom of decision; protection against persuasive technologies, whose purpose is to detect users' preferences with the intention of guiding their conduct towards certain pre-established outcomes; protec-tion against information overload and the right to opt-out. Here aspects such as the degree of control of the user's involvement by the provider, the level of product customisation, the reliability and credibility of the information provided, the user's level of self-understanding with respect to the pursued purpose and the ease or difficulty in fostering ethical values and facilitating moral deliberation in the relationship come into play (cf. Rughiniş et al., 2015). It is not sufficient for the agent to be free to decide; he/she must under-stand that this freedom includes deep-seated reasons for acting as a conscious, free human being (cf. Sen, 2010, 18).

In the home, users must protect themselves against digital technologies' far-reaching influences on people, particularly on those who are most vulnerable, specifically children, the elderly and the disabled: for example, giving greater value to online connections over face-to-face conversations, listening and empathy; dispersal over attention; impatience over waiting; the drive to con-trol over acceptance of reality; noise over silence; automated consumerism over critical reflection; or immediate attention to the barrage of information over deep thought (Severson and Carlson, 2010).

Sociability

The home is a place for privacy, but it is an accepted privacy, shared and facilitated by others. "The home is also the place where personal relationships are developed, in which each individual gives of him or herself to others and receives from them" (Argandoña, 2018, 14). Technology can be a means for facilitating these relationships, both inside and outside of the home, but it also carries the risk of isolation when it is used inappropriately. And it can have a destabilising influence on the social processes that take place within the home and with its surroundings, for example, by causing situations of addiction or dependence, or lack of protection from external threats. On the positive side, it should empower the home's members and open up opportunities.

One conclusion that we can draw from all that we have said in the previous paragraphs is that, beyond technology's technical, economic and social qualities and benefits, and the progress that has been achieved through the use of digital technologies, the active involvement of well-informed professionals and users will always be necessary because ethical decisions are always human decisions, hopefully bringing to bear useful knowledge, understanding of specific situations and certain skills that cannot be replaced by the use of computers (cf. Coeckelbergh, 2013; Morek, 2006; Paradice and Dejoie, 1991).

Putting ethical principles into practice

The independent algorithms that will contribute to shaping human decisions, or which will make them in humans' place, must include moral criteria because the goal is "to create a machine that follows an ideal ethical principle or a set of ethical principles in guiding behavior" (Anderson, 2011; cf. also Anderson and Anderson, 2007; Wiegel and van den Berg, 2009). This raises the problem of the consistency of the criteria used by people and machines, insofar as they must always act in accordance with the same set of ethical principles – although it may be difficult to define the principles followed by humans in their decisions, and even more so to translate them into computer language.

One frequently used solution is to have expert (often multidisciplinary) groups draw up ethical codes of best practices, protocols or principles with the purpose of influencing the design, development and application of machines and software. In April 2019, Morley et al. (2019) had found at least 70 collections of ethical principles applicable to AI; by August 2019, there were more than 90 (cf. Algorithm Watch, n.d.), including documents prepared by companies, governments (Montreal Declaration, Lords Select Committee, European Commission's High-Level Expert Group) and academics (Future of Life Institute, IEEE, AI4People, among others).

These collections of principles are usually developed in accordance with the "ethics of action" (Floridi, 1999). They are abstract normative principles which must be observed in these technologies' design, production, distribution and use, sometimes in the form of prescriptions for artificial agents, even if no ethical responsibility is ascribed to them (Floridi and Sanders, 2004, 368): for example, when it is stipulated that a loan application evaluation programme must not discriminate unfairly on the grounds of gender, race, religion or political ideas. However, ultimately, they are moral precepts intended for the people who design, develop or apply these programmes. Consequently, they address the action directly, and only derivatively the people who perform the action, who are considered morally responsible for what they do or do not do. Opinion is not unanimous about how many principles there should be and what they should say, not even whether they should be based on traditional ethical principles or developed *ex novo* (cf. Anderson and Anderson, 2007;

Bello and Bringsjord, 2012). However, they usually prioritise the protection of the individual (privacy and explainability) over the interests of the community (efficiency and profitability).

Their enforceability is based on (1) universally valid rational ethical criteria (deontology); (2) social agreements (contractualism) often backed by law, which can have a major impact, as became apparent with the introduction of the EU General Data Protection Regulation (GDPR), in May 2018; or (3) the determination of advantages and disadvantages (consequentialism). They suffer from the typical limitations of the ethics of action: for example, being abstract principles, it is not always clear how they can be applied practically, because they do not take into account the circumstances of each specific case: "it is impossible to standardize or universalize what constitutes the ethically correct actions in technology design and research contexts, not least because we cannot predict what will happen as a result of our choices" (Markham et al., 2018). And when there are conflicts between principles (e.g., the right to privacy versus public security, or the freedom of speech versus protection against offensive information), clear criteria for settling them are not always available. In short, they are a form of "ethics by design" which tends to restrict agents' decisions paternalistically to force them to comply with a type of behaviour defined "from outside" (Morley et al., 2019), which may facilitate social acceptance of the principles but not their application to specific cases.

In the case of the digital technologies, these principles are associated with other difficulties:

- They may impair human agents' sense of responsibility, if they can offload their agency or intentionality onto computer systems, or delegate responsibility to these systems (e.g., by thinking that an incorrect decision is just a computer error).
- The passive agents who suffer the action's consequences may seem abstract individuals, without any face or name, who are reached by online interactions, much in the way that monsters are killed in a computer game (Floridi, 1999, 39–40).
- The sense of responsibility for a relationship generated, mediated and/or controlled by a computer may be lost as a consequence of anonymity and conceptual distance. As Floridi complains (1999, 40):

> The increasing number and variety of computer crimes committed by perfectly respectable and honest people shows the full limits of an action-oriented approach to CE [computer ethics]: computer criminals often do not perceive, or perceive in a distorted way, the nature of their actions because they have been educated to conceive as potentially immoral only human interactions in real life, or actions involving physical and tangible objects. A cursory analysis of the

justifications that hackers usually offer for their actions, for example, is sufficient to clarify immediately that they often do not understand the real implications of their behaviour, independently of their technical competence.

- There is also the risk of

  an "anything-goes" startup attitude that pushes technology designs into the market without adequate scrutiny for their potential impacts, glacially slow updates to conceptual and regulatory guidelines, a push for ever-more precise profiling of people at any cost, and a continued rapid pace of technological transformations that continually change the rules of the game.

  (Markham, 2015; cf. Markham and Buchanan, 2015)

In spite of these limitations, drawing up lists of ethical principles is not a futile exercise, because it forces experts to undertake a process of reflection that accommodates different ways of viewing the problems, in accordance with the disciplines involved and the different positions of the stakeholder representatives taking part: users, regulators, designers, manufacturers, distributors, innovators and policymakers (Durante, 2010). The important thing is not just whether or not the principles are applied, but whether they are applied frequently, and whether the algorithm systems to which they are applied are tested and reviewed. Briefly, the goal is to advance from an "ethics by design" system to a "pro-ethical design" system, which nudges agents to behave ethically while giving them freedom to decide otherwise, if there are reasons for doing so (Morley et al., 2019): speed bumps on roads are examples of ethics by design, which force drivers to brake to avoid damaging their vehicle; speed cameras are a form of pro-ethical design, which encourages drivers to slow down but leaves open the possibility of exceeding the speed limit, not to flout the regulation but because the regulation cannot take into account all possible driving situations. In other words, the idea is to broaden the perspective of ethics of action so that other ethics are taken into account.

For example, Polo (1995) proposes an ethics with three dimensions: (1) one focused on the purposes or goods of human action; (2) another with a normative or prescriptive value, that is, rules, and (3) a third dimension aimed at perfecting the human being, the ethics of virtues. These are not proposed as three alternatives but, in fact, the ethics includes all three. For example, the professional who intends to develop a software program should seriously consider his/her action's purposes or intentions; he/she must follow the rules set by law and ethical principles, and he/she must always seek his/her personal improvement, in both technical and moral aspects, accepting his responsibility and striving to live by the corresponding virtues. And the same can be said of other agents, such as manufacturers, distributors, supervisors and users.

When considering the person's development through ethics, this should not be seen as limiting the freedom of decision of the technology's agents, in the same way that the side barriers on motorways do not restrict motorists' true freedom.

In any case, even when the list of ethical principles has been made, it is not immediately applied to a machine or algorithm. The example of the driverless vehicle that interacts with its environment (the city, the road, other vehicles, road signs, physical obstacles, the people who are travelling in it and those who are outside, etc.) may be useful here (Etzioni and Etzioni, 2016, 2017). The driverless vehicle must be capable of making ethical decisions, that is, decisions that in a human person could be defined as good on the basis of its users' needs, the driving's effects on them and on other people and objects, the provisions of traffic laws and the rules of ethical standards, etc.

This can be done basically in two ways: (1) using a top-down approach, which states the principles and applies them, down to the level of specific actions, and (2) using a bottom-up approach, which starts with the actions of a good driver, his technical and moral preferences and their results, and then generalises the principles (Asaro, 2006, 15).

Conclusions

Ethics must be present in all the stages of development and use of digital technologies, particularly when they are used in the home, because it has always been the best place for people's moral development. It is people, not technologies, who deal with ethical problems. Therefore, designers, producers and distributors must ask themselves what are their underlying intentions, what actions they are going to perform and what consequences their decisions will have for themselves, for users and for society in general. Ethics should not be seen as a constraint on people's freedom and autonomy. On the contrary, it helps identify a series of problems that go beyond the merely technical; it helps find the right solutions that take into account all the relevant aspects and not just the technical or economic aspects (concerned with efficiency or profitability, for example); it provides criteria for evaluating alternatives; it helps make the decisions and – last but not least – it helps put them into practice.

Ethics does not have an answer for every problem: that is why it must work with all the scientific and technical disciplines involved in the decisions on digital technologies. It is focused on people, but people are relational beings, so it also considers the home, the family, the firm, the team, the local community and society as a whole.

Experts and practitioners in digital ethics have produced several lists of principles that have been proposed for people to consider and for machines and programs to include. There is no general agreement on what these principles are, because the number of situations in which problems can arise is potentially infinite. The important point is that designers, manufacturers and distributors are aware of their moral duties towards the users of these technologies, for example, in the home, and that these same users are aware of the risks, threats and problems that may lie hidden in their devices and programs. It is not an easy task but it is possible, because humankind has already devoted thousands of years trying to find solutions to similar challenges.

References

Algorithm Watch (n.d.). The AI Ethics Guidelines Global Inventory: https://algorithmwatch.org/en/project/ai-ethics-guidelines-global-inventory/ (accessed 20 January 2019).

Ananny, M. (2016). Toward an Ethics of Algorithms Convening, Observation, Probability, and Timeliness. *Science, Technology and Human Values*, 41(1), 93–117. doi: 10.1177/0162243915606523.

Anderson, M. and S.L. Anderson (2007). Machine Ethics: Creating an Ethical Intelligent Agent. *AI Magazine*. 28(4), 15. doi: 10.1.1.430.1790.

Anderson, S.L. (2011). Machine Methaethics. In M. Anderson and S.L. Anderson (eds.), *Machine Ethics*. New York, NY: Cambridge University Press, pp. 21–27. doi: 10.1017/CBO9780511978036.004.

Argandoña, A. (2018). The Home: Multidisciplinary Reflections. In A. Argandoña (ed.), *The Home: Multidisciplinary Reflections*. Cheltenham: Edward Elgar, pp. 8–31. doi: 10.4337/9781786436573.00009.

Asaro, P.M. (2006). What Should We Want from a Robot Ethics? *International Review of Information Ethics*, 6, 9–16.

Asimov, I. (1942/1950). Runaround. In The Isaac Asimov Collection (ed.), *I, Robot*. New York, NY: Doubleday, 1950.

Bambauer, J.Y. (2012). The New Intrusion. *Notre Dame Law Review*, 88, 205–275.

Bello, P. and S. Bringsjord (2012). On How to Build a Moral Machine. *Topoi*, 32(2), 251–266. doi: 10.1007/s11245-012-9129-8.

Boden, M. (ed.) (1990). *The Philosophy of Artificial Intelligence*. Oxford: Oxford University Press.

Boden, M., J. Bryson, D. Caldwell, K. Dautenhahn, L. Edwards, S. Kember, P. Newman, V. Parry, G. Pegman, T. Rodden, T. Sorrell, M. Wallis, B. Whitby and A. Winfield (2017). Principles of Robotics: Regulating Robots in the Real World. *Connection Science*, 29(2), 124–129. doi: 10.1080/09540091.2016.1271400.

Bogroff, A. and D. Guégan (2019). Artificial Intelligence, Data, Ethics. A Holistic Approach for Risks and Regulations, Working Paper, Department of Economics, Ca' Foscari University of Venice 19/WP/2019.

Bostrom, N. (2003). Ethical Issues in Advanced Artificial Intelligence. In I. Smit and G.E. Lasker (eds.), *Cognitive, Emotive and Ethical Aspects of Decision Making in Humans and in Artificial Intelligence*, Vol. 2. Windsor, ON: International Institute for Advanced Studies in Systems Research/ Cybernetics, 12–17.

Bostrom, N. (2014). *Superintelligence: Paths, Dangers, Strategies*. Oxford: Oxford University Press.

Boyd, D. and K. Crawford (2012). Critical Questions for Big Data. *Information, Communication and Society*, 15(5), 662–679. doi: 10.1080/1369118X.2012.678878.

Brey, P. (2015). Design for the Value of Human Well-Being. In J. van den Hoven, P. Vermaas and I. van de Poel (eds.), *Handbook of Ethics, Values, and Technological Design. Sources, Theory, Values and Application Domains.* New York, NY: Springer, pp. 365–382. doi: 10.1007/978-94-007-6970-0.

Bryson, J.J. (2010). Robots Should Be Slaves. In Y. Wilks (ed.), *Close Engagements with Artificial Companions: Key Social, Psychological, Ethical and Design Issues.* Philadelphia, PA: John Benjamins Publishing Company, pp. 63–74.

Bryson, J., M. Diamantis and T. Grant (2017). Of, for, and by the People: The Legal Lacuna of Synthetic Persons. *Artificial Intelligence and Law,* 25(3), 273–291. doi: 10.1007/s10506-017-9214-9.

Burkert, H. (1997). Privacy-Enhancing Technologies: Typology, Critique, Vision. In P.E. Agre and M. Rotenberg (eds.), *Technology and Privacy: The New Landscape.* Cambridge, MA: MIT Press, pp. 125–142.

Burr, C., M. Taddeo and L. Floridi (2019). *The Ethics of Digital Well-being: A Thematic Review.* www.researchgate.net/publication/331231431_The_Ethics_of_Digital_Well-Being_A_Thematic_Review (accessed 18 December 2018).

Burrell, J. (2016). How the Machine "Thinks:" Understanding Opacity in Machine Learning Algorithms. *Big Data and Society,* 3(1), 1–12. doi: 10.1177/20539517 15622512.

Burton, E., J. Goldsmith, S. Koenig, B. Kuipers, N. Mattei and T. Walsh (2017). Ethical Considerations in Artificial Intelligence Courses. *AI Magazine,* 38(2), 22–34. doi: 10.1609/aimag.v38i2.2731.

Calvo, R.A. and D. Peters (2014). *Positive Computing: Technology for Wellbeing and Human Potential.* Boston, MA: MIT Press.

Capurro, R. (2009). Digital Ethics. In The Academy of Korean Studies (ed.), *Civilization and Peace.* Seongnam-si, Korea: The Academy of Korean Studies Press, pp. 203–214.

Coeckelbergh, M. (2013). E-Care as Craftsmanship: Virtuous Work, Skilled Engagement, and Information Technology in Health Care. *Medicine, Health Care and Philosophy,* 16(4), 807–816. doi: 10.1007/s11019-013-9463-7.

Damiano, L. (2021). Homes as Human-Robot Ecologies. An Epistemological Inquiry on the "Domestication" of Robots. In A. Argandoña, J. Malala and R.C. Peatfield (eds.), *The Home in the Digital Age.* Abingdon: Routledge, pp. 80–102.

d'Entremont, A. (2018). Spatial Relationality and Domesticity: Reality and Functions of the Home from a Human Geography Perspective. In A. Argandoña (ed.), *The Home: Multidisciplinary Reflections.* Cheltenham: Edward Elgar, pp. 163–175. doi: 10.4337/9781786436573.00021.

Durante, M. (2010). What Is the Model of Trust for Multi-agent Systems? Whether or Not E-Trust Applies to Autonomous Agents. *Knowledge, Technology & Policy,* 23(3–4), 347–366. doi: 10.1007/s12130-010-9118-4.

Epstein, R.G. (1997). *The Case of the Killer Robot.* New York, NY: Wiley.

Ess, C. (2009). *Digital Media Ethics.* Cambridge, MA: Polity Books.

Etzioni, A. and O. Etzioni (2016). AI Assisted Ethics, *Ethics and Information Technology,* 18, 149–156. doi: 10.1007/s10676-016-9400-6.

Etzioni, A. and O. Etzioni (2017). Incorporating Ethics into Artificial Intelligence. *Journal of Ethics,* 21(4), 403–418. doi: 10.1007/s10892-017-9252-2.

Floridi, L. (1999). Information Ethics: On the Theoretical Foundations of Computer Ethics. *Ethics and Information Technology*, 1(1), 37–56. doi: 10.1023/A:1010018611096.

Floridi, L. (2004). Open Problems in the Philosophy of Information. *Metaphilosophy*, 35(4), 554–582. doi: 10.1111/j.1467-9973.2004.00336.x.

Floridi, L. (2014). Smart, Autonomous, and Social: Robots as Challenge to Human Exceptionalism. In J. Seibt, R. Hakli and M. Norskov (eds.), *Sociable Robots and the Future of Social Relations. Proceedings of Robo-Philosophy 2014*. Aarhus, Denmark: IOS Press, p. 11.

Floridi, L. (2015). The Onlife Manifesto. In L. Floridi (ed.), *The Onlife Manifesto: Being Human in a Hyperconnected Era*. Heidelberg: Springer. doi: 10.1007/978-3-319-04093-6.

Floridi, L., J. Cowls, M. Beltrametti, R. Chatila, P. Chazerand, V. Dignum, C. Luetge, R. Madelin, U. Pagallo, F. Rossi, B. Schafer, P. Valcke and E. Vayena (2018). AI4People – An Ethical Framework for a Good AI Society: Opportunities, Risks, Principles, and Recommendations. *Minds and Machines*, 28(4), 689–707. doi: 10.1007/s11023-018-9482-5.

Floridi, L. and J.W. Sanders (2004). On the Morality of Artificial Agents. *Minds and Machines*, 14, 349–379. doi: 10.1023/B:MIND.0000035461.63578.9d.

Floridi, L. and M. Taddeo (2016). What is Data Ethics? *Philosophical Transactions Royal Society A*, 374(2083), 1–5. doi: 10.1098/rsta.2016.0360.

Fung, M.L. and D. Gale (2021). Digital Home: The Missing Element for a People-Centered Digital Future. In A. Argandoña, J. Malala and R.C. Peatfield (eds.), *The Home in the Digital Age*. Abingdon: Routledge, pp. 15–37.

Gipps, J. (1995). Towards the Ethical Robot. In K. Ford, C. Glymour and P. Hayes (eds.), *Android Epistemology*. Cambridge, MA: MIT Press, pp. 243–252.

Goldberg, D.E. (1989). *Genetic Algorithms in Search, Optimization and Machine Learning*. Reading, MA: Addison-Wesley. doi: 10.5555/534133.

Hacker, P. (2018). Teaching Fairness to Artificial Intelligence: Existing and Novel Strategies against Algorithmic Discrimination under EU Law. *Common Market Law Review*, 55(4), 1143–1186.

Hellstrom, T. (2013). On the Moral Responsibility of Military Robots. *Ethics and Information Technology*, 12(2), 99–107. doi: 10.1007/s10676-012-9301-2.

Hildebrandt, M. (2011). Legal Protection by Design: Objections and Refutations. *Legisprudence*, 5(2), 223–248. doi: 10.5235/175214611797885693.

Hildebrandt, H. and J. Koops (2010). The Challenges of Ambient Law and Legal Protection in the Profiling Era. *Modern Law Review*, 73(3), 428–460. doi: 10.1111/j.1468-2230.2010.00806.x.

Himma, K.E. and H. Tavani (eds.) (2008). *The Handbook of Information and Computer Ethics*. Hoboken, NJ: Wiley. doi: 10.1002/9780470281819.

Horvitz, E. and D. Mulligan (2015). Data, Privacy, and the Greater Good. *Science*, 349 (6245), 253–255. doi: 10.1126/science.aac4520.

Johnson, D.G. (2000). *Computer Ethics*, 3rd edn. Upper Saddle River, NJ: Prentice Hall.

Johnson, D.G. (2015). Technology with no Human Responsibility? *Journal of Business Ethics*, 127(4), 707–715. doi: 10.1007/s10551-014-2180-1.

Johnson, J.A. (2014). Ethics of Data Mining and Predictive Analytics in Higher Education. *International Review of Information Ethics*, 21, 3–10. doi: 10.2139/ssrn.2156058.

Karppi, T. (2018). "The Computer Said So": On the Ethics, Effectiveness, and Cultural Techniques of Predictive Policing. *Social Media + Society*, 4(2), 1–9. doi: 10.1177/2056305118768296.

Keane, J. (2019). La nueva era de la revolución de las máquinas. *Letras Libres*. www.letraslibres.com/espana-mexico/revista/la-nueva-era-la-revolucion-las-maquinas (accessed 10 December 2019).

Kitchin, R. (2016). Thinking Critically about and Researching Algorithms. *Information, Communication and Society*, 20(1), 14–29. doi: 10.1080/1369118X.2016.1154087.

Kraemer, F., K. van Overveld and M. Peterson (2011). Is There an Ethics of Algorithms? *Ethics and Information Technology*, 13(3), 251–260. doi: 10.1007/s10676-010-9233-7.

Kranzberg, M. (1986). Technology and History: Kranzberg's Laws. *Technology and Culture*, 27(3), 544–560. doi: 10.1177/027046769501500104.

Latour, B. (1994). On Technical Mediation: Philosophy, Sociology, Genealogy. *Common Knowledge*, 3(2), 29–64.

Latour, B. (1999). *Pandora's Hope: Essays on the Reality of Science Studies*. Cambridge, MA: Harvard University Press.

Lin, P., K. Abney and G. Bekey (2011). Robot Ethics: Mapping the Issues for a Mechanized World. *Artificial Intelligence*, 175 (5–6), 942–949. doi: 10.1016/j.artint.2010.11.026.

Macnish, K. (2012). Unblinking Eyes: The Ethics of Automating Surveillance. *Ethics and Information Technology*, 14(2), 151–167. doi: 10.1007/s10676-012-9291-0.

Marino, D. and G. Tamburrini (2006). Learning Robots and Human Responsibility. *International Review of Information Ethics*, 6(12), 47–51.

Markham, A.N. (2015). Producing Ethics [for the Digital Near Future]. In R.A. Lind (ed.), *Producing Theory in a Digital World 2.0: The Intersection of Audiences and Production in Contemporary Theory*, Vol. 2. New York, NY: Peter Lang, pp. 247–256.

Markham, A.N. and E. Buchanan (2015). Ethical Considerations in Digital Research Contexts. In J.D. Wright (ed.), *Encyclopedia for the Social and Behavioral Sciences*. Waltham, MA: Elsevier, 606–613.

Markham, A.N., K. Tiidenberg and A. Herman (2018). Ethics as Methods: Doing Ethics in the Era of Big Data Research – Introduction. *Social Media + Society*, 4(3), 1–9. doi: 10.1177/2056305118784502.

Markowetz, A., K. Błaszkiewicz and C. Montag (2014). Psycho-Informatics: Big Data Shaping Modern Psychometrics. *Medical Hypotheses,* 82(4), 405–411. doi: 10.1016/j.mehy.2013.11.030.

Matthias, A. (2004). The Responsibility Gap: Ascribing Responsibility for the Actions of Learning Automata. *Ethics and Information Technology*, 6(3), 175–183. doi: 10.1007/s10676-004-3422-1.

McQuillan, D. (2018). People's Councils for Ethical Machine Learning. *Social Media + Society*, 3(2), 1–10. doi: 10.1177/2056305118768303.

Mittelstadt, B.D., P. Allo, M. Taddeo, S. Wachter and L. Floridi (2016). The Ethics of Algorithms: Mapping the Debate. *Big Data & Society*, 3(2), 1–21. doi: 10.1177/2053951716679679.

Morek, R. (2006). Regulatory Framework for Online Dispute Resolution: A Critical View. *The University of Toledo Law Review*, 38(1), 163–192.

Morley, J., L. Floridi, L. Kinsey and A. Elhalal (2019). From What to How: An Overview of AI Ethics Tools, Methods and Research to Translate Principles into Practices. https://arxiv.org/abs/1905.06876 (accessed 20 October 2019).

Newell, S. and M. Marabelli (2015). Strategic Opportunities (and Challenges) of Algorithmic Decision Making: A Call for Action on the Long-Term Societal Effects of "Datificaton". *Journal of Strategic Information Systems*, 24(1), 3–14. doi: 10.1016/j.jsis.2015.02.001.

Ocnarescu, I. and D. Sciamma (2021). Homes through the Design Shift in the Digital Age. In A. Argandoña, J. Malala and R.C. Peatfield (eds.), *The Home in the Digital Age*. Abingdon: Routledge, pp. 103–119.

Paradice, D.B. and R.M. Dejoie (1991). The Ethical Decision-Making Processes of Information System Workers. *Journal of Business Ethics*, 10(1), 1–21. doi: 10.1007/BF00383688.

Patrão Neves, M. (2018). Self and Others: Home as a Cradle of a Non-Violent Relationship. In A. Argandoña (ed.), *The Home: Multidisciplinary Reflections*. Cheltenham: Edward Elgar, pp. 57–76. doi: 10.4337/9781786436573.00012.

Polo, L. (1995). *Ética. Hacia una versión moderna de los temas clásicos*. Madrid: AEDOS – Unión Editorial.

Ringle, M. (ed.) (1979). *Philosophical Perspectives in Artificial Intelligence*. Atlantic Highlands, NJ: Humanities Press.

Rughiniș, C., R. Rughiniș and S. Matei (2015). A Touching App Voice Thinking about Ethics of Persuasive Technology through an Analysis of Mobile Smoking-Cessation Apps. *Ethics and Information Technology*, 17(4), 295–309. doi: 10.1007/s10676-016-9385-1.

Russo, D. (2014). Domotics and Robotics. *Dolentium Hominum*, 84, 137–144.

Samuel, A.L. (1960). Some Moral and Technical Consequences of Automation – A Refutation. *Science*, 132(3429), 7421–7422. doi: 10.1126/science.132.3429.741.

Santos, M. and F. Toni (2021). Artificial Intelligence-Empowered Technology in the Home. In A. Argandoña, J. Malala and R.C. Peatfield (eds.), *The Home in the Digital Age*. Abingdon: Routledge, pp 38–55.

Schermer, B.W. (2011). The Limits of Privacy in Automated Profiling and Data Mining. *Computer Law and Security Review*, 27(1), 45–52. doi: 10.1016/j.clsr.2010.11.009.

Sen, A. (2010). *The Idea of Justice*. London: Penguin.

Severson, R.L. and S.M. Carlson (2010). Behaving as or Behaving as if? Children's Conceptions of Personified Robots and the Emergence of a New Ontological Category. *Neural Networks*, 23(8–9), 1099–1103. doi: 10.1016/j.neunet.2010.08.014.

Sharkey, N. and A. Sharkey (2012). The Eldercare Factory. *Gerontology*, 58(3), 282–288. doi: 10.1159/000329483.

Sheliazhenko, Y. (2017). Artificial Personal Autonomy and Concept of Robot Rights. *European Journal of Law and Political Sciences*, 1, 17–21. doi: 10.20534/EJLPS-17-1-17-21.

Singer, P. (n.d.). Ethics. Philosophy. *Encyclopaedia Britannica*, www.britannica.com/topic/ethics-philosophy (accessed 27 January 2019).

Sloan, R.H. and R. Warner (2019). Algorithms and Human Freedom. *Santa Clara High Technology Law Journal*, 35(4), 1–34. https://digitalcommons.law.scu.edu/chtlj/vol35/iss4/2 (accessed 13 November 2019).

Sullins, J.P. (2005). Ethics and Artificial Life: From Modelling of Moral Agents. *Ethics and Information Technology*, 7, 139–148. doi: 10.1007/s10676-006-0003-5.

Sullins, J.P. (2006). When Is a Robot a Moral Agent? *International Review of Information Ethics*, 6, 24–30.

Tene, O. and J. Polonetsky (2012). Privacy in the Age of Big Data: A Time for Big Decisions. *Stanford Law Review Online*, 64, 63–69. www.academia.edu/28487186/Privacy_in_the_age_of_big_data_a_time_for_big_decisions (accessed 12 January 2019).

Turilli, M. and L. Floridi (2009). The Ethics of Information Transparency. *Ethics and Information Technology*, 11(2), 105–112. doi: 10.1007/s10676-009-9187-9.

Vallée, T., K. Sedki, S. Despres, M. Jaulant, K. Tabia and A. Ugon (2016). On Personalization in IoT. In *2016 International Conference on Computational Science and Computational Intelligence (CSCI)*, vol. 1, pp. 186–191. New York, NY: Institute of Electrical and Electronics Engineers.

Vallor, S. (2010). Social Networking Technology and the Virtues. *Ethics and Information Technology*, 12(2), 157–170. doi: 10.1007/s10676-009-9202-1.

van Wel, L. and L. Royakkers (2004). Ethical Issues in Web Data-Mining. *Ethics and Information Technology*, 6, 129–140. doi: 10.1023/B:ETIN.0000047476.05912.3d.

Verbeek, P.P. (2006). Materializing Morality. Design Ethics and Technological Mediation. *Science, Technology and Human Values*, 31(3), 361–380. doi: 10.1177/0162243905285847.

Vinge, V. (1993). The Coming Technological Singularity: How to Survive in the Post-Human Era. In G.A. Landis (ed.), *Vision 21: Interdisciplinary Science and Engineering in the Era of Cyberspace*, NASA Publication CP-10129. Cleveland, OH: Lewis Research Center, pp. 11–22.

Wiegel, V. and J. van den Berg (2009). Combining Moral Theory, Modal Logic and MAS to Create Well-Behaving Artificial Agents. *International Journal of Social Robotics*, 1(3), 233–242. doi: 10.1007/s12369-009-0023-5.

Wiener, N. (1960). Some Moral and Technical Consequences of Automation. *Science*, 131(3410), 1355–1358. doi: 10.1007/BF02837160.

Index

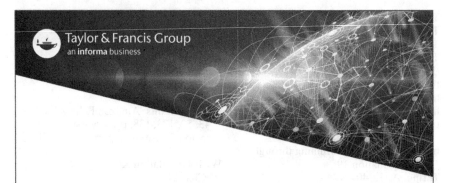

Printed in the United States
by Baker & Taylor Publisher Services

Printed in the United States
by Baker & Taylor Publisher Services